Software That Sells
A Practical Guide to Developing and Marketing Your Software Project

Software That Sells
A Practical Guide to Developing and Marketing Your Software Project

Edward Hasted

Wiley Publishing, Inc.

Software That Sells: A Practical Guide to Developing and Marketing Your Software Project

Published by
Wiley Publishing, Inc.
10475 Crosspoint Boulevard
Indianapolis, IN 46256
www.wiley.com

Copyright © 2005 by Wiley Publishing, Inc., Indianapolis, Indiana

Published simultaneously in Canada

ISBN-13: 978-0-7645-9783-1
ISBN-10: 0-7645-9783-3

Manufactured in the United States of America

10 9 8 7 6 5 4 3 2 1

1B/SV/QV/QV/IN

For general information on our other products and services or to obtain technical support, please contact our Customer Care Department within the U.S. at (800) 762-2974, outside the U.S. at (317) 572-3993 or fax (317) 572-4002.

Wiley also publishes its books in a variety of electronic formats. Some content that appears in print may not be available in electronic books.

Library of Congress control number: 2005012599

About the Author

Ed Hasted has worn most of the T-shirts in computing. He was introduced to his first computer in the days before PCs were delivered by the postman. Having completed a course in Engineering Mathematics at Bristol University in England, he went on to become the youngest PC dealer in the U.K. The firm soon grew to supply hardware to almost all of the country's government departments.

At the start of the 1990s, Ed set up a communications software house to write e-mail and groupware, pioneering the use of the Internet. The software was implemented by companies of every size. It was one of the first products to be sold electronically online. Ed saw products through from inception to release, brought in 80 percent of the sales, and pioneered the use of teleworkers. On a roll in the late 1990s, he sold out to a U.S. corporation.

Since then, he's worked for Wang, helped run some of the largest networks in Europe, organized the system builds for London's Metropolitan Police Department, and instigated best practices in Internet Operations.

Book writing aside, Ed now works as a consultant, covering everything discussed in this book.

Ed restricts himself to one wife, two children, and an unlimited number of PCs.

Credits

Acquisitions Editor
Katie Mohr

Development Editor
Marcia Ellett

Production Editor
Gabrielle Nabi

Copy Editor
Kim Cofer

Editorial Manager
Mary Beth Wakefield

Vice President & Executive Group Publisher
Richard Swadley

Vice President and Publisher
Joseph B. Wikert

Project Coordinator
Erin Smith

Graphic and Layout Technicians
Jonelle Burns
April Farling
Denny Hager
Julie Trippetti
Mary Gillot Virgin

Quality Control Technician
Laura Albert
Amanda Briggs
John Greenough
Leann Harney
Brian Walls

Proofreading and Indexing
TECHBOOKS Production Services

Introduction

Christopher Columbus didn't just point his boat at the sunset to discover America.

He'd heard an old fisherman in the Azores (about a third of his way into the Atlantic) tell of a vast land to the West. The fisherman knew because he had seen it when a ferocious easterly blew him off course several years before. With this scrap of information, speculation became certainty and the rest was history.

Software's a trifle more complex. When I first began to write software in President Reagan's era, I knew I was doing something no one else had done. I thought I was alone. I didn't even know what I didn't know.

Creating software is still pioneering, but only a masochist tries to create it unaided. To end up where you want to be, you and your team must navigate many crucial passages. There's nothing difficult in any of them. As the chapters of this book explain in simple language, it's mostly common sense.

This book is accordingly organized like an Atlas, with pages to guide you from one area to another. So start at the part that concerns you and take it from there. The more you understand the A to Z of it, the healthier your project's chances, which is why I hope that you will eventually read the whole book. Others have gone through ulcers, divorce, bankruptcy, firing, executive jets, and Las Vegas to put this information in your hands.

Let their hindsight be your foresight.

Conventions Used in This Book

Software That Sells: A Practical Guide to Developing and Marketing Your Software Project uses a simple style and employs the following icons to help you pinpoint useful information:

 The Note icon marks an interesting fact—something I thought you'd like to know.

 The Tip icon marks things you can do to make your job easier.

The Caution icon highlights potential pitfalls. This icon tells you: "Watch out! This could produce unexpected and/or undesirable results!"

 The Cross-Reference icon points to places in the book where you can find further information on a mentioned topic.

Sidebars

Sidebars are used throughout the book to highlight interesting, non-critical information. Sidebars explain concepts you may not have encountered before or give some insight into a related topic.

For feedback, visit www.software-that-sells.com.

Acknowledgments

Any author's name on the spine covers a multitude of omissions—never more so than here.

Long before I put finger to keyboard, I dwelled on the subject until a strong and encompassing framework emerged. Before I took the monumental step of interrupting my career for nine months to write the book, I outlined the concept to a neighbor, who happens to be one of Europe's foremost publishing gurus. Jackie Douglas told me I didn't need to be certified to proceed. Through highs and lows, Jackie has been my guardian angel, dispensing support, direction, and the occasional quizzical look.

As fast as I could draft each chapter, I sent them over to my father, who edited them in real time. My greatest single "Thank you" goes to him. Having retired from running the first international Creative Consultancy, he took it upon himself to teach me the rudiments of writing. With his skill, quagmire was turned into crystal. For his support in this and everything else in my life, I am eternally grateful.

Before I dared show the manuscript to my publisher, individual chapters were vetted by colleagues on both sides of the Atlantic. The best recognition of their input is the incorporation of almost every point advanced.

Jonathan Graham, Mark Speller, and Philip White gave salutary feedback on finance from the funder's viewpoint.

Nick Alton, Martin Chesbrough, Nigel Cornwall, Charles Lecklider, Judith Maidens, Robert Neuschul, Mark Stanton, and Roger Wilson used their hundreds of years' experience to double-check the chapters on IT.

Clive Francis and Chris Miles similarly drove their way through the section on distribution.

A super heavyweight team comprising Nick Crossman, Tony Douglas, Jonathan Fisher, Stewart Hasted, Jeremy Spiller, and Peter Watson refined the sections on marketing, research, and selling. Together they helped condense what ordinarily covers hundreds of pages into the lucid distillation here.

And Chris Rowland checked the design issues all on his own.

Only then was I prepared to put my head above the parapet. Katie Mohr, my acquisitions editor, had the courage to run with the book. It gave me the greatest pleasure to sign with Wiley, vindicating her faith. And finally, the book was only fit to go to press after development editor Marcia Ellett waved her magic wand, or rather her editing pen, over it.

Together we produced what you read today. But without the endless patience, support, and coffee from my wife, Lis, the book would never have happened at all.

Chapter 10: Scoring with Words 139

Chapter 11: Before You Say "Go!"—The Release Process 149

Contents

Contents at a Glance

How Winners Spot Winners

Anyone can have a good idea. Don't let anyone talk you into thinking otherwise. It is just that novelists, inventors, and composers have developed the knack of leaving their creative taps on. Even then, ideas don't exactly gush. They tend to appear when your attention is elsewhere, tiptoeing into consciousness, so to speak. At the germinal stage, they easily vanish. A harsh word or shrug is sometimes all it takes. Even as they disappear, you may sense a loss of some merit. So do not to be too hard on your thoughts, however ungainly. Gather them reverently, and allow them to settle and find a niche. Once you have enough, you are in a position to pick and choose. Sometimes a concept arrives like a scissor blade, useless in itself. Other times, ideas surface in installments. Occasionally, they arrive fully-fledged. When the right one comes, you'll know. Even before friends stop saying *"Bah!"* and start saying *"Oh!"* and you begin to get positive reactions, give some thought to your destiny. There's absolutely no point in having an idea if you don't do something about it.

Where Winners Find Their Ideas

Getting a good idea is one thing. Recognizing it is another. All good ideas come from the crucible of what you know already: your knowledge and experience. Scientists who have studied the formation of ideas say there are two sources:

✦ Ideas that appear spontaneously are thought to come from the right side of the brain, your so-called *creative* subconscious.

✦ Ideas that are built up logically are thought to come from the conscious, left side of the brain and are described as *synthetic*.

The words psychologists use don't matter. You just have to know that ideas come in two parts. If you know how you did it, it's *synthetic*. If you don't, it's *creative*. It's what Thomas Edison described as "perspiration and inspiration." Edison was strong on perspiration. His invention of the light bulb was completely synthetic. Edison labored 16 hours a day for years at his famous laboratories at Menlo Park. He tried every conceivable physical condition and chemical element until he arrived at a truly illuminating combination.

> **Note**   Edison tried over 6,000 combinations before he perfected the incandescent light bulb. He used to joke that he *had* to succeed, as he'd tried everything else that had failed.

In contrast, Archimedes, the ancient Greek mathematician and inventor, got a one-step solution. His idea for the Principle of Displacement came when he leaped into his bath. That idea is held to be creative.

Most marketable ideas are a combination of spontaneous thoughts that have been optimized by polishing. Gene Roddenberry did just this. His inspiration came from a 1961 movie called *Master of the World*, in which Vincent Price as "Robur" went around the Earth in a giant airship to explore strange new worlds, to seek out new life and civilizations. The perspiration was drawn from Roddenberry's experiences as a bomber pilot, policeman, and his consummate plot and script-writing ability. The result was *Star Trek*.

How to Bottle Eureka

As previously mentioned, ideas that materialize in a flash can evaporate just as quickly. If you've ever awakened from a vivid dream from which you can remember the feeling, but you just can't recall the substance, you will know what I'm talking about.

Creative ideas come from the subconscious part of the brain. Unless they are copied onto the conscious brain, they are prone to submerge and may not resurface.

Take a tip from people who make their living from ideas: keep a pencil and paper by your bed, in your car, wherever. When you get an idea, jot it down immediately. Use just enough key words to help you recall the notion, but nothing too detailed; there may be other thoughts to come.

Step 1 – Sit Down

The early green pasture days of IT, if they ever existed, are over. You will want to avoid the pitfalls that have snared so many of your predecessors. History hasn't recorded how many promising ideas fizzled out for poor presentation. Thinking things through is now the only way to win. Keep the following in mind:

✦ Bosses want solutions, not problems.

✦ Investors can't afford half-baked ideas.

✦ The public won't tolerate software that doesn't work properly the first time.

To succeed you must develop a successful idea. So the last thing you want to do is rush in on your boss. Imagine being the person who dreamed up the concept of the Web browser and dashing into your vice president's office saying, "Hey, I've got this idea of viewing Web pages through a software program!"

What do you think the likely response would have been? He'd probably have looked up from his desk and growled, "What's a Web page?"

If you had thought the idea through in advance, you might have explained that you had come up with a unique idea that would supersede print, which would allow total global information to be accessed from anywhere.

Then he might have been more likely to have said, "Pull up a chair and tell me more!" If he had any sense, he'd be counting the dollars before you'd even finished and asking how to patent it.

Step 2 – Stretch Your Idea

Latex, the main constituent of rubber, had been known to the South American Mayan Indians since 1600 B.C. It was naturally sticky in summer and brittle in winter. No one knew quite what to do with the stuff. Then in 1839 Charles Goodyear accidentally spilled some sulphur into a vat and averaged the attributes. With a second stroke of luck he found that heat was the missing ingredient and vulcanized rubber was born.

New ideas not only need to be cultivated, but exercised as well. Having half an idea is less than half the battle. Whether your bottle is half full or half empty, customers will only buy a full one. You have to find the key extra ingredient to fill it up and turn your idea into a complete winner. So stretch your idea, tease it this way and that, chop out elements, turn it on its head, try it as expensive, try it as cheap. And remember McDonalds.

The humble hamburger had been served by German immigrants in North America for well over a century before Maurice and Richard McDonald (in 1948) began to give the recipe thought. Here's what they came up with:

✦ Get rid of waitresses.

✦ Persuade customers to eat standing up.

✦ Severely restrict menus.

✦ Fire specialist chefs.

✦ Develop cooking machinery that any employee can operate.

None of these ideas were winners in and of themselves. Yet together they built a worldwide, fast-food industry.

Even operating systems were nothing new when IBM commissioned Bill Gates to write the Disk Operating System (DOS) in 1980.

DOS was designed to be ported to other computers easily (remember there were many different types at the time and it took years before the IBM PC became the standard it is today). This appealed to the manufacturers, as it allowed them all to start from the same playing field. Bill didn't know who would be the eventual winner, but he knew that if he backed them all he couldn't lose.

Most new ideas are not entirely new. They are old ones with a twist. When the Gates, Goodyears, and McDonalds of this world are asked how they came across their ideas, they typically say, "'It was just under my nose."

 Note   The thought that turns a leaden idea into gold is often surprisingly close at hand. So scrabble, search, and twist.

Step 3 – Make Sure Your Idea Is Well Defined

If an idea is sound enough to persuade outsiders to back you, you have got to be able to explain it over the telephone or on the back of a postcard. All great inventors or developers can make the complex sound simple. Einstein said, "If you can't explain an idea to an eight-year-old child you probably don't understand it yourself."

Whether your idea is simple or complex, you are going to have to communicate it simply if you want anyone to finance you. If you can't explain it to a potential backer, they won't be able to explain the idea to their colleagues. And, if collectively they don't understand it, they will never allow the money to be risked in the first place. Backers have to be confident that you have a clear vision and direction.

The exercise of trying to encapsulate your idea, who will use it, and why in 30 words or less is salutary. You will either discover that it just can't be done, in which case your idea is almost certainly too complex to ever sell efficiently, or by trial and error with friends and relatives you will arrive at an explanation that everyone can understand. Your explanation should raise few questions and most people should find it satisfactory as far as it goes. Marketing people call this explanation *the concept*.

Step 4 – Open Up Your Concept

A good friend who runs a major U.S. corporation had a competition with another director to see which could make more money selling something they could get for nothing. His colleague thought he had struck gold when he started to sell pressurized water as a cosmetic product. My friend went one better and sold pressurized air as a cleaning agent for medical, hi-tech, and photographic equipment.

The idea of making your concept more attractive to more people is usually possible. Initially, think laterally from other points of view. A mosquito might be a pest to you, but you're a midnight feast to it. Consider all possibilities, no matter how bizarre.

The larger the audience a product can attract the better its chances. Could you, for instance, incorporate your embryo product inside another? Could it be part of a more significant package? Could it be sold on the back of other products? This is exactly what Mr. Dunlop and Mr. Gates did.

Mr. Dunlop took Mr. Goodyear's vulcanized rubber, which had been around for over 40 years by then, and turned it into an indispensable product—the pneumatic tire. Mr. Gates got his operating system incorporated into every IBM PC. We take many of these very smart moves so much for granted that we forget that they began as clever ideas.

If at this stage you are feeling held back by not having a finalized, killer name for your idea, just do what they do in Hollywood—give it a working title, something that's good for the time being and indicative of what you aspire to, such as "Project Everest."

Step 5 – Check the Concept against Your Own Experience

Right at the start, you have to face up to common-sense questions and have some idea of what is involved. Don't concern yourself too much about whether your idea is unique. Few good ideas are. They just have to be unique enough.

Pioneers who have "First Mover Advantage" are often able to charge a premium, however, this notional bonus is almost always swallowed by their promotional and educational costs.

Note

Software is rarely copied by stealing the source code; that's illegal and too easy to spot. What competitors do is look at your finished product and re-create something that is functionally similar and improve upon it.

Some ideas are brilliant but the development is staggering. The Internet would never be the universal IT backbone it is but for U.S. government funding of the ARPANET project since 1967. Not only did Uncle Sam give the developers money, he indirectly taught hundreds of thousands of people how to use it and gave major corporations and universities the incentive to adopt it as well. Bear thoughts like these in mind as you subject your concept to private and personal scrutiny:

✦ Has anyone had the idea in this form before you? Quickly check the Internet.

✦ Is it too far ahead of its market? Are you inventing the pneumatic tire before the automobile?

- ✦ Is it too easy for competitors to learn from? Get some kind of ballpark on secure coding and patents.

- ✦ Is it too difficult to explain? Take an educated guess.

- ✦ Can it be distributed efficiently? Could it be sold off the Web?

- ✦ Is the cost of development likely to be in any way unusual? Is the project likely to be small, medium, or large?

- ✦ How long could the coding take? Extrapolate from projects of similar scale.

- ✦ Have you got a moneymaking proposition? Is there a prima facie case for profit?

If the answers are satisfactory, give yourself a green light. If they are not, it isn't all doom and disaster. You just have to do a little more thinking. Go back a stage or two and consider how you can transform a limitation into a decided advantage.

Step 6 – Gather Your Inner Sanctum

So you've got your idea, expanded it, articulated it, and checked it with yourself. Now you need to pass it by a few close friends or colleagues. Try to pick a time when they are relaxed and receptive. At work this is much easier said than done; so it is probably best scheduled after hours.

For your sounding board, select people with relevant experience, potential users, and programmers.

Explain your concept briefly, cite its advantages, outline the way it fits with existing products. Then sit back, listen very carefully to what they say, and take notes. You will probably want to embody some of their ideas. Try not to interrupt until they have finished; otherwise you'll be tampering with the evidence.

If your previous surmises are sound, your quorum will probably confirm them, though almost certainly you will want to make some beneficial adjustments.

People with new ideas are a lot more secretive than they probably needed to be with hindsight. However, at this stage this is the smart policy. You can always let the genie out of the bottle later, but you can never put him back. Only discuss your idea with close, trusted friends and colleagues on a strictly confidential basis. If you do need to show the idea to people outside your inner sanctum, such as technical specialists for appraisal purposes, get them to sign a confidentiality agreement first. You only want your idea to enter the public domain when you're ready to put it there.

Step 7 – You Are Only Human

As you soar to paradise, remember, human error is the last thing to fall away.

However flattering people are about your idea, you are always prone to error. You can't even predict what your best friend will choose on a restaurant menu. They may always start the meal with shrimp cocktails. But don't bet on it. He or she is bound to eventually crave something else.

The only person whose actions you can begin to gauge in advance (and then not always) is yourself, and if you rely entirely on your own evaluation of your product's possibilities, you could end up with a market of one. The path to Silicon Valley is paved with self-declared geniuses who never amounted to more than road kill on the Internet Super-Highway. Your future, your time, your whole style of life deserves better than that. So don't skelter out with your golden idea. Be objective. Test the water, one toe first. You are only just coming out of the conceptual stage. It's time to do some proper research.

Why Development Pays

There is no copyright on having ideas. It is not uncommon for two people to have similar ideas, circumstances being what they are, often at about the same time. The idea that wins is invariably the one that has been thought through the best. That's why developing the idea matters, and the thought you put in now will pay dividends as you progress.

✦   ✦   ✦

What Successful People Ask

Developing even the simplest software on the fly has got some very high IQs into some sticky messes, not the kind they could actually spot before they became entangled, but ones that seemed to be signposted plainly enough when they reached firm ground again and looked backwards. This brings us to the theme of this chapter: hindsight first.

Many of us are so taken aback when we get a good idea that we tremble to ask people what they think of it. However, if we don't find out people's opinions in advance, we're guaranteed to find out afterwards; and by then we've spent our own and other people's money.

If you take all initial criticisms and rephrase them as positive suggestions, it is much easier to creatively build up an idea. And you might find that these further and better ideas are backed up by solid support. So, although it may require more spadework to build a bigger mountain, the results you want and the thrills you will get from success will give you a real kick.

The choice essentially is Russian roulette or a quick squint up the revolving chamber before depressing the trigger. I advise the quick squint. If you are going to develop software, you are going to be forced to take enough risks (essential management decisions). So it's sheer masochism to take more chances than you have to. To minimize your risks, you must, by hook or by crook, lay your hands on trustworthy information. You have to put the right questions to the right people in the right way. It is well worth careful inquiry. Your future is at stake. So before you start to do any code writing, you need to establish the sort of facts that shopkeepers a hundred years ago were able to glean from their customers directly over the counter. They called it chatting.

Being able to build a business on bedrock facts is a colossal, potential business advantage. I say "potential" because not only do you have to find out what the facts are, but you also have to be able to exploit them. Market research, which only really amounts to asking convincing questions, can give you a competitive edge because the majority of software developers still rush out, take a quick look at where the rocks are, and dive in before they've found the alligators. The time it takes to do a little careful probing is more than repaid by the increased speed and surety with which you will be able to make prudent decisions afterwards.

Before you even think of investing any serious money or time, you need to be able to answer the following:

+ Is there a demand for this software?

+ What features do users want?

+ How many want them?

+ What do they expect to pay?

+ What's the state of competition?

+ Where do people expect to buy it?

By the time you have asked enough people, you will have a much broader idea of whether your project is feasible before you have committed real money.

Any research worth its salt gives you practical answers with high degrees of probability. Elementary market research can enable you to streamline your coding schedule by telling you which functions and features customers are most likely to pay for. It can help you to discover how much you are probably going to have to teach the customers before they can appreciate your program. Although there can be vast differences between what people say and what they do, market research can supply the price slot most likely to attract purchases.

Major corporations value information of this kind so highly they would never consider launching a new product without first conducting exhaustive surveys. They also know that on-going research will enable them to assess the effectiveness of their competitors' activities and give them early warning of market trends. While it may be time-consuming, market research doesn't have to be expensive.

 Note   You don't have to consult thousands of people about their reactions. The outcome of any general election can be predicted to within 3 percent by analyzing voting changes in less than a dozen constituencies (largely thanks to the computers).

Who to Ask

The most important single fact that market research can supply is verification that enough people want a product like the one you envisage to justify its creation.

However, there is a catch-22 situation here. Who exactly are "the right people?" The people who use the product are not necessarily the people who make the purchasing decision; and neither the user nor the decision-maker is necessarily the person doing the buying.

Usually, it is the end user who sets the ball rolling (though it may be shrewder, if the program will benefit the whole organization, to approach the decision-maker first and set up a "Look into this!" directive from on high). The people who actually do the procurement are either accountants or professional in-house buyers. By and large, accountants have a strong power of veto. Professional buyers justify their existence by trading quantity against price, so be warned.

Where the product will be a corporate purchase, it is important to find out from the purchasing manager/CFO what protocols are required. There's no point in having customers eager for your offering only to find out that most of them are barred from using it because it doesn't comply with a state law such as being Y2K, ISO9001, or Euro currency compatible. Whenever you are in doubt about whom you should approach, conduct a pilot study by testing the water on a few dozen prospects, not the most important ones, of course, yet typical ones nevertheless.

To this quality dimension there is also a quantity dimension. The quantity dimension is like a series of concentric rings, with 20 percent of clients accounting for 80 percent of the turnover in smaller operations and 10 percent of the clients accounting for 90 percent of the turnover in larger ones. These are surrounded by a core of strong potential users, with secondary prospects on the fringe.

The trouble at the start is that you cannot know who will be your best customers. Interest among secondary prospects may be stronger or weaker than you anticipate. Your definition of strong potential users may, or may not, need an adjustment. Better indications may alter the priority you will later have to give to market sectors and necessitate some revision of product features.

How Many People Must You Survey?

If you think you've got a good idea, run it by half a dozen colleagues and you will probably get a quick idea of whether it's likely to be a clear winner or a flop. But very often the responses from a close circle of friends can polarize both ways. Statisticians think that if you put the question to two dozen of the right people you will get a reasonably indicative, initial reaction, which is fine if you are testing a drug as one body reacts much like another. However, if you are dealing with minds, reactions are highly individual. So the only way to be sure you are asking the right people is to ask a larger sample. What this larger sample gives you is never the right answer but an answer that is less prone to error.

The chart depicted in Figure 2-1 shows how many people you'd have to ask to get better than 90 percent reliable answers for various sizes of customer universe. In each case the sample allows for 5 percent of respondents giving wrong answers.

Market Size	5,000	50,000	500,000	5,000,000
Reliability	Number of Respondents Required			
90%	258	271	272	272
95%	357	381	384	384
99%	586	655	663	663

Figure 2-1: Predictor of required respondents.

Note how quickly the number of people required for a quorum levels as market numbers grow. When highly specialized software is being written for a limited number of potential users, you should aim to consult them individually. Because their appreciation of what you are doing is likely to be high, you can usually ask quite complex questions. They may also volunteer a lot of further useful information. But be very circumspect: while most are undoubtedly potential clients, a few may turn out to be competitors.

The Ethics

Many of us get frequent calls from household-improvement companies trying to sell their products under the guise of market research. So profligate has the practice become that it has a name—*sugging*, or sales under the guise of research.

If you are new to conducting a survey, the basic rules are common sense:

✦ Don't try to influence your respondent's opinion.

✦ Don't sell.

✦ Don't build canvassing lists to target sell from.

✦ Don't gather information to which you have no right.

While it is illegal in most countries to use research as a cover for industrial espionage or for prying into individual lives, there is nothing to stop you from contacting people who have shown a strong interest in your product later. However, the sole reason for speaking to them in the first place ought to be to gather information.

A Task for a Professional?

In the old days, when most shops were owned by families, it was easy enough to ask customers what they wanted across the counter. Now that everything needs to be done on a much larger scale, it is easy to forget that the same down-to-earth principles apply. As Table 2-1 makes plain, you don't necessarily need to know everything about market research to do a perfectly sensible job.

Table 2-1 The Pros and Cons of Doing It Yourself		
Aspect	**Professionals**	**In-House**
Cost	Fees and hourly rates usually restrict use to established companies.	Costs theoretically negligible but it takes staff away from other work.
Experience	Sensitive areas (sexual and political preferences, and so on) need sophisticated approaches by experienced researchers.	If you know your business, you should be able to phrase the questions and assess the answers.
Area of inquiry	Contractors need careful briefing in advance.	This is your forte.
Objectivity	It is easier for outsiders to be dispassionate.	There may be problems assessing marginal responses.

Young firms often go about research like this:

1. It costs nothing to ask a research company about a potential project. Unless they have studied statistical theory and worked as researchers, start-up firms approach a couple of likely research firms and explain what they want to achieve; ask how the research outfit would go about it; the costs; how they would interpret results, and how long the exercise would take.

2. Where the budget is limited, they often decide to conduct the interviews themselves. After all, they know their product. But they retain the professionals to specify the sample, frame the questions, and interpret the results.

3. If they can't afford professional help, they conduct the entire survey themselves. Many make a pretty good job of it.

There is no justification for fooling yourself into thinking that research is a luxury. If you think you can't afford to find out whether your project is likely to be profitable, you can't afford to develop it. Remember this true story. Not that long ago the operator at Capetown's fire department got a late-night call from a woman in a phone booth.

"Send an engine!" she shouted.

"Yes madam," replied the operator, "tell me your address."

"Never mind my address," shrieked the woman adding, "just send the fire engine!" as she slammed down the phone.

Try as she might the operator couldn't raise an answer from the phone booth. A week later one of the firemen cycling to work by an unusual route passed the ruins of a house in the Tamboers Kloof district razed to the ground.

If you don't provide all the pertinent information, your product is doomed to fail.

Framing the Questionnaire

How you phrase a question is crucial. For example, if a child you are on vacation with asks for a vanilla ice cream and the ice cream stand only has strawberry left by the time you get to the head of the line, do you return-empty-handed, or do you say, "Will pink vanilla do?"

What Might You Charge?

How much will users pay for your product? Ask them openly and they'll try and give you the lowest possible figure that won't raise a laugh. The way costs are usually handled is to give respondents a choice of standard software pricing bands, as demonstrated in Figure 2-2.

Less than $49.99	☐
$50.00 – $99.99	☐
$100.00 – $299.99	☐

Figure 2-2: Portion of questionnaire devoted to pricing.

It is advisable not to make the ranges too broad. You can arrive at a likely figure by averaging the answers. Alternatively, you can choose the most realistic price, bearing in mind your costs and their less optimistic expectations. Either method gives your people some ammunition to use if and when prospective purchasers question your prices.

Sales Potential

Trying to assess forthcoming sales by asking users if they'd buy the product based on a few articulate sentences is just asking for trouble. What is really being asked is, "Does what I've just said make any sense to you?" To begin to assess whether prospects are likely to be seriously interested in the software you are proposing, you will almost certainly need to ask a whole series of questions that make it equally easy for respondents to welcome the program, reject it, or sit on the fence.

Asking, "Would you buy the product as described?" might make the research company feel that they have done something to answer their client's question, but as previously mentioned, there can be a vast difference between what people say and what they do. It might be smarter to ask one of the following:

✦ "How much better is what has just been described than what is available at present?"

✦ "What additional benefits would be needed to interest you in purchasing a program of this kind?"

✦ "How much money would a program like this have to save your company in its first 18 months for you to strongly advocate its purchase?"

Competition

Going all the way through to production only to discover that there is serious competition is like being beaten to the South Pole. Why not ask the market researcher group about potential competition? What you really want to find out about is competition of which you are not currently aware or do not perceive to be competition (but maybe the customers do). To find out what may be lurking out there, cast your net wide by asking: Are you aware of any similar products? If there is a clear known leader, add "other than X?" This way they don't tell you what you know already.

Office Information

Information about the company that has commissioned the survey is usually better not revealed or declared in the preliminaries of a questionnaire where details of respondent can also be noted. Of course, it is easier to withhold the name of the commissioning corporation when you are working through a professional market research firm.

Sticky Questions

Questions that touch on politics, beliefs, or personal matters enter questionnaires from time to time. It's always safer to sidestep them if you can. If, however, they are essential to the inquiry, debate ways and means first. Place such questions towards the end of any questionnaire.

Types of Questions

The golden rule when framing questions is to make them simple. If you are conducting interviews by any intrusive medium such as the telephone, keep the number of questions down. Seven seems to be about the maximum tolerable to unsolicited callers. Fewer questions leave respondents wondering whether your inquiry is serious. More questions become tiresome.

If it is possible to interpret any question in an ambiguous way, someone will. People generally take each question at face value. Ask yourself what each question means literally. Avoid all potentially confusing meanings. Also avoid words that invariably trigger predictably unwanted reactions. If you color a question in any way, you will slant the answers and defeat the entire purpose of the survey. Questions should be phrased without giving any hint to your own preferences. This doesn't mean to say they cannot be lively.

It is essential to ask everyone the same question, not variations of the same question. "What features do you want?" is not the same as "What features do you expect?" There are five classes of questions:

✦ Open

✦ Direct

✦ Comparative

✦ Non-Comparative

✦ Likert

Note   The Likert scale is used to measure subjective issues such as attitudes, perceptions, and values. It uses a scale of statements that respondents may choose from.

Open Questions

Open questions allow the respondent to answer whatever they want (for example, "What do you like best about accounting software?"). Open questions are invaluable when the interrogator is trawling for ideas (for example, "Which features do you most frequently use?"). They are less successful when you want to find out which new features end users would like. Respondents are often at a loss to come up with sensible suggestions (even by their own standards). This is understandable, as people are asked about matters to which they have given little or no previous thought.

Direct Questions

Direct questions force respondents to choose a predetermined answer (for example, "Have you vacationed abroad in the last 12 months?"). This is useful when there are few practicable responses. There can be two or more options. Direct questions can also elicit answers to combinations of ideas, some of which may be probed further. Is blue a good color for a series of legal programs? If yes, which blue is best?

Comparative Questions

These are more useful in software research. They ask respondents to make an explicit comparison. Instead of asking, "What do you expect to pay," the researcher might offer the respondent a choice of pricing ranges.

It is advisable to make the ranges narrow enough for answers to be useful regardless of whether respondents pitch their replies towards the top or the bottom of the bracket. In other areas, the respondent might be asked to select one level from a scale, as shown in Figure 2-3.

Figure 2-3: Example of comparative question.

How Do You Rate Your New ABC PC with the XYZ 123?		
5	Vastly Better	☐
4	Better	☐
3	Similar	☐
2	Worse	☐
1	Vastly Worse	☐

Non-Comparative Questions

These simply ask the respondent to evaluate the subject according to a scale. These are very popular in political circles when people want to know how opinions are shifting between surveys. Used as isolated responses they are sometimes more useful as public relations ammunition than throwing any definitive light on a product's potential success. Figure 2-4 gives an example.

How Do You Rate Your New ABC PC?		
5	The Best	☐
4	Very Good	☐
3	Average	☐
2	Not Good	☐
1	The Worst	☐

Figure 2-4: A non-comparative question example.

The Likert Scale

More people are familiar with this scale than its name. The Likert scale is similar to the comparative scale, but responses are measured in degrees of agreement with a brief statement, as demonstrated in the examples shown in Figure 2-5.

I would like my next keyboard to be engineered to reduce miskeying.
   (5) Strongly agree   (4) Agree   (3) Neither agree nor disagree   (2) Disagree   (1) Strongly disagree

I would prefer a laptop screen that can display two A4-size pages.
   (5) Strongly agree   (4) Agree   (3) Neither agree nor disagree   (2) Disagree   (1) Strongly disagree

I would like a program that automatically returns me to where I last closed down.
   (5) Strongly agree   (4) Agree   (3) Neither agree nor disagree   (2) Disagree   (1) Strongly disagree

Figure 2-5: Questions applying the Likert scale.

Occasionally there are three or seven response options but five is the classic number. The Likert scale is normally introduced to assess the strength of reactions to ideas that are difficult to quantify, particularly intangibles such as attitudes, personal taste knowledge, perceptions, and values in general terms. Because of this, the Likert scale is widely used in qualitative research.

Pre-Testing the Questionnaire

It is fairly common for professionals to discover the questions they should have asked as responses begin to come in. Most times there is no immediate budget to take a second bite at the cherry. However, if you are conducting your own survey, you may be able to have a second go. This being said, there is no substitute for getting your questionnaire right the first time.

After you have agreed what questions you think you want to ask, consider very carefully what you are going to do with the answers. The exercise often reveals some questions as being surprisingly unimportant while others need a slight surgical rephrasing. You may also find some additional queries essential if you are to assemble data on which you can persuade others to act. It is a very sensible idea to pilot the questionnaire on a test sample before you send it out en-masse. This will alert you to omissions and questions respondents have trouble answering because of the way they were phrased. A sample of about 20 from the list is usually enough. If you are approaching respondents by mail it makes sense to ask for their telephone number so you can follow up on their answers.

If you don't get clear answers in the sample test, rephrase the question and try again until you elicit responses that produce a clear "Yes" or "No," but remember, there is a limit to probing. There are always respondents who have no views on anything. Results from the pilot should not be included in the overall results if the questionnaire is altered.

Methods of Contact

Have you ever been confronted by a market researcher who asks, "Do you mind if I have a few moments of your time?" and then produces a questionnaire that runs on for pages? It is not unknown for market research companies to combine questionnaires to keep down their costs. However, an experienced researcher may not ask his questions in strict, numerical order. He (or she) picks out the questions most likely to open up a general conversation and lets the respondent run with it from there. Some are so good at this they can get three quarters of their questions answered without further probing. When they do ask questions, the form follows the questionnaire verbatim but the tone is lightly conversational. If the response is ambiguous, they know when it is better to accept the ambiguity but usually they ask for clarification. It's an ideal way to draw out the facts.

Before you get to this stage, you should check that the respondent falls within your sample target. You will need to confirm the following:

- ✦ Their name and e-mail address if you don't already have it
- ✦ The type of operation they are working with (company, educational institution, profession, and so on)
- ✦ Their function within that working group

Very often you will want to volunteer your own and your company's name to foster an even-handed exchange. This can lead into a natural explanation of what your company happens to be doing. You may need to prime your prospect by describing your new software. Remember, anything new is news. For example, you might ask, "If there was a software program that did the following. . . would you be interested?" You need to be able to outline the program's function in just a couple of sentences.

You can explain more as necessary. Give a for instance if the prospect doesn't appear to understand. Then ask the following:

1. Would you or your company need such a product?
2. Which of these features would you expect to be most useful to you?
3. Are you aware of any similar products?
4. Where would you normally expect to buy such a product?
5. Is there anything else you would like to know?
6. Which of these prices would you expect to see on the ticket?
7. Would you like to be contacted when the product comes out?

Note Professional market research companies make a great play of anonymity of information. However, it is probably in your best interests to ask if you can add the recipient to your contact list for when your product is eventually launched.

The best way to gather the data is the one most appropriate to the questions and personnel. You can visit respondents, canvass them outside retail outlets, telephone them, mail them, or e-mail them via your Web site.

Personal Interviews

This is the most expensive form of survey. Direct meetings take time to organize and conduct. However, they do enable you to ask questions in considerable detail and probe qualitative issues. Personal interviews are best suited to customized programs where the deal is substantial and a number of people on the same site are involved in the buying decision.

Street Surveys

You'd be surprised how many people are prepared to give up a few moments and end up spending five or 10 minutes discussing your project. Many of us secretly take it as a great compliment when someone is interested in our opinions. Even so, keep the questionnaire short. If you decide to conduct your survey at a trade show, avoid the first day or last day when things are hectic, or times when everybody just wants to sidle off. A quiet intermediary day is best; often you'll find people in food and beverage areas taking a break. Asking for a few moments of their time is usually acceptable. But be aware, every competitor in the place will know what you are doing.

In practice you'll have to conduct the bulk of these interviews via telephone. Even so, do try and conduct some interviews face-to-face so you can see the recipients' body language and appreciate how your survey is being received.

Telephoning

Telephoning is the most immediate method, but you may find that many people are too busy to speak to you at length. It is often better to whet their appetite by explaining how this new product might be useful or by mentioning some incentive. Once motivated people will give you more time; but you can only count on this if your questionnaire is interesting.

E-mail and WWWing

These are the most commonly used means, particularly in combination with the telephone. To get a statistically valid sample you will almost certainly need to conduct at least 250 interviews. Many software houses can cut down the time that formal interviews take by introducing themselves by telephone and following up via e-mail or the Web. The great advantage of conducting the survey electronically is that it is faster and cheaper. All the data can be posted directly into a database for immediate analysis. This method is particularly recommended if your target market is also online.

When a questionnaire has to be long, you'll almost certainly have to include some incentive to encourage respondents to wade through it, so keep it short and sweet. You also need to personalize the cover letter that explains what the firm is doing and why. If personal questions have to be asked, guarantee anonymity and organize the questionnaire so they can complete it without having to identify themselves.

Contacting prospects via their e-mail address isn't the same as spamming them. It is advisable to include a preliminary message explaining that you are thinking of producing a new product that does such and such, and as someone who is involved with similar tasks, you'd appreciate their views. Ask them if they would mind if you sent them a short questionnaire.

Mailing

Unsolicited mail does not normally get a good response unless the introduction is skilfully written and the software topic is of genuine interest. If the survey follows a positive response to a telephone inquiry and you include a postage-paid reply envelope, the number of responses is improved and you can ask reasonably detailed questions.

Who to Contact

Whichever sampling method you choose, you will need a list of prospective respondents. Gathering around 500 names (you'll need extras because a proportion won't reply) takes about a week of very hard work. However, it's time well spent, as these could be potential clients.

If you aren't able to conduct the interviews yourself, find one or two bright personalities with a pleasing telephone manner to garner names and addresses (someone who isn't working that week perhaps or possibly a parent, partner, grown child, or friend, anyone who will make a credible ambassador).

Store the data in a database or spreadsheet from the start; otherwise you'll end up having to retype it. The place to start compiling your list is from your own records of business associates and leads your sales team has built up over the years. Further company names and telephone numbers may be garnered from telephone and trade directories. Once you have listed these, you will have to contact each company to solicit the name of the individual you want. Sending questionnaires out of the blue to unnamed chief technical officers or to whom it may concern just multiplies its chance of hitting the trashcan, and you will never know who to contact when your program is launched.

Companies are understandably wary of giving out employee e-mail addresses to strangers. If you want e-mail addresses, you will just have to comb the Internet.

How to Interpret the Results

"A lot of people use research as a drunk uses a lamppost: for support rather than illumination."

—David Ogilvy, founder Ogilvy & Mather, Advertising Agency

Research isn't designed to supply categorical, black and white answers. It is designed to establish the odds. The most positive response you can get is a strong likelihood that you *may be* on to a winner. The most negative response you will get is likely to be no appearance of any wide interest. Whatever you want the result of the survey to be, the biggest favor you can do yourself is to accept the results for precisely what they are. Interpreting an overall no as a maybe or a weak yes as a go isn't going to do you, your firm, or your family any favors.

Before you come to any decision, consider the responses you received to individual questions.

What Features Would You Like It to Have?

The quality of responses to an open-ended question like this is likely to be extremely scattered. At one end of the spectrum, you are likely to get off-the-cuff replies that are best ignored. At the other, you may get a few inspired ideas that give your whole project a boost. The bulk of the replies, however, are likely to be mundane. The most useful things to note are the incidence of popular mentions and those features that are largely ignored.

Non-Responses

If a respondent is reluctant to reply or will only respond in a form you can't understand, you can't play God and decide what they mean. You just have to strike that interview even though this increases the number of questionnaires you have to conduct.

Misleading Answers

The biggest query over any questionnaire is whether respondents are telling the truth. However scrupulously you conduct your survey, some people will give you the answers they think you want to hear, or supply an answer that conceals more than it reveals. This happened spectacularly in the 1993 U.K. General Election. The Labour Party had an 8 percent lead according to all the polls. When the results came in John Major (Margaret Thatcher's successor) won by 2 percent. How come? Basically, it was uncool to admit supporting Conservatives at the time. When questioned by the market researchers a large number of respondents fibbed.

What do you feel is a fair price? If you phrase a question like this, you will inevitably get less reliable answers than you seek. (Why should respondents make a rod for their own back and pay more?) If the prices suggested vary disconcertingly, consider analyzing them by type of company, position of respondent, geographical area, or whatever else you think might account for such a marked disparity. An obvious market division will often appear. Other times, you may arrive at a more useful figure (as already suggested) by averaging respondents' answers.

A post mortem may suggest that they have given you a realistic price within their authorized signing limit. Thus, the price suggested by a personal assistant might be understandably lower than a price suggested by corporation chiefs. Conversely, potential users may rate a program's concept more highly than their chief financial officer. In the end, you may have to go for a compromise between your historical costs and your prospects' expectations. Provided you have sound reasons for your price, you should be able to explain it satisfactorily to anyone.

Where Would You Expect to Find Such a Product?

Most times the answers are the ones you expect. Occasionally, they come as quite a surprise. Either way, the answers help you make distribution decisions on an informed basis.

Do You Know of Any Similar Products?

Although you are probably aware of any obvious competition before you start formal research, respondents will often tell you about obscure products that you never knew existed, products under development, and programs you may never have considered as direct competition. Don't write these off because they offer fewer features. Interviewees may be quite content with a simpler program. They may prefer a program that sells at a fraction of your anticipated price or one that works in a way they have grown used to. Investigate them all. Any one of them could turn out to be your worst enemy.

If you come across direct competition, especially from large or established branded opponents, think very seriously about aborting. Unless you have a hidden agenda, are privately funded with large pockets, are privy to inside information, or know that their program has some monumental flaw, my advice is to down tools, take stock, reflect, and do nothing. The sky is full of other products yet to be invented.

How Many Units Are You Likely to Sell?

The answer to this is the big one. Treat scaled up numbers with caution. What perhaps is most useful is the feel of the overall response. Are there, for instance, enough potential customers who are really keen on the product? Or do you sense that you are going to be in for heavy selling? Is the program a marginal one? Or will it in some significant way change their lives? Don't place too much faith in your personal powers to overcome the odds. When you are up against a host of other people, force of personality can only carry you so far. On the other hand, sheer guts and persistence have been known to turn a marginally difficult sales situation into a viable one, particularly when it is associated with an intelligent marketing strategy.

Reasons for a poor response to this question may by as obvious as someone has got there before you; or it may be subtle. Your idea may be ahead of its time and buyers feel unable to cope. If they think there will be a lot of new things to grasp they will almost certainly stick with what they already know and have. Whatever the explanation for the negatives, you need a second opinion. Talk the situation through with your friends or colleagues. Listen particularly to those who have both IT experience and sound judgment. If you haven't any such friends, consult a market research company. Offer to buy an hour of their time to help you interpret the facts. Nothing would be worse than making the wrong decision (whether to persevere or to stop) with all the information in your hand.

If the appeal verdict is another thumbs down, take a deep breath, and explain to your backers what has come up that is making your project unviable. And don't forget to tell those closest to you.

You will know almost immediately if shutting down the project is the right thing to do. If it is, you will regret deeply having to abandon all hope, but you will surprisingly feel better. You are being responsible. You are doing the mature thing. You are acting in the best interests of the entire project team. However disappointed they also feel, they will respect you for not going blithely on and gambling with their futures. Take some comfort from the thought that it's the soldier who doesn't get into a losing fight that survives. Sooner or later, you will likely have another, better idea that will succeed. And it is the one you win that really counts.

In the interim, there may be consolations. You'll know better how to go about developing software. You know who you would want to invite back on your team. You may even be able to sell components of your closed-down project.

Moving Respondents Nearer a Sale

Most market surveys go to some pains to avoid disclosing who is asking the questions, both to discourage competitors from getting wind of what a rival is up to, and to deter respondents from offering prejudiced replies (for or against a well known brand).

Software research, by contrast, is more up front. It tends to use the interview as a gentle opportunity to introduce the sponsor; but an introduction is where it stops. A solid survey merely gathers information. Even so, every well-chosen respondent is a possible customer in the future. Yet at the time they are being questioned, they know the questioner isn't in a position to sell, just as you know there is no point in anyone at your end being pushy.

Putting respondents at ease, as you will discover quite quickly, gets the most valid answers. By all means, be enthusiastic about the product, explain its promise lucidly, and listen carefully to everyone's responses. Reiterate their points and explain that you will definitely pass along their feedback. Once interviewees find themselves on the ground floor of a project, they are often keen to see the product when it comes out. Some even volunteer to be beta testers. When this happens, you are on your way to selling your product.

To Sum Up

Developing a program without undertaking any market research is like launching a submarine without a periscope. The independent facts you establish through market research provide the direction and substance to your business case. Drawing up a questionnaire and putting it to a valid number of respondents is more a matter of common sense and sweat than money and genius. Finding out what your chances are before you risk losing serious money is probably the most useful thing you can do to ensure that your effort is not wasted.

Sample Questionnaire

Following is a sample questionnaire. It is printed on two sides of a card, which respondents send back in the stamped addressed envelope provided. The front (see Figure 2-6a) introduces the product by its working title, states who is developing it, and with the aid of a picture enables respondents to visualize the product in a 100-word description. It outlines how the product might be used and invites recipients to complete the questionnaire on the back (shown in Figure 2-6b).

The Acme Wheel Project

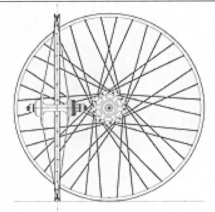

We have devised a revolutionary idea that will make transport easier and more efficient. It is called a wheel and is tentatively round. When they are attached to all four corners of a flat surface, wheels can form a platform for moving goods. These are expected to supersede the sledge, particularly in summer.

Wheeled platforms will enable animals to pull large loads over rougher surfaces. Not only is it more beneficial for us, but it will extend the working life of your animals.

In time, we anticipate that machines may be strapped to the wheeled platforms to propel these vehicles. Wheeled vehicles could eventually become so cheap that everyone will own one. You'd be able to visit friends, relatives and business contacts when you want, and not have to walk or ride everywhere or be dependent on others to carry you.

We predict you'll be able to go from Washington D.C. to New York in under a day. The wheel has numerous other possibilities.

If you could take the time to finish off the questionnaire overleaf and post it back to us in the stamped addressed envelope provided, it will help us work out what shape the wheel should take.

Yours faithfully,

Edward Spoke, Chairman, The Acme Wheel Company Inc.

Figure 2-6a: Front of the card.

Please read the information overleaf before you complete this questionnaire

The Acme Wheel Project

All information is strictly confidential.

1 Does the wheel appeal? ❑ Yes ❑ No

2 Would you buy this product? ❑ Yes ❑ Maybe ❑ No

3 What would you do with a set of wheels? (E.g., roller skates)

_____

_____

_____

4 Can you name a competitive product? (Ignore the hoop)

5 What price should it sell for? ❑ Less than $50
  ❑ $50–$00
  ❑ $00–299
  ❑ More than $300

6 Where would you expect to buy this product?
  ❑ The Blacksmith ❑ The Village Store ❑ The Post Office

Please inform me when the wheel is available. ❑ Yes

Name _____

E–mail address_____

Type of Company_____

Position _____

Respondent #: 123

Figure 2-6b: Back of the card.

The questionnaire is short, easily laid out, and numbered for checking.

Remember, programming is still at the stage of replicating by electronic means tasks that were until recently routinely accomplished with pencil and paper. A new software program is still news.

✦   ✦   ✦

Plan for Success

The last definitive survey of software developments in the United States (The Standish Group Report 1995) found the following:

+ Less than one in six projects succeeded.

+ Over 30 percent of all projects were cancelled prior to completion.

+ Over 50 percent went over budget (on average 189 percent over).

+ Less than 17 percent of projects were completed on time and on budget.

+ Among large firms, the success rate is even lower—just 9 in 100.

Never think you are too small to need to behave in a professional way, not until you are big enough to lose money.

If you are going to win where thousands of other program developers have fallen, you have got to do something they didn't, and we are not talking about raising more money. The best and richest resource you have is harnessed between your ears.

No good builder would dream of setting to work on anything but the simplest garden shed, until everything had been planned down to the last door knob. Architects don't say planning is okay for skyscrapers but not for a row of houses. The difference is in the scale—the laws of physics and Chapter Eleven apply identically to both projects.

So never consider yourself too small to plan. Small jobs in software writing are generally accepted as either tasks that take a couple of people less than a week or routines you are repeating. Anything more ambitious needs a plan.

If you want your project to succeed, you must conceive the word *before* you make it flesh. The plan should define, in straightforward language, what the program will do, how the user will operate it, and what benefits there are. The plan should also list the time writing is likely to take and the resources that will be necessary to see the task through. While most good plans are simple, they aren't necessarily short.

Shell had been successfully selling engine oil to garages worldwide for over 50 years when the company trainers decided that they needed to conduct a Human Resource Analysis. Their findings, much to everyone's surprise, grew to 38 pages of one-liners. From this they structured a new sales training program.

Not only were the new trainees more successful, but when salesmen fell short Shell was able to identify the specific part of the curriculum the salesman failed to apply. In one instance, they were able to trace a course member's omission to the exact point where the trainer was called out of the classroom to answer a call from his superior and resumed his lecture at a slightly different juncture.

A good plan is sufficiently comprehensive to enable you to spot and solve problems in advance. The planning process produces the blueprint on which every contributor is agreed. It simply and clearly states all of the following:

+ What the product is
+ Why people want it
+ What it will do
+ How it will work
+ How long it will take to develop
+ What resources are required

Planning reduces the scope for hit or miss. Instead of creating stresses through the As not knowing what the Bs are doing, planning enables you to build up sound working relationships with those who are experts in fields other than yourself.

 Note   If for any reason you are unable to draft a plan yourself, find someone else who can.

Planning has big advantages. For a start, you are not making mistakes with real money. You are just making them with paper.

Improving Your Odds

With such staggering odds against you, what can you do to improve them? Learn from other people's experience rather than your own, and learn those lessons in advance.

Planning Takes Time Yet Saves Time

If you start writing as soon as you have an idea, the project will take longer because the only way to forge ahead is by trial and error. People who have tried to develop software both ways will tell you that unplanned projects end up taking longer, cost more and, most damning of all, they have a significantly greater incidence of failure. On the other hand, if you spend too much time planning in endless detail and not enough doing, you may miss your window of opportunity altogether. So planning is a trade off; you just have to keep a sense of proportion.

Planning enables you to think in a focussed way about your project, discuss aspects of it with people whose opinions you value, and to consider alternatives before you dive in.

Generally speaking, the answers tend to come out of the problem. Snags that may otherwise never come to light until you are up to your armpits in development have a way of surfacing when the water is only up to your ankles. Issues that sometimes drown projects once programmers get stuck can often be side stepped altogether with a well-planned route.

Some people make a big deal about planning inhibiting their freedom and prefer a Russian roulette method of creativity. The truth is, nothing inhibits freedom more than failure. What planning does impose is a certain self-discipline, not just for you, but for everyone you are going to involve in your project and invite to back you with money. The success of all good software designs hinges not on what everyone knows can be done, but on how well the designer handles things within their limitations; in other words, by making better use of the rules, as opposed to breaking them.

Think Backwards

The aim of planning is to work out what is required to make a product. Once the project is completed, hindsight will tell you all the answers to the key questions you should have asked at the start. But how do you get a handle on all these important questions *before* you begin?

A great trick here is to use *pre-operative hindsight*. Mock up the completed project in your mind, view it dispassionately, and then list the issues that will eventually arise. You probably have a good idea of the principal questions already, but here's a starter list:

1. What will the program do?
2. What are its benefits?
3. What hard evidence is there of a need for this program?

4. Is there any competition?

5. If competition exists, why will people want this product?

6. Who are the users and who are the buyers?

7. How many users and buyers are there?

8. How much will buyers pay?

9. How many potential users may be converted?

10. What new things will users need to be taught?

11. Do you have a complete synopsis of the program structure?

12. Is there a frame-by-frame storyboard of screen usage?

13. Is there a storyboard for startup and closedown?

14. What programming problems are foreseen?

15. How do you know you can solve them?

16. Which components can you buy in?

17. How many programmers are required?

18. What particular skills must the programmers have?

19. For how long will you need the programmers?

20. Is this program feasible?

21. What is the deadline for the launch?

22. What are the risks?

23. Do you have the development money?

24. Is this program potentially profitable?

25. In a sentence, what's your proposition to buyers?

You won't have answers to all these questions at the outset. However, you should gradually be able to fill them in as you obtain market soundings and your thinking develops. The aim of planning is to confront everything that is required to make your dream come true.

Consulting Potential Users

One of the biggest differences between people who succeed and people who flounder is that those who succeed are constantly questioning and examining. They are continually polling others for advice, and while they don't always take it, they do keep the array of views in mind and keep a running scorecard.

Early programmers, by contrast, were often self-sufficient loners who, in the recesses of their parents' garage, were reinventing the world on a screen. Even today, end users often find it hard to avoid a feeling that computer programs are written for those who write them rather than those who are intended to use them. We have all been frustrated by at least some of the following:

✦ Search lists that don't return you to base

✦ Word processors that have no concept of leading or settings

✦ Graphic programs that produce weird textures but not wood grains, concrete, knits, or glass

✦ Financial programs that cannot multiply

✦ Help systems that don't employ the conventional terms and offer little real help

Developers usually get themselves into such positions because they never consult the people whom the program is supposed to assist before they frame their specifications. The classic defense to such complaints is a) "There's nothing wrong with my program," b) "I didn't know anybody to ask," or c) "I didn't want my idea to be swiped." These really boil down to the fact that the developers didn't know or bother to learn about their market. If you don't know any potential users or buyers, it is all the more essential that you find some.

Use your instinct. Take some users into your confidence a little or find a way of questioning them obliquely. This may call for a little ingenuity. Most of the time people will be delighted to help you.

If you are developing a program for supermarket checkouts, work with their cashiers for a day. Ask them to tell you their greatest problems and what innovation could help them most. Then repeat the process with the store manager and head office. People empathize with products all the more when they have made a contribution. Successful software is always a team effort.

Divining the Sales Cycle

Working out how long your product will take to sell is essential, even in the early stages. Financial realities tell you that there is no point producing the product only to find out that it takes 12 months to make your first sale. You might go bust waiting—many do. Remember your budget does not stop when development finishes the first version.

Calculating the sales cycle for upgrades and replacement software is obviously easier than doing so for new software, as you have existing data. For new products one technique is to find comparable products and draw parallels. Another is to poll your sales and marketing teams. Try and make the process as accountable as possible.

Look at similar products, and use from/to criteria to try and nail down your options. Beware of inexperienced staff that give you the answer they suspect you would like to hear.

Creating the Plan

All artists begin with preliminary sketches. You too need to begin with an outline plan. A good way to tackle this is to break the project down into four bite-size pieces.

1. **The reason for being**—Why the product should exist.

2. **The business rationale**—Who wants it? What do they want it to do? How many will buy it? How much will they pay? How long will the product last? What side benefits, in terms of deliverables and so on, are there?

3. **The mechanics**—The architecture and main components. How will they link? What snags are foreseen? How to stop and start the program.

4. **The presentation**—The way that screens will work. The face of the product. Its name, packaging, and support material.

You can then begin to flesh out your skeleton:

✦ **The reason for being**

- What the market is looking for and why
- What the product offers
- The product's development title
- Why there isn't any direct competition

✦ **The business rationale**

- The group(s) at whom the product is aimed
- What they are prepared to pay
- How it surpasses alternative products
- The ceiling of development costs
- How this breaks down into overheads, salaries, bought-ins, and third-party workers' time
- The price range allotted for these
- The number of units that have to be shipped (in the first six months or a year)
- How they will be distributed

- How they will be promoted
- Cost of production broken down by overheads, materials, labor, and so on

✦ **The mechanics**

- What the program does and how it does it
- The operating system(s) the program will work on
- Minimum hardware requirements
- Environmental constraints

✦ **The presentation**

- The product name, technical description, and logo
- The tag line
- Product attributes the program must have
- What the program has to be seen to do to deliver these attributes
- The User Interface, how it looks and how it responds
- Advanced Programming Interface (API), if appropriate
- The startup sequence
- How the screens will perform
- How the session will close
- The deliverables—the product labels, packaging, manuals, Help system, discs, downloads, and so on

It should come as no shock to you that most of these questions will have already been supplied by your initial market research. The main task of planning is to bring together everything that the team believes from experience needs to be done to create a sellable product. In the process of fleshing out your plan you will find yourself sorting out priorities and finding ways around pitfalls.

So that everyone on the team knows what they have to do, you should draft your plan in a *development plan*. A development plan is not the same thing as a list of software requirements. The spec is about what; the development plan begins to focus on the how.

- ✦ How to go about it
- ✦ How long it will take
- ✦ How much it will cost

With a coherent development plan everyone should begin to get an overall picture of the project in a single comprehensive document.

Note If you need to exclude sensitive areas such as financial details from some copies of the development plan, just remove them.

Let's now take a closer look, from your customer's point of view.

Know the Difference between Ideal and Perfect

Inevitably, when you begin to assemble a plan, you suddenly find yourself with an impossible list of absolutely essential attributes. So bear in mind that while a product can never be too good for its purpose, it can be too good for its market.

Software code is imperfect until the last string is fitted perfectly in place. Then it suddenly starts working as planned. As such, programming calls for a great degree of patience from managers, and programmers who want to see their project completed are wise not to defend themselves but to explain what they are doing.

When programmers finish compiling their code early, they will (given the opportunity) almost certainly use the time left to polish their writing and clear up loose ends. It's essential to have a coherent development plan in place so everyone is on the same timeline and not questioning when the project is actually finished. Programs such as Word, WordPerfect, and Corel have been fantastically successful because they provide quality functionality within limits.

You should acquire this profound marketing insight in advance. No program is ever going to be 360 degrees perfect. And like every product from lifeboats to lip salve, it will evolve throughout its commercial life cycle. The time to draw a line under the development plan is not when it's perfect but as soon as the perceived value of the program's benefits outweighs the anticipated retail price.

So, aim high, but don't trip over the balcony. You can always introduce fixes later. The point at which you plan to sign off on the project should be determined by whether the program will be easy to update. Most of the software programs used on office PCs are revised periodically by programmers trying to iron out their technical wrinkles. This is par for the course.

Caution Firmware, which is embedded for good into chips, is non-upgradeable. If you are producing upgradeable software you can plan improvements gradually, but if you are producing a program that is necessarily fixed for the life of the product (five to 10 years), your program has got to be viable for the life of its host and right from the start.

The Unified Development Plan

Over the years, various schools of developers have standardized their approaches to planning. While many of these have very real strengths, there is a good deal of technical exclusivity that isn't always an advantage to anyone else. Generally speaking, each method helps the project for which it was originally designed. Many developers cherry pick their approaches, a bit of this, a bit of that, and a bit of their own. With the idea being that form follows function, the longer developers contemplate their project, the more likely it is that the most appropriate format will surface.

For large, sophisticated projects, there are a number of complex, tiered, established procedures (for example, Prince2). Unfortunately, they don't scale down well as they tend to be managerially top-heavy and abstruse. So it isn't surprising that project management sometimes mushrooms into a function that threatens to dwarf the program development itself. Small and medium-sized projects need an approach that doesn't take up too much time yet addresses all key issues. This is where a template called the Unified Development Plan (UDP) comes in handy.

The UDP is designed to be short, unambiguous, and understandable, a practical document into which marketing, research, technical specs, design, and financial inputs are all streamed. It is essentially a functional document that brings together managers, technicians, and anyone else involved in the project.

A UDP differs from similar documents in as much as everything is contained in a single coherent document much like a corporate manual. Every member of the development committee contributes to it, approves it, and signs up to support it. The initial advantage of a UDP is that every participant learns to appreciate his colleague's contributions. And because it's written in plain English, arguments have to stand up for themselves. There is no hiding behind gobbledygook.

Any member's partner should be able to spot a flaw and any financier of the project should immediately be able to appreciate the plan's real strengths. Group heads should be able to easily explain the plan to their team so programmers grasp the importance of their work to the end users.

Once things flow on functional lines, there is less need for paper checks and more time and resources to get on with the job. However, the UDP is not a static instrument. It is more like a policy log that develops with time. Each of its sections is updated and explained as modifications are agreed. One excuse you should never hear is, "X had no idea what was going on."

The sharing process is amazingly simple if you take the following steps:

1. Take the initial marketing specification and verify it.
2. Identify the main components.
3. Calculate the gamut of resources required.
4. Draft, circulate, and redraft the document until there is general agreement.
5. Keep it up-to-date.

Assume the Widest Readership

You never know who will need to read your Unified Development Plan—a subcontractor who is being considered for his specialist skills; a financier wanting to fund you; a potential client or government agency checking your specs, or the board reviewing the projects. As well as having a grasp of broader issues, there are times when they need to be able to appreciate why certain trivial things are important. Remember, the more clearly you tell it, the more surely you'll sell it.

Working in Sit-down Groups

If you have ever had the privilege of watching a good chairman in action, you know they are a joy to watch. They understand the subject sublimely, and they make everyone at the meeting feel that their presence is welcome. They steer the discussion without any noticeable leverage and bring in relevant people who might have not piped up and courteously move the subject forward when the meeting is stuck in a rut. The agenda is well planned and can be followed to the letter, and the meeting ends at the planned time with everyone knowing what they have to do and feeling confident that their time has been well spent.

How do these people do it? They are obviously consummate professionals and they have probably had a lot of practice, but the most important thing is that they have a realistic idea of how to get where they are going. They try to coordinate the team so the whole is greater than the sum of its parts.

Gathering Opinions/Feedback by Committee

Don't think if you are small, you are unimportant and therefore you don't need to behave in formal ways. The important thing about formality is that it is businesslike. So take your cue from the successful and take yourself seriously.

A good committee will normally take a show of hands at every point on the agenda and then publish the meeting's decisions in subsequent minutes. However, what seemed a good idea on a spontaneous show of hands sometimes makes no sense later on, especially when participants from differing disciplines such as marketing and programming strive for fusion.

To avoid conflicts later when decisions are more carefully examined, I suggest a minor innovation. At the end of each team meeting, the chairman or minute taker reads out the collective decisions. Any potential conflict between hand-raisers and non-hand-raisers can then be aired and sorted out then and there. This reprise should not be used to rake over old ground, but it can bring to light the real reason a minority didn't raise their hands at some particular point and shed light that helps to clarify a quandary. It may also serve to clarify priorities going forward, where participants need approval or directives, what should be done first, or who needs to liaise with whom.

A Few Tips on Writing Plans

Plans are meant to be used by a variety of people. You can hardly write one plan for programmers and another for the lawyer and another for the people who will lend you money. You have to find a single way of communicating with them all, and that means using a vocabulary that everyone can understand. Research shows that keeping technical wording to a minimum increases the readers' ability to assimilate ideas. This even applies to technicians reading papers on their own specialty. The reason for this is very obvious. The average developer has had 20 or more years' head start using plain English before they begin to acquire technical dialects, like computerspeak.

To carry the largest number of people along with you, use technical phrases only when there is no common equivalent. When you have to use technical jargon, don't overload your sentences or you won't give the reader time to absorb what you are saying; you'll just smother them to a standstill.

Insincerity has a way of showing through. If you don't believe in what you are writing, stop and come straight out with what is really on your mind; you can always phrase it more tactfully on your second draft. Readers are more perceptive than you might think. When something troubles you, work out why and swap the word or phrase for some alternative. Discuss it with family or colleagues and then redraft it.

You are not trying to out-write *War and Peace*. The more succinct your sentences, the more effortlessly your document will be remembered and the less room there will be for ambiguity. The average sentence length is 11 words, and anything over 16 is in danger of becoming too complex. Remember, a well-written document is widely understandable, unambiguous, and inspiring.

How to Get Projects Completed on Time

There are only fives core items that you need to make any project happen. The lack of any one can spell doom.

1. People (programmers, managers, testers)
2. Things (computers, office space, pizzas)
3. Money (enough to make it happen)
4. Time (how long is enough)
5. Process and methodology (how to make it happen)

It all comes down to having the necessary resources and using them wisely. Gone are the days when one computer programmer knew it all. Project managers could do much worse now than invest the greatest part of their working time finding, briefing, and orchestrating a complete band of specialists. The best way to get any project completed on time is to employ only programmers who have current experience in the areas you need. This way, you are not paying for people whose sole strategy is trial and error. They know the tricks and the traps. Code will flow from their fingers because they are in their element. Your prospective product may be leading edge, but if the components that make it work are already tried and tested, its chances of coming out on schedule skyrocket.

 Cross-Reference   Further ways of managing the development process are discussed in Chapter 6.

What do successful program developers do that unsuccessful ones don't? They follow these guidelines:

+ Involve end users from an early stage
+ Assemble a clear specification of the program's requirements
+ Plan thoroughly
+ Cultivate support on the way
+ Respond positively to changes and suggestions
+ Have realistic standards
+ Know how long things will really take
+ Enjoy clear visions and objectives
+ Communicate vertically and horizontally
+ Enjoy competent, well-motivated, hardworking staff
+ Set up regular milestones and reviews
+ Turned experience into sound judgment
+ Don't leave anything to luck

Gathering Apostles

However brilliant your concept, however well your project is planned, your program will never see the light of day unless you bring the right people together. The more ambitious the project the more crucial people will be. Yet even with a modest project, you will need responsible beings to fulfill four basic functions:

+ Technical creativity
+ Marketing
+ Coordination and progress
+ Resource accounting

These form the steering committee, some of whom may wear two hats. Keep the development team lean. Additionally, you may need an end-user representative or market researcher plus anyone who has experience on a similar project. Make sure that every department that should be represented is represented.

When making your selection, remember it is vital that the people get along together. Introduce them in a social setting and see what happens. If they gel, you can look forward to shorter meetings with more agreement, and you will find it surprisingly easy to arrange times for them to meet. Figure 3-1 provides an illustration of how the process should flow.

Write an individual job description for each member and go over it with each. Revise and agree on the details before you hold your first meeting. If the result leaves you with a lean hand of trumps, discard the wrong suits and pick suitable replacements from the pack.

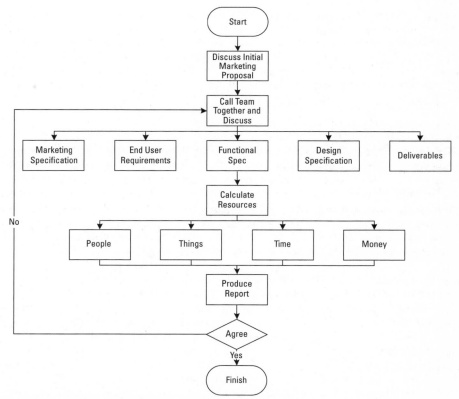

Figure 3-1: Project development team flowchart

If you are the chairman, your job is not to do all the work but to coordinate the rest of the steering committee. Each member should be invited to explain his role to the rest. Thus, the business case for the project should be advanced by the marketing manager. It is his or her job to convince the others of the relevancy and importance of the proposed project. It is everyone else's role to question the marketing manager until the case is sufficiently refined for agreement so the meeting can move on.

The technical representative should give a rundown of the main components of the programmers' work, explaining where the writing is straightforward or may be bought in, and where they anticipate future difficulty. The purpose is not to sow doubt but to dispel any unrealistic expectations.

The person responsible for day-to-day progress should explain how he will be setting up milestones and monitoring progress, what he will do if a key programmer drops off the project, or how they will tackle items they would like to buy in but are precluded from by some conflict of patents.

With project meetings it is vital to keep the momentum going. When everyone else has made their case, the Chairman should sum up and make a statement on behalf of the highest level of management expressing why they believe in the project and giving highlights of the resources they are putting at the committee's disposal. The meeting can then turn toward organizing a development schedule, penciling in from and to dates, and setting up progress meetings with the aim of coming together within a few days to create the product development plan.

Dealing with Killjoys

We've all met the dour pessimist who turns up discontentedly and makes it clear from his countenance that he has better things to do and then delivers some deflationary point just as the rest are getting enthusiastic. The best solution in dealing with killjoys is to win them over. In fact, you should be worried if you run projects where too many people are in continual agreement. It could mean that only one person (not necessarily you) is doing the bulk of the work. When there isn't enough debate, the group isn't stretching itself and introducing fresh concepts, which is exactly what should be happening at this planning stage.

The best thing to do with a killjoy is not to put him down in front of the rest of the group. Far better is to get to know him and discuss the situation privately. Find out his views. Killjoys often have very valuable views but are unduly afraid that no one will take any notice of them. They utter in all embracing terms, "This project will never work!" instead of being specific and saying something along the lines of, "Please explain how this program will integrate with the accountancy system mainframe." If they're jumping to conclusions due to insufficient or incorrect information, set them straight. Then ask them what their views are now. They'll appreciate your attention and may return to the group with a more positive attitude.

Always take the following steps in dealing with someone whose attitude seems to be dragging the rest of the group down:

1. Speak to them privately.

2. Establish that they are working from a correct set of facts.

3. Find out what really concerns them. It may not be the first explanation they give.

4. Address their concerns.

5. Make them feel a wanted and valued member of the project. (It's why they were invited to be a member of the group in the first place.)

Personnel

The number of tasks involved in producing software may seem overwhelming. At one extreme there may be hundreds of programmers working on thousands of crucial steps. At the other extreme, you may find yourself doing everything. When planning a project, consider all the human skills required, even if you are going to perform most of them.

There are two ways to get good specialists: hire them or grow them yourself. Project management is a skill. If you have a brilliant programmer who displays no aptitude for management, do not promote him beyond his capabilities. You are better off leaving him with what he does best. Training may help in bridging the gap but don't rely on short-term training to overcome a natural human limitation.

People behave better in better circumstances, so your first thought should be how you organize the lines of communication and the basic working rules. How you manage your team depends on its size, the complexity of the project, and the individuals. Small teams prefer direct lines of communication and find it easier to understand and be responsible for specific tasks. Resource requirements boil down to how many, how long, and how much. Write down the answers and put them in your Gantt chart.

Note   Gantt charts displaying how parts of a project interlink are discussed later on in this chapter.

Human Character

People bring many things to a project, but bear in mind that certain traits seem to go along with each role. For example, the business manager, for obvious reasons, usually has the best overview as they are constantly balancing short-term expenditure against future payback. It is vital that this person has complete confidence in the project at all times.

Financial people are normally very focused on their task in hand. During development they double-check every penny as if it was their own money, especially if you suggest that the project requires additional cash. (Once the product gets to market, they will look at the revenue likewise.)

Technocrats tend to be absorbed with producing ideal code. Managers have to temper this laudable aspiration against production schedules. While titles and roles are often combined, the key players are as follows:

- ✦ **Business managers**—Instrumental in defining, steering, and signing off a project. They will typically liaise with top management (or clients) on major issues. Money is always a major concern.

- ✦ **Project managers**—They are responsible for liaising between other middle managers and the teams doing the work. They must be able to organize and motivate staff as well as work with them and solve problems. They must retain the confidence of their staff and know the way forward at every stage. It is their job to monitor progress and take management initiatives.

- ✦ **Product manager**—Although not used as much as might be useful, the product manager bridges both camps combining marketing savvy and good technical knowledge. Such people often help put together the product definitions as well as acting as the product ambassador for it at launch.

- ✦ **Programmers**—These may be full-time encoders or specialists brought in part time to develop specific components. Make sure all programmers are capable of doing what they say, and that they understand their role and its level of importance.

- ✦ **Installers**—It is extremely desirable for a member of the internal team to build a test rig at an early stage in development. This enables initial builds to be checked quickly under realistic conditions. The installer's inside knowledge of the products' intricacies makes it easier for the other programmers to accept and respond to unexpected problems.

- ✦ **Quality controllers**—This isn't the same task as testing the product. The quality controller ensures that the development technique produces stable solutions, reduces bug creation, and tracks down problems, if and when they occur. He or she also develops test plans for the product and runs all alpha and beta tests. The results are then fed back to the project manager for further refinement.

- ✦ **Documentor**—Writes the manuals and help systems. The documentor may also coordinate and prepare copy for the Web site, support, training, and so on.

- ✦ **Release Controller**—When the product is ready for release this executive takes control to synchronize the rollout. For most projects this is a non-time-consuming task, so it is common for this person to be performing another role the rest of the time, most often that of quality controller.

Equipment and Space

Members of the team should have access to a decent computer to work on, all the necessary development software, ancillary hardware, and secure Internet connections.

If the machine requires regular and intensive compiling you will need a fast machine to avoid continual down time. Find out if there is additional software that could possibly help you.

Time and Money

The longer any project takes, the greater the investment. Time has to be considered seriously. It isn't just computer projects that take longer than anyone anticipates. Most innovative products tend to finish late. Keep in mind, though, that you aren't working out a train timetable. You can't say how long every task will take. You can't foretell how things will be delayed if a key man falls ill or a piece of vital external kit is unobtainable in time. However, you can with some probability estimate the minimums and maximums of coding design and duration and devise, in conjunction with the other departments, fallback strategies.

It is much better to build in a measure of flexibility from the outset than find yourself the victim of an ironclad timescale you can neither control nor escape from. The man who falls out of an aircraft doesn't need more altitude; he needs a working parachute.

The Doomsday Scenario

If your blueprint says you need 20 people, six months, and $500,000, your problems start when those things are given to you. If you come back in week 27 and say you are behind schedule, need another couple of programmers, and another $50,000, you are over budget and have three strikes against you. If you discover that their plan is going to be compromised this early on, you have two options:

✦ Accept the limitations of staff, time, or money.

✦ Explain the danger and redraft the plan.

Failing this, the only honorable course is to withdraw from this particular project. In the end, no one is going to remember how many times you fail, but the one time you win big. So, if you have to withdraw from the project or abort it later, treat it as a learning experience. You haven't lost when finances force closure. You haven't lost when your staff goes over to your competition. You haven't lost when your program takes a dive. You have only lost when *you* say you have.

However, even with faith in yourself intact, it still takes courage to stand down the troops, especially when they are all eager for the fray. It is infinitely wiser to disengage than be driven into the ground. Acting early is likely to conserve a portion of your resources that may later form the basis for a better springboard.

In addition, if you have good reason to shut down, everyone around you will understand, provided you call them in, explain the situation frankly, and allow them to ask questions and talk through the situation so that they can see for themselves that there is no other choice.

Common management reasons for one third of all IT projects aborting include the following:

+ Costs outrun budgets

+ Failure to complete

+ Lack of adequate personnel

+ Competition

On the programmer's side, there are equally valid though less widely understood reasons for failure:

+ Lack of management confidence

+ The financial precariousness of the firm (if the project doesn't come in on time, it could take the company down)

+ The absence of any budget or plan

+ Too many technical hurdles

All of these can be valid reasons for curtailing a project. If you are worried, discuss the situation with a colleague privately. It is not an indication of failure. It is a sign of profound concern and responsibility to the company, the project, and everyone involved.

Planning

It isn't just bigger bombs for which we have to thank military research. Occasionally they come up with something useful to all of us (such as the non-stick frying pan). One of their useful developments was the Program Evaluation Review Technique (PERT). It was introduced to develop the Polaris Submarine Nuclear Missile project in 1958. PERT allows you to plan a complex project in a way that ensures that all resources are being used evenly and to forecast where bottlenecks can be expected to occur. The initial technique was such a success that it reduced the anticipated development time by two years.

The way we most commonly see this planning schematic is on a Gantt chart. This familiar chart often used for evaluating projects was developed in 1917 in the U.S. by Henry Gantt to help schedule his workshop's jobs. You don't have to have a military-sized budget to afford this technique. It is available over the counter in the form of Microsoft Project or Linux equivalents.

+   +   +

I Want to Work Here!

At startup, most IT projects become so concerned with funding and development that all other issues get side-lined. Be aware that during those heady, early days, whatever procedures, style, and practices you adopt as you go have a habit of petrifying into permanent policy.

It's only human to concentrate on the most important issues. However, if you don't get the main components as you really want them at the start, it can be a long hard slog to change established working patterns. As with a garden, it pays to set up the right environment and guidelines at the start. Creating an atmosphere that others want to be part of will pay for itself again and again.

Eight key areas particularly deserve consideration:

1. People

2. Company ethos

3. Communication

4. Working environment

5. Staff relationships

6. Spreading the benefits

7. Corporate stability

8. Freeing the human spirit

People

Like Robin Hood, no company can begin to succeed until it brings the right people together. Initially, this is a matter of some chance. No matter how well the founders or key players know each other, their personal strengths are less conspicuous initially than their intelligence, energy, or skills.

When you begin to take on other people you have to choose with even more care. The interview technique is notoriously difficult, even among experienced interviewers who are generally considered to be excellent judges of character. A person's motivation for wanting the job and what people they have previously worked for say about them may be the most positive indications of their future performance.

Inspiring, enthusiastic people make for a great working environment. Even so, you don't want all yes men or the pros and cons will never be properly debated. Be careful also to distinguish healthy assertiveness from bullying. Look carefully to see whether the applicant is truly positive minded and supports the groups to which he or she has previously belonged. Drop a sourpuss into the mix and suddenly everyone's trying to get another job.

Taking on people is similar to "perimeter security." You control who is allowed into the firm. Careful screening increases the chances of newcomers being net contributors to the team. You want people who will enjoy the challenge, get along with the others, and add to the environment.

The fewer of you there are, the more you are susceptible to personalities. Human quirks don't usually themselves even out until you have engaged 25 or 30 people.

Affirm the Company Ethos

Firms with destiny have a buzz about them. They know where they're going, the staff know the route, and everyone pulls in the same direction. Great working environments are established around a shared purpose, whether it is building the Pyramids or getting out XP. Tap into this and your operation gathers cohesion and coordinates its actions. You also benefit from vastly improved productivity.

In the 1990s every organization believed they were undressed without a "Mission Statement." They felt publicly humiliated and corporately inept without one. Unfortunately, Mission Statements got trivialized as it became the fashion to reduce them to the length of a sound bite or an advertising slogan. What Mission Statements did do was make firms think about what they really did and the biggest benefits they gave their customers (more about this in Chapter 14).

Founders normally have vision, guts, and a sense of destiny. They are inspiring people. Their firms start off with strong ideas and sound reasons for existence. It is highly desirable for the founders to record their aims at the outset so that everyone who comes on board afterwards knows where the firm intends to go. These *raison d'êtres,* as the French call them, may help you to differentiate your firm from others with similar aims. They certainly make it clear to applicants what kind of firm they would be joining, if invited.

An introductory company résumé doesn't have to be long but it probably should tell newcomers the following:

- ✦ Who founded the firm and why
- ✦ The market they are after
- ✦ What they want from their staff
- ✦ Ways they feel customers should be treated
- ✦ Their aspirations for the product and the company
- ✦ The kind of reputation they wish to earn

Speaking the Same Language

Most organizations simply let communications evolve. They think that once they have established a common language and set up a working e-mail, fax, and telephone system nothing but milk and honey will flow. All they have done is put the mechanics in place.

Communication is more about the traffic than the media. Good communication is clear, largely predictable, and systematic, both internally and externally. Although everyone knows this, it's frightening how many of us forget it.

Just because everyone speaks English, don't assume that everyone speaks the same language. There are many Englishes. The standard vocabulary comprises over 880,000 words. The Shakespeares of this world typically use 30,000 in print.

Managers and marketing people rarely use the same vocabulary and idioms as programmers, and vice versa. Each sometimes assumes that this separation in word use conveys some kind of superiority born of exclusive knowledge. However, silence born of bewilderment on the part of the recipient is not the same as understanding.

Always use the vocabulary of the lowest common denominator in your audience so that *everyone* understands and feels included. In other words, describe everything you possibly can in plain English. If you have to use words exclusive to your specialty, accept that the onus of education rests on you. Explain what the technical word means *before* you bring it into the conversation. Make sure the other person understands your explanation before you speak further. Gradually, simple bricks of mutual understanding will assemble into long fluent strings and all sides will wonder why there was ever a problem at all.

Meetings

Another problem is that, in all the hubbub, people sometimes feel too busy to communicate at all. How often have you learned something important about your organization from a client or supplier? Rarely is the omission intentional. It usually occurs because a suitable opportunity to share never offered itself on a plate.

Analysts have found that companies that manage to hold regular meetings are more frequently successful than those who don't.

In small companies and teams, everyone is so busy doing everything that the hardest thing to arrange is often a meeting. Something always seems to crop up or interrupt. Two aborted meetings and you're lost. The solution is to set in stone, on the highest authority, regular, group, or company-wide meetings, once a week. Always have it on the same day, always at the same time, always in the same place—then no one can say they didn't know the venue.

It must be clearly understood in advance that these internal meetings *always* take precedence over everything else, including urgent individual meetings, inquiries by the taxman, and crucial appointments with the client. You come first. The rest of the world comes second. Once people get used to internal meetings having priority, it is amazing how deftly they are able to schedule outside appointments around them, switch off their telephones, and let their faxes pile up.

Use the most powerful meeting chairmen in the firm to set the process off, even if that doesn't happen to be you. Regular meetings correct two common misunderstandings:

+ Meetings waste valuable development time.
+ They just drag on.

Firms that hold regular meetings say that just by pulling people together you build collaboration, reduce duplication, and iron out ambiguities that typically waste significantly more time than the combined time of those assembled. Meetings are an excellent opportunity to motivate and publicly acknowledge the contributions made by individuals.

Meetings certainly just drag and lose focus if you haven't had a meeting in ages and open without an agenda. Everyone wants to air everything they've been storing. They have no idea when there will be another opportunity. Regular, structured meetings mean short meetings.

Circulate the News

If you don't communicate with staff at reasonable intervals they soon feel left out. This demotivates them, their focus wobbles, they start to gossip, have time to grow two heads, and so on.

Efficient project managers often find it useful to circulate notes of what is going on and indicate the progress achieved each week. Even if you are working on your own, write yourself a short progress log regularly. You will then be able to look back and draw (sometimes surprising) lessons from your progress. If it's good enough for James T. Kirk . . .

Working Environments

Louis Henri Sullivan knew a lot about buildings; he was the father of the modern skyscraper. He also coined the precept "Form follows function," which has been the vade mecum of architects and designers ever since. You have only to look around you to see why.

Some offices are bright, uplifting, and everyone blossoms. Others are so depressing they stifle.

Surprisingly, the difference isn't a matter of money; it's more a matter of mood.

We've all visited corporate offices where the interior design has been backed by a budget to die for. Yet for all the latest chairs and high-tech security systems and meant-to-be-impressive artwork, the staff are housed like executive battery chickens. By contrast, other offices working on a shoestring can have a real buzz about them.

Place plants in a healthy environment and they blossom. Place them in a poor one and they wither. Same stock, varied conditions produce completely different results. Why would you expect people to behave differently?

Narrow-minded managers feel that if you employ someone and pay them at the end of each month, their productivity and quality of work should be tops despite everything else. Sensitive, creative people, whether they are managers or programmers, are not that thick skinned. People are a software firm's largest single investment and by far its most important one. So it is vital to do everything possible to encourage your staff to give their best.

Creative people don't need to work in the Ritz. They just need to be somewhere where the lighting is pleasant, they are sufficiently warm and comfortable, and it's quiet enough to concentrate without external distraction.

When it comes to planning your office space it may help to employ a technique used by interior designers. They categorize working spaces into the following four types:

✦ **Hives**—Found in call centers where people are undertaking intensive, routine work, need little room to work, and social interaction is considered counterproductive.

✦ **Cells**—Often used by lawyers and accountants (and ideally suited for programmers) where intensive work is undertaken in small mutually supportive groups.

✦ **Dens**—Group larger numbers of people by function, such as sales or accounting teams. They used to be called departments.

✦ **Club**—Environments are not owned by anyone. Clubs are found in communal areas such as meeting rooms and refreshment areas.

Once you know the functions you require, it is easy to plan suitable spaces. The determining factors are the degrees of interaction and supervision that people require to perform their tasks. Table 4-1 shows an example.

Table 4-1
Interaction and Supervision Grid

Category	Interaction	Supervision	Example
Hive	Low	Low	Support
Cell	Low	High	Programming
Den	High	Low	Sales
Club	High	High	Meeting Room

If, like many software firms, you are starting from home, it is a good idea to differentiate between home and work by making the color scheme and the feel of your study, office, or work corner different. It's easier then to disassociate the two and not let work and home merge.

With office rents and rates so high, it is understandable that firms try and pack as many people into their spaces as possible. Current practice allocates 130 sq. ft. per person per desk for conventional work. This is reduced to 90 sq. ft. if the space is being used flexibly (for example, where employees share communal workspaces). The square footage is continually being raised with prosperity. At the beginning of the 1980s, leading designers advised 100 sq. ft. per person, although they knew the average office space per person was usually closer to 80 sq. ft. Such allowances include reception areas, passages, break rooms, bathrooms, and so on. There are no fixed rules.

Most job roles in software development are similar to their equivalents in management, accounting, human resources, and production. However, two activities specific to IT deserve special attention: programming and support.

Programmers need peace and quiet to work. Time and motion people calculate that they lose 20 to 40 minutes of production time each time they have a serious interruption. If they are interrupted 10 times in the course of a day, don't be surprised if they accomplish zilch.

The best way to ensure productivity is to give programmers their own enclosed workspaces. These needn't be large or lavish. To prevent your programmers from becoming too insular, you can engineer it so that they have to use gregarious communal areas, such as around the coffee machine or lunch area.

These techniques also work for support and sales staff.

Staff Relationships

Allowing relationships to develop organically is leaving your greatest asset to chance. Staff relationships matter. They can make or break a company, especially small ones. Work out at the outset how you will manage others.

Some people are born managers. Others are able to manage with training and support. Most prefer to be led. Quite often the people who have the ideas prefer to just carry on with development. They are often the first to admit it if they aren't natural leaders.

If you don't have the time or inclination to deal with your staff, appoint someone who does. It leaves you free to concentrate on what you do best and, if you have chosen your partner(s) wisely, it strengthens your project.

While there are hundreds of books on management that can help you hone your skills, always keep one thing in mind: People who are natural managers have one thing in common. They like and respect the people they work with. This doesn't mean the manager always has to agree with them, or that in an adverse situation employees shouldn't be fired; but it does mean that the manager intuitively understands what makes people tick and can tap into a common bond between your needs and theirs and, with a deft touch, generally bring out the best.

Couple this with strong organizational and communication skills and you have a real buttress to your business.

Sharing Success

Companies that work well perform as teams. In sport, if the team wins everyone wins. It's the same at work. Make it clear that when the firm wins everyone benefits.

When You Don't Have the Cash

Sometimes when you're just starting out, you don't have the funds to reward your employees with financial bonuses. That doesn't mean you can't find other ways to show your appreciation. Perhaps a swivel chair would improve an employee's comfort level in a narrow office. Perhaps a team wants to help with a fundraiser for a medical charity that is close to one of their hearts. Create a fair, achievable, and proportionate target for them to deliver, and when they do, get that chair or join that fundraiser. Everyone benefits, and you are seen as both generous and magnanimous.

The incentive should be proportionate to the achievement. It might be a beer at closing time or a chocolate cherry cake on their birthday. Your thought and recognition will be remembered long after the chair is worn and the cake is no longer even a smudge around appreciative mouths.

Proportionate rewards are especially important where the form of recognition is financial. Your accountant will be asking some very pertinent questions if you show signs of being philanthropic. Yet bonuses (for completion ahead of schedule or sales targets met) need to be clearly separated from salary. In most instances bonuses are more productive than a pay raise. Increases in salary quickly become taken for granted. They diminish the link between work and achievement and become a fixed cost for years to come.

It's your task to choose the right balance between the security of guaranteed income and the reward of the further financial benefit. Salaries provide cake. Bonuses are the icing on that cake.

Although share options go in and out of favor as the stock market fluctuates, anyone who is interested in long-term employment has hitched their destiny to that of the company. Share options can be a just and fitting reward. They give loyal staff much greater faith in the company's sense of fair play beyond the actual value or equity disbursed.

The key issue is the selling of the shares. If firms are publicly quoted, shares acquired as options can be sold (or indeed bought) in the usual way over the Internet or through a stockbroker. If your firm is unlisted for the time being, you must set in place some index from the start that generates a rational value (for example, a percentage of the last audited profit) against the share, so that they can be sold at pre-agreed times.

Share options work least well when they are introduced later as a result of staff pressure. They provide the strongest motivation when they are introduced at a very early stage.

Corporate Stability

If the firm is dicey, don't assume that only you and your accountant know it. Your suppliers will know about it. Your clients will know about it. Even the office cleaner will know about it. Potential instability saps morale, particularly among those who place a premium on security.

At any time, a certain percentage of ventures are financially unstable. If their main client suddenly leaves, a fire guts the premises, or a major competitor sets up shop next door, they may not have the cash reserves to weather the storm.

Until you are really established, being periodically short of cash is unfortunately the norm. The corporate bank balance usually oscillates like a roller coaster between investment and payback. With experience as a project leader or company boss you learn to live with this and put mechanisms in place to manage it.

As soon as you see that finances are beginning to dwindle take the matter seriously. Have the cashflows presented to you daily or weekly so you can take the earliest counteraction.

While you don't want to worry your staff with the details of these financial responsibilities, it's unwise to misrepresent the long-term picture. Once your staff gets a hunch that there are problems (imaginary or true) they'll understandably become worried. Their work will start to fray, their timekeeping will become erratic as they embark on a series of job interviews, and gossip can grow from embers into a bushfire in a matter of hours. The best of your staff will be able to find other jobs easily enough, and with key members of your team missing and no money to recruit replacements, your schedules will be torpedoed.

It's always better to take a view that every software project will hit financial uncertainties at some time during its lifespan. You've got a good product. The real problem is completing the development on time. So work out in advance how you will deal with the cash ups and downs. The best defense is to shield your staff from everyday management issues and provide the stability they need to get on with their job. It's your job to protect them and their job to deliver the product.

 Note These are important issues and not to be pushed aside. See Chapter 18 for more on financial issues.

Freeing the Human Spirit

The purpose of your business should be, to some extent, to improve the human condition. In the process, everyone should get a raise in funds and self-esteem. Everyone in some way or another should grow. In other words, your business activity should be an enriching experience. This isn't idealism. It's the only way the economics can work. Any firm that doesn't make economic headway has no management steerage.

Many of us were brought up by pressured parents in an authoritarian style. "Don't be late!" "Eat your food!" "Brush your teeth!" "Don't hit your brother!" Not surprisingly, we tend to come out with the same management style in later life, issuing orders in a similar vein: "Where were you?" "Finish that report!" "Refill the photocopier!"

Children don't like it. Adults don't like it either, which is why it doesn't work. Every adult resents being spoken to like a child.

Some managers reprimand people for being late regardless of the fact that the person is one of those who work late and over weekends when there is a panic. The victim feels unappreciated. His or her colleagues feel the manager is unfair. They think why should they bother? He doesn't care.

Managers get better results and much less stress by assuming that their staff are responsible adults and by addressing them as equals. There's more to management than showing respect and encouraging others to behave maturely, but making this small shift in attitude can have significant results. When you enable them to give to you, self-motivation and productivity increase. The management time required to monitor responsible people diminishes.

Responsibility is to all intents and purposes, respondability.

✦   ✦   ✦

CHAPTER 5

Raising Cash and Kind

The pioneering spirit that drove settlers west to the lush Silicon Valley is alive and well. The idea of heading off into uncharted territories and discovering unknown landscapes and mining untold riches sets our minds alight. So much so that too many people still take the pioneer spirit literally and try and do everything themselves.

Some are afraid the ordinary public won't understand what they are doing. But if that's the case, are they likely to rush to buy the final offering? Some feel they don't have to communicate with others or justify their actions. Yet, they are going to have to talk to others when the time comes to do the selling. Some are scared of their idea leaking out, but eventually they'll have to trust someone. To a certain extent, all these concerns are prudent, but carried to extremes they ultimately prove to be counterproductive.

Creating a program, selling it, and managing the resulting operation requires a combination of skills and resources that few individuals possess. Help comes in many forms and sometimes from unexpected sources, and money is only one aspect, although it is the most pressing one.

Contrary to many people's personal intuition there are IT engineers, business managers, and bankers out there who *are* prepared to help. Whether you are a one-man band, an isolated programmer, IT manager, part of a small team, or a student feeling your way for the first time, you need never be alone. There is help out there if you know where to look and are willing to accept it.

Andrew Carnegie knew this. Son of a weaver in Scotland, his family emigrated to the U.S. in 1848 when he was 12. Through a succession of jobs he eventually set up the Carnegie Steel

Company, which he went on to sell for over $10 billion at today's prices. One of his maxims was, "Why spend a hundred hours of your time doing something if you can persuade 100 people to do an hour each themselves?" He had a shrewd understanding of his fellow men and appreciated that what he was getting wasn't just help, but a network of people who wanted to spread the word about what they were doing (a bonus you would never reap if you'd spent 1,000 hours doing it alone).

Advice

Running anything is a solitary activity. No matter how close you are to the people around you, there are some decisions you must make by yourself. These are usually the sort of things you can't discuss comfortably with anyone else, such as:

+ Is so-and-so pulling their weight?
+ Should they be sacked?
+ Is there enough cash in hand for next month's wages?

Having friends outside your business, particularly those who may have gone through similar experiences, is worth its weight in gold. Most often such people have no other vested interest than wanting someone else to avoid the pitfalls that were so hard for them to climb out of. A person whose judgment you respect, someone who you can level with, discuss situations with, and try solutions out on is invaluable, if you are astute enough to learn from another's experience instead of discovering everything at your own expense.

The most important areas to get advice about are obviously those areas you know least. It might be market research or the legal side. Build up a group of contacts you can call on.

Tip   Help like this is unstructured and sometimes presents itself when you least expect it. You just have to learn the knack of switching into a receptive frame of mind instantaneously.

Money

Money is normally the most pressing concern for developers, though it isn't the be-all and end-all of program development. It's amazing what has been accomplished with very little, but clearly without enough, just as with a lack of oil in an engine, the operation will seize and grind to a halt.

There are normally three things that worry people about money:

✦ They haven't got it.

✦ They don't know how to get hold of it.

✦ They don't know how to spend it when they do get it.

When starting out, most of us are not very experienced buyers, sellers, and book-keepers. Few of us have ever been in a situation where lack of money has never been a problem. And although we may have a very shrewd idea of how to techni-cally accomplish our chosen task, we have absolutely no idea how to persuade oth-ers to trust us with their cash. The combination is understandably scary. Yet most of our fear is simply fear of the unknown.

Irrespective of what the ups and downs of the stock market infer, the world is signif-icantly more affluent than it has ever been. This, coupled with the historically low interest rates in the western world and a wider choice of cash sources than ever before, has resulted in a situation where it has never been easier or more affordable to get financing. Some sources of funding might even be closer to home than you thought.

Unless you are sitting on a personal cash pile, money is available by three routes:

✦ Cash you will have to repay

✦ Cash the business will have to repay

✦ Cash invested in the business

Whichever the category, they are all Other People's Money (OPM) and include the following:

✦ Personal loans (friends and family)

✦ Credit manipulation (credit cards)

✦ Institutional loans (banks, mortgages)

✦ Business Angels

✦ Venture capital

Cash You Will Have to Repay

This is the easiest form of money to raise because you are the bottom line. Whether the product succeeds or fails, you will repay it or you'll be declared bankrupt.

Personal Loans

The quickest funding method is to get a friend or family member to write you a check. While this solves the immediate problem, you have to be aware of the responsibilities and rules that go with it. When accepting money from friends or family, make sure they can afford it, should the worst come to pass and they lose the loan. You also need to ensure that a loss will not wreck the relationship. The fallout is often wider than just the person with whom you did the transaction. If you can't satisfy both these criteria, don't ask for or accept a loan, even if it's offered.

Set down in writing the fact that the money is a loan and what the interest rate and the repayment terms shall be. Additionally, agree what the procedure is should the money need to be called in at short notice. The best time to iron out such details is in advance, before you accept a penny. If there is risk associated with the loan, consider issuing shares against the money. The inherent risk is then often better understood than a straight loan that someone might naïvely presume to be watertight or secured.

Credit Manipulation

Unlike current bank loans, credit cards carry high repayment charges. The monthly interest rate is often four times higher. Yet used judiciously, credit cards can be a quick way to purchase goods and indirectly fund your business.

Using your credit card as a source of finance makes complete sense, provided the retail price (after all bad debts) is well ahead of the total production costs plus all likely interest. Credit providers are delighted to extend your credit if you have a good payment record. However, you should only use them to deal with cashflow against known monies coming in, and be sure to build the interest into the price you receive. Otherwise, the rates are heinous.

Bank Loans and Mortgages

If you have real collateral, such as a house, banks and mortgage companies are more than willing to lend money against it. Loans can be surprisingly quick to set up, especially if you know your bank manager and have a clean credit history.

An IT World Prime Example

The most notable instance in the IT world of using credit cards to fund big business is now one of the largest firms on the planet. In their early days the founders, Len Bosack and Sandy Lerner, a couple of married Stanford academics, wanted to swap e-mails. They used their credit cards to buy their gear and build routers. Others soon heard about their clever idea and wanted one as well, so they used their credit cards again and again. This went on for longer than they expected. The pair had to approach 76 financiers before they finally got funded. Luckily for them, demand was so strong that customers paid promptly. Now everyone has heard of Cisco.

Mortgages take longer to arrange, typically 4 to 6 weeks. Don't hesitate to approach several companies to get the best rate and motivate them to give you the best deal. When loan rates are attractively low, this is an option well worth considering. However, bear in mind that interest rates change with time, so be prepared.

If you successfully receive a bank loan, discuss with the bank manager what the repayment process is. Banks normally have a clause that allows them to call in any loan at zero notice. Innocuous though the statement looks, it has been used in recent times when the bank's head office is low on credit themselves or worried about the economy. They issue an edict to call in particular categories of loans and bank managers just have to oblige. I have seen a number of long-established businesses go under when their credit facilities were withdrawn at zero notice. Make sure you know the procedure and have a mechanism in place for coping with it. If your bank manager gives assurances that are above and beyond the standard statements, have them put it in writing, get both parties to sign them, and affix signed copies to both copies of the loan. Although bank managers are becoming an endangered species, a good one not only can unleash the purse strings in times of difficulty, but from training and experience in dealing with hundreds of other business customers they have a practical understanding of the problems that you are likely to encounter. They can usually explain the best course of action.

Tip   Don't take your bank manager for granted. When lending money against businesses bank managers still expect to see good, well-written, and preferably short business plans.

This route makes sense if you have an existing job or income to cover the repayments. Maybe the firm is generating a solid surplus to cover these costs. I strongly recommend against this approach if you have family and dependents. To say nothing of the stress, loss of sleep, and personal issues that can arise, dreams can be jeopardized if success doesn't happen to plan.

Cash the Business Will Have to Repay

Unless you already have an established record or your firm has some obvious asset, lenders are unlikely to be interested in your firm as security. Even if they are, they won't be willing to risk a fortune. However, this method does exist. If you can raise capital by using your company as security, seriously consider it. Then if anything goes wrong, it is the company that is liable; you and your family are protected.

Cash Invested in the Business

This form of investment can take the most effort to obtain but it can also be the largest should you require significant funds. Invariably it is a swap for equity, shares in your company.

Business Angels

Business Angels are wealthy individuals who invest personally. Not only can they provide the capital and make the decisions quickly, but they often bring management advice and contacts from their own successful careers. Sometimes they group together into a small investment group to spread out the risk and increase the management expertise they can bring to the table.

If a Business Angel route is to work, you need to make sure you get along with them and you won't be treading on each other's toes.

Unless you have a stash of Angels, try typing "Business Angels" and a location into your favorite search engine.

Venture Capital

Typically used to provide larger funds than Business Angels traditionally give, venture capital (VC) is the form of funding most widely associated with Information Technology ventures. However, it is a popular misconception that during the Internet/IT boom of 1997–2000 venture capital was freely available with no questions asked—it never was and never will be.

VC is designed to prime and nurture the initial strategic growth of companies that have the potential to rapidly become a dominant market force. Historically, venture capitalists were prepared to take a higher risk; this was offset by their exclusive interest in firms with potentially lucrative rates of return and obtaining disproportionately higher stake holdings. VC typically delivers the crucial investment in return for a large equity stake.

One of the reasons why VC funding is so attractive to IT entrepreneurs is that the cash is unsecured; if the project fails you don't lose your car, home, and other assets. VCs also provide you with enough money to pay yourself a fair salary.

Venture capitalists typically invest in companies in five classic ways:

✦ **Seed capital**—This is provided to develop the concept of a product or service and is often used to fund patents and trademarks, as well as establish the marketing, business, and future funding requirement in detail. Amounts to nurture a good idea are small.

Since the Internet/IT boom ended, nearly all venture capitalists have stopped funding start-ups. They want you to take the initiative, demonstrate that the idea works, and come back to them when you have some initial sales experience. If seed capital is ever offered, remember, it's best used to make the case for additional funding.

✦ **Start-up capital**—Enables the business operation to be set up, initial staff to be hired, and enables the product or service to be launched.

✦ **Early expansion capital**—Allows firms to gear up for increasing development and sales.

✦ **Development capital**—Used to expand the business, fund a buyout, or clean up the shareholding. By the time you are ready for development capital, your business will be well established with a sound, saleable product, proven market, and productive staff.

✦ **Turnaround finance VCs**—Used more and more to restructure good firms that are faltering. This has to be done quickly to work. With the funding normally comes a rethinking of the management, marketing, and product to correct inherent problems.

Although venture capitalists are prepared to take high risks, often investing where others fear to tread, they extract the highest price. During the Internet boom they used to send out scouts to talent spot potential ideas and pioneers at conferences and financing shows. Now they reduce their own risks by concentrating on sectors such as IT, Biotech, or Retail. Some only invest in firms at particular stages of development or in a particular geographical region. Ask them what they are looking for, how much they have in funds, how many projects they have invested in during the past 12 months, and what is the minimum amount they like to invest.

Sending in unsolicited business plans is the least likely course of action to succeed. Referrals to VCs by professional advisors such as attorneys, accountants, bankers, and even other VCs are more successful. To have any chance of success even then, your business plan must demonstrate the following:

✦ A strong marketing need for the program you plan

✦ You can develop and sell it at a profit

✦ You have the right programmers and managers in place

✦ You have a win-win exit strategy

Even at the height of the IT boom, only one in a hundred business plans would attract an investment. Table 5-1 lists the culls that VCs usually follow:

Table 5-1		
Stage	*Number*	*Percentage*
Business plans (BPs) received	2000	100
BPs fully read	400	20
Invited to present	200	10
Invested in	20	1

According to John Nesheim, author of *Hi-Tech Start Up* (Free Press, 2000), for every startup that receives money only one in 10 goes Public. In addition, the McKinsey analysis of U.S. Census data from "Secrets of Software Success" (Harvard Business School Press, 1999) says that 60 percent go bust or leave minimal residual worth.

You are going to need a superlative business plan, a great product, and adroit management if you are going to end up in the final 1 percent. From your very first contact with a venture capitalist, you will need to demonstrate strong business acumen, exemplary market knowledge, and a confident and succinct way of making each point. When you are eventually invited to an interview, stage a 3-minute elevator pitch.

Note   Most countries have VC Organizations that can provide you with lists of funders, their areas of specialization, and typical size of investment.

The Business Plan

Business plans force you to lay out in writing the roadmap and mechanism by which you believe your product can succeed. They are also the key to securing funding from any financial institution.

There's a myth that if you write a perfect business plan, the gates will open and untold riches will flow just because you put the right words down in the correct order. Unfortunately, like so much in life, nothing is guaranteed; but clearly the better your business plan, the better your chances.

Entrepreneurs often spend too much time on planning and too little time in action. In getting too bound up with planning, they lull themselves into thinking that the business plan *is* the be-all and end-all. They then underestimate the importance of being business-like and doing something about it.

Business plans, even for experienced formulators, take time. If you haven't written one before, allow at least a month. You will never write the perfect plan on your first attempt. Be prepared to redraft it multiple times. Use trusted friends and contacts who will give you candid feedback whenever possible. Only release your business plan when you are proud of the finished product. Don't worry about your lack of writing expertise. Business plans sound the most convincing when they are written by their proponent. Although they are primarily pitched at investors, they end up being read by a diverse set of scrutinizers with extremes of technical and commercial understanding. Even so, your plan must seem a winner to them all.

The Management Team

Venture capitalists only have to go through their in-box each morning to be reminded that clever ideas are a dime a dozen. They also know that plenty of people can dress up a good idea into a beauty of a programming proposition, but that few can make even the best ideas happen.

The first place venture capitalists look for real strength is in the applicant's management team. A good management team has the experience to make any sensible company work. What they really want to know is the caliber of the people you have with you, what they have achieved, and how well they know the industry. It is usually regarded as an advantage if some of them have worked together before. It helps immeasurably if these include any known names, as they dramatically reduce the uncertainly associated with a speculative startup.

Opportunity

An independently calculated mammoth opportunity offered by market circumstances is a better indicator of a project's prospects than any set of marketing figures. Most VCs look for emerging markets that are likely to boom. In the early '80s everyone knew that PCs were going to be massive—although they weren't able to put an exact figure on it, the orders were of a magnitude that couldn't fail. It has been a similar story with Internet and Web growth recently. Conversely, try to avoid venturing into saturated or highly competitive markets.

You then need to explain how you are going to make success happen. How much is it going to cost to develop, test, launch, distribute, and sell your product? In this area, VCs are looking for strong repeat sale signals—products and mechanisms that encourage customers to come back for more.

You must back up your thinking with figures. These are all the more interesting to VCs if they ride on a surging trend. However, VCs are wary of month-by-month breakdowns. They know from sad experience that such figures are almost always overly optimistic. Your figures should show that you can produce and sell the product at a profit. Make sure you know what you have to do to break even, when this is likely to occur, and what key inputs will alter these figures up or down. Additionally, make sure you have realistic cash flow summaries that provide for realistic time delays between supply and payment for both suppliers and clients. Assume and include the current industry allowance for bad debts.

Many business plans presented to venture capitalists affirm that theirs is a completely unique proposition and that the proposed product has no competition. This is very unlikely. Even when Netscape announced their browser, there were several others under development. If yours *is* a unique proposition, you are still in a weak position. The burden of educating the market is likely to be beyond the budget of any single startup company.

Circumstance

External factors, which are beyond your control, are often key to getting people to advance cash. The government might have introduced some enticing tax breaks. There might have been a flood of highly publicized hack attacks and you are going to market an industrial-strength firewall or a super-secure Web server. The economy may be riding a crest like that of the late 1990s. You couldn't create such circumstances if you wanted to. Yet they could make your proposition relevant and bring it to the top of the pile. If you are presented with such a fortunate opportunity, seize it with both hands.

Changing Trends

Since the downturn in 2000, venture capitalists have been unwilling to take overt risks and are investing more like merchant bankers. None of the guides will tell you this, but VCs are typically looking for the business whose pre-tax profit in three years equals the amount they put in. The investee must be able to sustain a growth rate of 30 percent for the first few years and the total funds invested should not exceed four times the expected annual profit or four years to return of investment. The business must also come across as being very low risk.

Reward (and Risk)

Researching for your business plan should give you a strong understanding of the financial outgoings. The hard part is anticipating your income.

- ✦ How will you handle major risk?
- ✦ What happens if a key deal falls through?
- ✦ What will you do if a supplier or subcontractor begins to run late?
- ✦ How will you handle it if you are preempted by an unexpected competitor?

Good strategists prepare contingency plans that cater to most foreseeable circumstances. Look the factors in the face and develop an alternative plan. The best Plan Bs are designed so they can kick in at zero notice. If investors know that you are protecting your business by facing potential problems in advance, their confidence in you will grow because they know that in protecting your business, you are also protecting them.

The most attractive reward to potential investors is the ability to take a firm to market because it makes their investment tradable as well as more significant. Some businesses are easier than others because of their product or marketing style. Ultimately, your business plan is a picture of how you believe the business will go. Good business plans are flexible and foresee changes that enable management to switch strategies and maximize opportunities as situations change.

Structure

There is no universal definition of the right structure for a business plan. The right business plan for your project is the one that works, raises the capital you need, delivers the goods, and scoops the profit. However, the business plan should ideally be less than 30 pages long. Supporting documents such as market research, detailed financial projects, and so on are usually best placed in a separate appendix so the plan doesn't appear overwhelming. Business plans that work are clear, simple, fair, and show an understanding of the business, the commercial environment, and investor concerns and aspirations. They are flexible so they adapt with the environment.

Architect your business plan to suit your story. Ensure that each section further develops your message so that by the end the reader is hard-pressed not to agree. All business plans should cover the following:

1. The contents

2. The company

3. The team

4. Its product/services

5. The competition

6. Foreseen obstacles

7. The marketing strategy

8. Funds required

9. Progress schedule

10. Exit strategy

The Executive Summary

The executive summary is a snapshot of the business plan. It's the 30-pager on a post card. Venture capitalists need to be able to see at a glance whether your project is likely to interest them. They can only do justice to so many business plans per month.

Although the executive summary is always read *before* the business plan, you should deal with it after completing the full plan because it is easier to cut down a proposal than to inflate a summary. In a sentence or paragraph of not more than 30 words, the summary should explain the product and why it is a genuine marketing opportunity. Briefly introduce the management team. Explain how you will get from Silicon Valley to Wall Street. Outline the timetable. Suggest the return on investment, and say how much money you need.

Good Executive Summaries are rarely longer than four pages. Most run to two. So don't repeat anything. Although it's a précis of your business plan, it shouldn't steal the business plan's thunder. The two should tell the same story in different words.

The Elevator Pitch

Imagine you get an elevator and by chance you bump into your mythical investor. You only have three minutes on your way up to the 39th floor to convince him to buy into your product, covering everything in your executive summary plus the exit strategy you will adopt. Rehearse and hone your pitch until it is Oscar-worthy. You will only ever be able to give one performance.

 Tip   Remember, you are trying to sell the whole business, not just the product.

Initial Placement Offering

When talking about VCs, the term Initial Placement Offering (IPO) comes up frequently. That's what the offer is called when a firm needs to raise capital from the sale of shares of its "Authorized but not yet issued stock."

If this is the first time they have been offered to the public, it is known as an Initial *Public* Offering. If privately offered, it is an Initial *Placement* Offering.

Is It Worth Going After Venture Capital?

Let's be frank. It takes about a full month to research, write, polish, and rehearse a good business plan. It will take a further two months to contact, dispatch, and await preliminary judgment from the VCs that you approach. The business plan is not to be undervalued as it provides the thinking and roadmap of how your operation is to operate anyway; but the level of polish required for external acceptance is dramatically different from the worksheet that can be used internally.

With only a one in a hundred chance of success, it makes sense to approach VCs if and only if there is no other recourse or you have a contact within a VC (preferably a number of VCs) who can fast-track your submission and give you firsthand feedback if your application is unsuccessful. I've been on both sides of the VC table. Winning investment requires you to put yourself in the funder's shoes. Make sure you are prepared, presentable, credible, interesting, and your figures add up. Work out who is the key VC representative; it is essential that you win them over.

Help in Kind

Ask most people for money to help your big idea on its way and they'll show you the door, never speak to you again, or phone the local hospital and warn them that you suffer from delusions. Most people only part with money in a known transaction, such as buying gas from the local filling station or food at the local supermarket. Investing, if someone has never done it before, seems a lemming-like leap of trust. However, ask them for some physical items that they don't want or aren't using and they can be more than obliging. When I started my firm, my previous employer was downsizing their U.K. operation. They let me use my old office for a couple of months while the firm was set up. My technical manager at another job got a load of first-rate Internet routers, servers, and racks from his previous employer when they overhauled their massive, internal infrastructure. This enabled him to set up a test network on which to evaluate his software without having to reconfigure his machines or compromise them if anything went awry.

If you don't ask you won't get. When providing it doesn't overtly cost the person anything and there is no conflict of interest, you'd be surprised how often they'll acquiesce to a fair and polite plea.

Do It Yourself

Do you really need outside funding? A group of experienced IT directors in Europe were starting a new venture using some software that had been in hibernation for about six months. The previous owners had gone bankrupt and the product was finished but needed launching. It was a blue chip product that enabled companies to put together secure and potentially complex Web forms in $1/10^{th}$ the time it took normally. Everything looked great except that they felt very insecure without regular salaries during the startup and refused to make a move without the backing to provide it. Writing a Wall Street standard business plan took time, but given the odds and timing, nothing was forthcoming. If they had used the same time to court the numerous leads they had between them, they'd have gotten their first orders under their belt and the product could be living again.

Funding solves the money question, but not for very long. Access to funds may seem prodigious on day one, but a false sense of security can insulate you from the real world. What you have isn't wealth; it's a wealth of debts. Being forced to sell your product from a very early stage, on the other hand, brings you continually into contact with customers and makes the firm customer-centric. Pick your customers carefully so the product's destiny coincides with the customers' requirements; otherwise, you'll be pulled in every direction by each one of them wanting specials. If nothing else you'll end up with a lopsided product. Remember, they're meant to be subsidizing you, so keep your eye firmly fixed on your own targets while remaining ever tactful.

Ironically, this technique of getting the project started against real orders is becoming the base requirement for a number of VCs that want to see an initial track record before they invest. This is after you have taken the greatest risk. The beauty of it is that you do not have to give equity away. The trick is not to be greedy at the start.

✦　　✦　　✦

Development

You may not know what makes a development successful, but you know what makes for trouble:

- ✦ Unfinished plans
- ✦ Hazy objectives
- ✦ Trite planning
- ✦ Unrealistic timescales
- ✦ Insufficient funding
- ✦ Too long or too short development cycles
- ✦ Having the wrong people on the team
- ✦ No real support from higher up

For all the talk about planning and fundraising that has gone
on before, *development* is the point where software turns from
a dream into reality. Essentially, development is about the production and management of the software, but it doesn't work
unless the timetable, the team, and the techniques gel.

A well-considered and well-structured project plan will make
development a much more straightforward exercise. Once the
resources, sequencing, and milestones have been worked out
in detail, you can motor ahead for much of the time at a fairly
constant speed. You do not have to make key decisions in
mid-flight.

However, just as the simplest computer routine can be complex, so can development. As formally taught, it requires you
to keep your eye on four balls simultaneously: people, product, projects, and process. What follows is a practical hands-
on guide to juggling without dropping the balls. Fortunately, if
you have been following the advice in this book thus far, you
have done a lot of the work already.

The First P Is People

For all the specific positions you hear bandied about, there are fundamentally only two roles: managing and developing. One administers the process and the other does the work. Specific job titles vary according to the scale of an operation. The terminology also varies from firm to firm. At the time of writing, some job descriptions that go with management and planning include the following:

+ Project managers
+ Chief technical officers (CTOs)
+ Technologists
+ Architects
+ CEO engineering

Counterparts on the programming side include the following:

+ Senior developers
+ Developers
+ Testers
+ Documenters

There is nothing to stop people from having a role in both managing and programming, or indeed handling more than one task area. However, it is as unusual for information technologists to excel at management as it is for managers to be more than pedestrian programmers, unless they have had considerable experience. So be realistic about your own capabilities. Don't bite off more than you can chew.

Get the Right People

With all programming projects time is at a premium. The last thing you can afford is to hire people who will waste time. The first thing you should be looking for is people who are familiar with the type of application and the critical programming issues. So if you are writing a design program, applicants who have trained and worked in graphics are heaven-sent. If specialist expertise is critical for your program, you must employ an applicant who has previous experience.

Such people can bring an intimate knowledge of the program application and coding solutions that an outsider could never guess. Their experience not only forms a fund of solutions to technical problems, it also enables them to code solutions in a form that customers expect. This avoids considerable rewriting if discovered in time. Otherwise, the software publisher has to convince prospective customers to live with an aberrated program. When programmers understand the application field, it is also much easier for them to implement client improvements and ward off suggestions that offer the end users no real advantage.

If you are initially unable to recruit staff of the caliber and background the project deserves, persevere. Do not advance from Go until you find them. You are always better off waiting for the right people to become available than attempting to make headway with incompetents. Everyone you hire should understand what the product does and why it's needed. If any person cannot see its justification or is morally or emotionally uncomfortable with the concept, it would be unfair to invite them to join the team.

> **Tip**   As you take each person on, take care to invest your money where your needs are.

The Project Manager

You obviously need top people in the skeletal team from a very early stage, and the project manager is a key position. The project manager is your full-time product champion, whose task it is to supervise the encoding and assembly of the program so it matches up to its specification in word and spirit. In an embryo firm, it's usually the marketing manager who assumes this role.

Having a great project manager is your best way to ensure that your project will come in on time. He or she will know how to manage and schedule your project. In addition to doing his own share of the coding, he will help and advise programmers with new approaches and techniques, as required. Equally important, the project manager enables everyone to focus on the same dream and ensures that less tangential coding is accidentally produced.

The project manager holds the pearls of wisdom about what the product does, how they're going to write it, and why it is so important. He interprets the company's vision of the program for the programmers in relation to screen layouts, screen messages, and displays of the corporate and product logo. He also sees that only the authorized version ever gets out of the programmer's room.

Some firms believe, with good reason, that the more sensitive parts of this role are better managed by a senior person who is not directly involved in day-to-day coding. This person may also be tasked with supervising beta testing.

The caliber of person you can attract for this role depends very much on the size of your organization and what you are able to offer. It also depends on the job's implicit opportunities and rewards.

How Do You Recognize a Good Project Manager?

Any project manager worth his salt should be able to research a project, schedule its development, add something creatively, and keep everyone focused and happy. A project manager should be part of the team and never above it.

To fulfill these tasks, project managers need a foot in both camps. They need to know and understand the development process (if they don't, they can't help the developers) and be good managers as well. While most people cite endless energy, telepathic insight, and the motivational skills that can move ants to conquer Everest, the following are other core qualities you should be looking for:

- ✦ Organized
- ✦ Ability to solve problems
- ✦ Consistent communication
- ✦ Deft touch with people

All good technical managers, irrespective of their rung on the ladder, have to be more than theorists. It is essential that they have extensive first-hand experience of the technologies they must employ. It is only by having worked as a programmer that they can know where the tricks and traps lie. The management part of the job calls for trained skills in addition to natural abilities. This should include experience in reviewing team progress and negotiations. Those who are strong conceptual and strategic thinkers are natural leaders providing they can communicate adroitly.

Note   It might come as a surprise that a bad project manager is rarely the converse of a good one. He's unlikely to be rude or badly organized.

Bad managers often interview well (otherwise you wouldn't take them on), but when they commence the job, their limitations quickly show. At the start of a project, providing the project plan is well constructed, it will practically run itself. You'll only become aware that the manager is out of his depth when a problem occurs. It's at this point you are likely to discover that they don't know how to handle people sympathetically or cleverly. They seek to blame instead of solve. The organization begins to react and communication becomes lax or unclear. People begin to bury their problems. A project manager who simply reacts is likely to fail.

Tip   If you find that you have a bad project manager and need to replace him or her at short notice, your best bet is often to temporarily promote a senior programmer who will know the project and what is involved. Provide him or her with some admin backup to perform both tasks. It's rarely a long-term solution but it does give you time to locate a replacement.

Twenty years ago, hardly anyone on any PC software project had management experience. Now so many people have been through the mill that small firms are often professionally managed by people who began working solely as programmers. So the question now is not can you manage and write the code, but should you try both? The answer is probably not, if you have any choice.

Programmers

The more demanding the task, the more vital it is to have good programmers. If you were looking for a good architect, engineer, or designer, you would probably put more value on what they'd created than what they said. This is a good strategy with programmers, too. Check out prospective programmers' recent projects, look at a few excerpts of their code, and have them explain what they've done. Rogue coders can bring down an entire project, so if a programmer is unable to demonstrate the competence they promise, act on your instinct and draw back.

If you do hire a dud programmer (and many of us have done it), you'll end up with unusable code, a sour team, lost time, and your budget shot to ribbons. All you can do is show him the door as fast as you can and put his code through the shredder. When you have a good person, you'll know it, and so will the rest of the team.

Tip In choosing a programmer, if you have to weigh niceties to arrive at a decision, you are already on to a loser.

The following are signs that a programmer may be less competent than they purport:

✦ They hold a view that the answers usually pop out during coding.

✦ They get bogged down in seemingly trivial tasks.

✦ Their work is indifferently documented.

✦ They are slow learners.

✦ They prefer to deal with bugs afterwards.

✦ They demonstrate an inability to supply satisfactory explanations.

✦ They use eloquence to mask weaknesses in their work.

✦ They never admit mistakes.

✦ Their production rate is unexpectedly low.

✦ Their code regularly fails quality reviews.

Contrary to the popular myth that good programmers are unintelligible geeks, they are normally quite the reverse. A strong analytical mind means they can communicate complex ideas simply as well as consider problems from many different perspectives. Good programmers possess the following skills:

✦ They have excellent abilities to plan structurally.

✦ They work fast.

✦ They document their progress systematically.

✦ They have thought out the answer before they begin.

✦ Their vision is based on knowledge.

◆ They debug on the fly.

◆ They rarely need to redo their work.

◆ They care about the quality of their code.

◆ They know from experience when to take a risk.

◆ They produce the goods.

Table 6-1 lists the positions you should fill given the size of your software house.

Table 6-1 Positions Commensurate with Company Size					
Size of Software House	**Programmers**	**Project Managers**	**CTO/ Technologists**	**Development Manager**	**Contractors**
Individual	Yes (it's you)				
2–12 (Small)	Yes	Maybe			Maybe
2–12	Yes	Maybe	Almost certainly		Maybe
18–30 (Med)	Yes	Yes	Yes either/or	Probably	
40–1,000 (Large)	Yes	Yes	Yes	Yes	Probably
1,000+ (Corporate)	Yes	Yes	Several	Yes	Probably

Managerial Roles

The IT industry borrowed the title chief technical officer (CTO) from research industries during the late 1970s. At the same time the field of IT exploded as new products, ideas, and disciplines hit the scene. This made it increasingly hard for the person in charge of a project to be conversant with all aspects of programming. The CTO was accordingly pushed into the crow's nest. His primary function is to know what technologies and products are coming over the horizon and to map out the capabilities required.

As you will have noted in Chapter 5, venture capitalists like to see an eminent technical expert on the board of any firm in which they are considering investment. As they see it, firms that have a technician at the top demonstrate vision and an awareness of the importance of maintaining a technical edge.

Good CTOs are rare because they have to understand the present *and* guess the future. On the other hand, you may not need one full time. Look for someone who has a good working knowledge of the technologies the program is going to involve as well as its ramifications. Such a person should be able to pilot you through those areas of technology where you do not have knowledge yourself. They should also be able to help you exploit those techniques that are new to you.

CEO Engineering

For large projects, this title is often given to a professional heavyweight who oversees the technical infrastructure of the components to ensure overall compatibility.

Development Managers

Development managers are mainly found in organizations that develop several programs simultaneously. Usually they report to the department head or CEO. Unfortunately, there aren't too many experienced ones, so there is a tendency to promote anyone who shows promise. Many development managers attain the title with relatively little experience. The development manager is sometimes referred to as the CEO engineering, but their role is wider.

Systems Engineers, Architects, or Technologists

Although these titles are often used interchangeably, as a rule, technical engineers and architects usually concentrate on the framework of a solution while technologists specialize in the features that slot into the niches.

Contractors

There is little point in employing someone full time when their specialty is only required for a brief period. Hire subcontractors for specific subprojects. Keep track of star players for future works.

A Wise Precaution

Employ great people and you stand a real chance of becoming a giant. People rarely leave great teams. But you should not count on this. If yours is a short, time-critical project, it is not unreasonable to ask for an understanding before you invite anyone to join you that they not move jobs during the course of the project. Explain, if you can, that this is in everyone's interest. If, for example, there is a $5,000 bonus for each member of the staff if the project comes in on time and a single person leaves to take a job paying $10,000 more than their current project salary, they are only $5,000 better off and they have won the lifelong resentment of all their former teammates.

Small Is Beautiful

Large teams don't work. They grind. Fundamentally, because so much effort is expended keeping everyone up to speed with what is going on, more time is spent on management than production. You are invariably better off with several small teams than one great monolith. So break down the task into distinct teams of three to seven people whenever you can. Tales of woe indicate that nine is the maximum you should consider. Each project team should have its own manager who liaises with the other groups and keeps in touch upwards. Figure 6-1 shows an appropriate team structure.

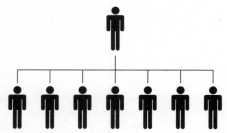

Figure 6-1: Team structure reflecting appropriate number of members and a manager.

Note   It might come as a shock but the computing and software business is hitting its half-century. Many of the early innovators, such as Dr. Wang, who helped invent RAM type memory, are no longer with us. Also keep in mind when forming your teams that while youth brings energy, age brings experience. Older programmers know how to avoid mistakes, so don't count them out.

The Last P Is Process

The *process* is the mechanism of getting from the start to the end of the coding. Nearly everyone has their own theory about it. The most important thing is to pick a working method that gives you the best chance of winning. A lot of the components typically associated with process, such as project feasibility, risk assessment, team structure, and project schedules, have already been sorted out in the project plan.

Process in reality is often a succession of developments that cover the lifetime of the product. The initial process produces the first release and subsequent processes produce its successors. The merit of using a process is that, once it has been explained, everyone understands their responsibilities and knows who is doing what.

The golden rule about starting is not to rush in. Go over your project plan and check carefully that nothing needs to be brought up-to-date. All sorts of things can creep in between the time a project is first planned and the time everyone is ready to start. So walk yourself through it. Some changes that necessitate adjustments will stand out like sore thumbs. Perhaps you have eight people to complete a task envisaged for 10. Perhaps the timeframe has been shrunk by a couple of months. Perhaps there is less money in the kitty than you thought. Items like these are easy for you to spot, but make sure that you also double check that nothing subtle and or apparently innocuous has been altered.

Caution   Read carefully through all the contracts into which you have entered. One of the backers of one public service project added a sentence just towards the end of a very long plan that said, "This project must be undertaken using the following proprietary software . . ." Inserting this without telling anyone wasn't very clever; the entire architecture of the solution had to be reconfigured.

As a standard precaution, the project manager should e-mail each member of the team asking if he or she is aware of any changes between the original project plan and where you stand now except those that everyone has already been made aware of (and list changes you are already aware of). Do not proceed until you receive categorical replies from all members and are agreed on what should be done.

Negotiating Change

Approach change with extreme caution. All projects will change; the final product will differ from the original spec, but the better the project plan, the less change is normally required. Treat late-in-the-day, good ideas with considerable caution. Once you are seen to alter anything, everyone will want to add their two cents. If you allow change to proceed unhindered, it is only a question of time before you will find yourself going round in circles.

Where an idea is of radical significance, consider its effect on your architecture, functionality, procedures, scheduling, and budget. Get everyone to sign off on the consequences before you make a move. The best practice is to leave those ideas for a subsequent version.

Note   Management often feels it has the right to make changes, and so it does. However, by the same token, everyone else has a right to demur.

If circumstances beyond the company's control have altered substantially since the plan was agreed upon, it is not a good idea to introduce arbitrary changes. The most therapeutic thing you can do is bring all the affected parties together, explain what has happened, and ask for help. After all, everyone involved shares the same objective. Between you, you should be able to work out the best way to handle the changes. This is far better than announcing summarily that fewer programmers are going to be employed without allowing the remainder extra time. Pressured managers don't always appreciate the side effects of their decisions.

It is much better to sit down together and talk through the implications. There may be an acceptable way to take out the thorns. If there isn't, agree only to what you honestly believe you will be able to deliver. If, for any reason, you are overruled, be courteous, calm, and log your reservations. Explain how it may compromise delivery; then hope like hell that you are wrong.

Keeping Problems at Arms' Length

The following sections detail strategies for warding off problems that can arise during the course of your project.

Risk Management

It's unrealistic to expect that if you have planned and prototyped the project well, there will be no risk. Computing is not like that. Risk management has many heads, as this lengthy section demonstrates. Before you get caught up in programming, it is vital to be aware of the uncertainties and know how to keep your eye on them. The only way to address risk is to accept it, quantify it, and confront it.

The Time-Money Quantum

Delays that are expressed in terms of time can be equally well expressed in terms of money, which is why every member of your team needs to keep a beady eye on the way the golden hourglass drips. The accounts people measure each item of expenditure. The managing director is concerned with the bottom and finishing lines. The project manager is concerned that he doesn't go over his ceiling in time or money. The staff are concerned that their expenses don't exceed their allowance and that they deliver on schedule. On a software project everyone has to pace their resources.

The five most common reasons why projects go over budget follow:

+ The specification changes.
+ There is a delayed realization of what the project really entails.
+ People leave and have to be replaced.
+ Additional software technologies are required.
+ The estimates were inept.

The ramifications of going over budget can be scary: Marketing windows are missed, key functions have to be dropped, or the project has to be scrapped. And in the worse scenario, it takes the firm down with it. Everyone on the team, from the most senior to the most junior, has to understand the importance of money, the seriousness of overspending, and that ultimately no firm, not even a rich one, has unlimited coffers.

Senior managers are usually wary of disclosing contingency budgets as they presume that project and team managers will factor it into their thinking. Nevertheless, managers should be equally wary of starting any project where the budget is absolutely rigid. Barely one in six projects comes in on time and on budget. It is statistical suicide to start a project without some leeway.

Whether your main strength is on the business side or the programming side, you still have to manage your time. Sometimes this is harder than managing others. The trick is to make a short list of all you intend to accomplish today before you check your e-mail. Clear the decks so you can devote as much time during the day as possible to productive work.

Make yourself a short list such as the following:

- ✦ Meetings today—is anything outstanding?
- ✦ What do you need to achieve today and are there issues to resolve from yesterday?
- ✦ Do you need a formal discussion with anyone? If so, arrange it.
- ✦ Is there any admin to do?
- ✦ Are you on schedule?

Rules to Block Disruptions

Once people appreciate that every time a programmer is interrupted he loses half an hour, they soon desist. Providing programmers with their own spaces to work in (discussed in Chapter 4) stops spontaneous chatter; however, going to this expense is a complete waste if people are going to bombard them indirectly. Here's a starter set of rules:

- ✦ Turn your cell phone off before you start work.
- ✦ Disable Internet chat systems.
- ✦ Only check e-mails during breaks.
- ✦ Anyone who has to contact you urgently during working hours should use the normal phone.
- ✦ Other members of the staff who wish to contact you should only do so via your project manager.

What to Do When Writers Stall

This is usually the first sign of trouble. Sometimes the programmer knows exactly what the problem is but not how to wriggle out of it. Coding blocks, for instance, are hard to define. They're not easy-to-spot objects with "trouble" written in big letters. Normally, it's something that just won't work correctly. It often takes a while for a programmer to realize that he or she may not be able to resolve it on their own.

It's a good rule of thumb that if a writer has spent more than half an hour getting nowhere, he should start using Plan B, even though it may mean interrupting his colleagues. The first thing he should do is talk the problem through with his project manager—it's what he's there for. If the project manager can't solve the problem, the pair should work out who (inside the team or outside the organization) is most likely to know the answer. If that doesn't yield results, they should put out a newsgroup message. The response time can be surprisingly prompt, but delays of up to four hours are common. If a programmer takes this route, he will naturally get on with something else in the interval, pausing to check every hour for a brainwave to emanate from the Internet.

 Note   Being shy, polite, or embarrassed isn't going to shift writer's block. Talking to someone else will. Whenever anyone's stuck, more heads are better than one.

Leave Grazing to the Project Manager

Nothing is worse than a stuck programmer delving into the Internet, finding a bit of code to get him around a problem, embedding it into the program, and plodding on. You have no idea of the implications of quality, source, support, updates, and copyright, to say nothing of the licence fees. You can't expect new programmers to understand these issues. Finding solutions via the Internet is a black art and uses up a lot of time. It's far better that the developers tell the project manager what the problem is and for him to find, screen, and assess any potential solution. This is an excellent topic to bring up at your weekly meetings. With many people around the table, they might already know of solutions that they have used on previous occasions. Who knows, your organization might have a valid license to use it already.

Handholding

Although few do it, one of the most important tasks of a project manager is to hold his programmers' hands whenever they get stuck. To be effective, the project manager has to be conversant with the languages and techniques being employed. The project manager can then work alongside the programmer, get him or her to explain the problem, discuss solutions, and together work through the answer.

Don't be wary of splitting the coding up and undertaking part of it yourself. Apart from being an excellent bonding exercise, you'll develop a better understanding of and respect for each other as you bring that tricky part of the project back on schedule.

Handling Adverse News

Perhaps the supreme challenge of self-discipline is how you react to bad news. If every time someone blurts out that they've dropped the team another day behind schedule you do an impersonation of Krakatoa, all that will happen is that everyone else will instinctively lie low. Far from sympathizing with you, they might feel that your reaction is even more upsetting than the news.

You will get a much more supportive reaction if you take a deep breath and think through the implications, which is what everyone else is striving to do. I'm not suggesting that you shouldn't let off steam later, but it's better, especially if you are a leader, to help others to come to terms with the setback. This will earn you considerable respect.

Whistle Blowing

Programming is essentially like a one-track railway. If anyone gets stuck, at some point, it's often hard for the whole team to get much further ahead. It's vital, therefore, that the obstacle is resolved in the minimum time possible. Don't imagine that if the person who encounters the problem pretends it isn't there the problem will resolve itself or that they will suddenly think of an answer. Tinkering usually makes matters worse. As soon as anyone hits a problem they must blow the whistle for help and ask their colleagues, the project leader, or anyone else in the organization who can lend a useful mind. If no one else can suggest an answer, post a newsgroup message ASAP. Don't be afraid to ask for outside help. If there is an answer (and there usually is), someone somewhere knows it.

 Tip   If you look at your schedules, you should know what you are working on the next day. If your are doing anything with which you are not familiar, post a newsgroup question the night before asking for general advice and the best approach to issues that give you concern. Next morning there's normally a queue of spot-on advice. This way you won't waste a day.

Keep an Eye on That Clock

Things don't always go according to schedule. Applying yardsticks from other fields, such as printing, plumbing, or manual calculations, is no guide to how long it will take to write the code to computerize a routine. What is easy to describe can be complex to code, and what might seem monumental can be a cinch. For example, to extract every individual word in Shakespeare's ascribed works can be written in as little as three lines of code. The answer is 29,066. To write and populate a Web form that allows you to use conditional dropdown menus to take you from country to town to street to house number, by contrast, can take an experienced programmer eight working hours.

Programmers can often supply guesstimates, and these are given in good faith and assume the code works as planned with no ramifications. However, the code they have just typed may affect a routine elsewhere in the program. Cause and effect can be the very devil to trace. So, while it is sometimes possible to affect a day's work in a minute with a computer, at other times it can take a day to do a minute's work. Monitoring and managing the operation is the only mechanism you have to bring this activity under control.

Pace Yourselves

All other things being equal, the biggest difference between a programming team that succeeds and one that falls short is that the winning team paces itself. As a group and individually, the programming team sets achievement targets for each day. Each person makes a vow that they will achieve so much by the end of the day. Five minutes before they shut down, the development manager asks every individual, in the earshot of others, how he or she got on. The responses are noted but no one makes a comment, not even for praise. They just let the situation sink in. The development manager then asks everybody to reflect overnight on what they intend to achieve the following day. First thing next morning, he asks for each member to announce his target in front of the others. These targets should not be ambitious. The aim isn't to break records; it's to succeed as a team. The focus is on quiet determination.

While each member will want to demonstrate to his peers that he is pulling his weight, the target he sets himself has to be achievable. The development manager will at this stage lend a hand to anyone who is lagging behind his own schedule. When the situation warrants it, he may ask other members for their help.

Clever teams realize that it is only a matter of time before they experience setbacks. So they build up a safety lead from the start by stretching themselves, trying to pack an extra 15 minutes of coding into a seven-hour day until they have a healthy lead.

Crucial to pacing is the preparation of the project steps. Unless this is done, programs of any ambition always seem to take longer than the length of their parts to complete. There's a FUD factor (fear, uncertainty, and doubt) about them that daunts new and junior members of a team, in particular. Project managers, therefore, break down the project into self-contained bites. Initially this is done on a functional basis. They then subdivide the main sections into reasonable weekly targets. Further subdivision is then left to individual programmers. Between the start and finish of a page for a Web site, for example, the following main steps might be listed:

1. Agree on content.
2. Mock up the proposed look and feel.
3. Choose the appropriate technology.
4. Design the template.
5. Commission artwork.
6. HTML it.
7. Test it.

You can then monitor progress component-by-component as your team gains in confidence, meets each challenge, and closes each subsection off.

The result is that you will have a working product to show for your efforts sooner.

Monitoring Progress

Much like a ship's captain, you hold the master chart. It's the one with the title, "Product Development Plan." You know where you are starting from, where you want to get to, and the route you need to follow. To keep track of your progress you must plot your daily position. Even if you are working on your own, remember to tick off the milestones as you pass them. Psychologically it will do you good and remind you of the genuine progress that you are making.

Ideally you need to keep two charts: a simple public one that shows progress against the major milestones and a detailed one available only to the team. This can be updated at the end of each week and used as a visual aid at the Monday morning meeting (see Figure 6-2).

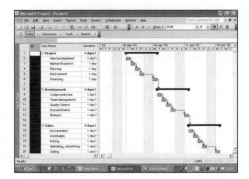

Figure 6-2: Project Development Schedule example.

Note If you are uncertain what style of chart you need to monitor your progress, I recommend a standard Gantt format. Most people are familiar with them even if they do not know the name, and they are very easy to understand.

There is a belief that developers hate progress reports because they tell you how behind you are. Good developers are never so shortsighted. Progress reports are essential to let everyone know the overall progress of the project. Without them, it's like trying to sail to America without plotting your daily position.

How to Inspect

Remember, you never get what you expect; you only get what you inspect. From the outset, progress and issues should be reviewed at the end of each day. If, for any reason, you miss the end-of-day check, take a good look at what's been achieved first thing the following morning. Never miss two days in a row.

Programmers will be more frank with you if they find you supportive. While they may not always be able to please you, they always want to. So always approach them in a relaxed manner. If you know they are working on something complex, agree on a convenient time to meet; otherwise, just pull up a chair for your daily chat. You want to discover three things:

+ Is there anything that you can help them with?

+ Have they got any concerns?

+ Have they completed today's task?

If anyone's working from home, call them up and have the conversation, get them to e-mail you any changes that need checking, or remote connect to their PC to see what they've been working on. Wherever your employees are working, don't just talk. Look at the code and ask to see how it's behaving. Offer comments. When deserved, give praise. Before you say goodbye, run through the tasks for tomorrow.

Doing daily updates means your programmers never have to confess they are a month behind schedule. The longest you can be informed about is a single day.

Weekly Meetings

Although development is a team effort, the actual act of programming is solitary. Regular weekly meetings are the best way to keep team feeling alive, bring everyone up to date, discuss current problems, and review progress. It's also a good time to discuss the wider picture. Weekly meetings are an ideal opportunity for developers to ask questions and for project managers to make everyone aware of what else is at stake.

Meetings are best held first thing on Monday mornings. The team will be fresh from the weekend and have had time to reflect on the previous week's accomplishments.

Brainstorming

If you haven't got any big thinkers on your team, brainstorming sessions are the answer. Ideally, the entire team should attend and someone from marketing should be present so they are kept abreast of progress and can clarify questions that impinge on salability. Local telecommuters should also be invited. If they are based some distance away, set up a videoconference link or fly them in as common sense dictates.

The crucial thing about a brainstorming session is that no idea is wrong. The chairman may acknowledge the wackiest contribution. He may ask the contributor to elucidate. Anything further tends to be counterproductive.

Each idea should be recorded in a succinct and clear manner without comment. Arguments against the ideas tend to speak for themselves and one thought, in a free atmosphere, leads to another. The project manager should verify and sign the minutes and distribute them to all concerned.

Larger projects benefit from a short report at the end of each week noting progress and issues. Such reports, normally prepared by the project manager, do not have to be overtly formal and can either be handed around or distributed by e-mail.

Containing Entropy

Every so often, your programmers are going to run into a brick wall. For some reason the program won't accept the next increment, and no one can figure out why. They then have to go back to the previous version. In the course of a program this may happen several or many times.

To avoid getting hopelessly confused, you should have some decent version control software. It stores old copies, indexes changes, and tracks who did what and when. This electronic librarian allows you to screen an earlier version of a program to compare differences between one cut and the next. It's particularly handy when you can't pinpoint what has made your program go ape.

The simplest version control programs just store and manage a sequence of charged files. The more sophisticated ones allow for coding concurrent changes, automate the build assembly, enforce regression testing, and can even create and compile the final product. Whatever level of complexity you need, don't code without installing version control software; and make sure your subcontractors and telecommuters have a compatible version.

Regular Builds

The sooner you can start testing the product, the sooner bugs can be discovered and squashed. The sooner the developers know that their coding integrates and works, the sooner your product can be launched. Clever engineers construct their project for prefabricated assembly. This way they can get the embryonic product working as quickly as possible. Another advantage of this technique is that they can produce demonstration builds for management and clients at a very early stage. Ninety-four percent of successful companies use daily or weekly builds. Unsuccessful ones assemble their code at monthly or even longer intervals (*Secrets to Software Success,* Detlev Hoch et al).

Backup Code

Before any project begins you need to have a mechanism that automatically backs up the code. Copies should be stored off site, away from theft and fire. Either store them physically elsewhere or e-mail or use File Transfer Protocol (FTP) to transfer them securely. Remember to include telecommuters' and contractors' contributions. Secure back up is the responsibility of the project manager.

Demonstration Builds

What will determine the selling success of your program isn't how good you think your program is. It's how easy it is for users to set up and use. So give a small panel of prospects a chance to try out your program as you get close to the end. Listen carefully to their comments. If, for instance, panel members do something unauthorized and your software doesn't even beep, you will realize that they've no idea what they ought to be doing. Give them a visual or audible clue. Improved customer confidence is the key to recommendations and cascading sales. Easy-to-use software is always easier to sell.

There is no substitute for being able to show a prospective user a working model of your program. Describing the product may enthuse him. Going into detail may get him interested. Writing an inspired project plan may tempt him into dipping his hand in his pocket. Mocking up key screens may even evoke suggestions, but there is no substitute for being able to demonstrate your program in action. Only then can it become real in the user's mind. Only then can he raise those devastating, sneaky questions that make you wonder why this or that had never occurred to you. Only by incorporating good answers can you turn objections into sales.

Commissioned Projects

If the project is a commissioned one, the longer the gap between starting a project and delivering the finished product, the more prone you are to the client's problems. If the client is inexperienced, take longer with them to make sure they understand the process (maybe get them to read this book), and take special care to make sure the issues are prioritized in the order they require them rather than the sequence that is most expedient to you.

Having ironed out the specs and released an injection of money, the client has a great deal of time to reflect on what he should really have asked for. He will often try to insinuate subsequent changes at no extra cost. Changes in legislation, economics, or the client firm's own internal circumstances can also alter a client's requirements. However, even without pressures like these, few clients are able to visualize what it is they really commissioned. That is why you are developing the program and he is the client.

Clients certainly know what they dislike when they see it and will articulate. Sometimes they exaggerate because they fear you will ignore them otherwise. Sometimes they may not hit the nail square on the head. Listen very carefully and take notes on the spot, writing down all the key points verbatim. Listen not just to what they say but also to what they may be trying to say. When you get back to your desk, think it through from their point of view and work out what is to their best advantage.

By far the most compromising situation for a middle management client is when he or she gets taken literally. They realize things aren't working as they should. They may also realize that the software is working exactly as they specified. They are also aware that someone else higher up in their organization is bound to spot the deficiency and blame them. The criticism may be trivial or it may be a showstopper. My advice is not to make a fuss. Volunteer there and then to put the matter right. Afterwards, augment the bill fairly but discreetly. The person you are dealing with will appreciate that you have got them off the hook and that your company has provided what their company needs. They are very likely to be grateful.

However, be aware that mistakes may also be laid fairly and squarely at your door. You aren't infallible either. If you find that you have indeed made an error, accept responsibility and put the matter right as soon as possible. If, on the other hand, what is being asked for is a genuine change, remind your client tactfully that provisions were made for additional costs when the specs were agreed upon. It was to minimize the need for extras that you carefully read through each item together. Do your best not to get into this situation in the first place. If you do, iron out the problem at an early stage by showing the client the program as you build it.

Showing the client builds as you go is a bit like showing expectant parents photographs of the fetus inside the womb; it's not such a surprise when a boy or a girl arrives. Whenever a client asks for anything new or novel, clever software houses win their client's approval on an installment basis by demonstrating progressive builds or prototypes. The client will then appreciate from the outset that you cannot deliver a bull's eye the first time any more than he can give you a complete brief in every respect. Sharing progress makes clients feel that they are part of the creative process, and once you have got them on your side, you may be surprised how imaginative and supportive they can be.

Unless the solution is highly technical, the best person to demonstrate builds to a client is usually the project manager. He usually has the greatest understanding of the client's needs and the software being developed.

Whenever a client asks for a novel feature, appreciate that by producing it you may also be solving other people's problems too. Consider whether it is in your best interests to charge your current client for the entire development or to share the cost among others yet to come. Consider the extra time it will take to produce a standalone and what else your firm may wish to do with its time. Give thought also to what the market will bear.

Data Prototyping

A similar procedure is often useful when you are developing an intensive data system. If you are uncertain of your ability to manipulate the required volume of data, construct a prototype to test it. I found this invaluable when asked to investigate whether some of the early PC networks could work fast enough to replace the predominant mini-computer-based systems for equity trades. We thought they could but some members of the client's team were highly skeptical, especially the managing director (MD). The solution was to build a prototype with a server that generated several hundred of thousands of changing numbers per minute (mimicking the stock market in perpetual heavy trading) and a workstation displayed these in the standard dealer's grid colors. It was then possible to demonstrate that the PC network system was able to cope with the heaviest data load 14 times faster than the older, more arcane mini-computers.

Never Underestimate the Learning Curve

Do you remember how long it took you to become conversant with your first computer language or to develop your first database program or interactive Web site? Getting up to speed with any new computing technique takes time, to find out how it works, to locate and understand the options, and to acquire a near automatic proficiency. Even then you need enough experience to know when it's best to use the tool.

You'd be unwise to expect your programmers to become fully acquainted with any major new item in less than a month. You should allow three months for them to be able to write basic code with any semblance of speed and six months before they are able to make genuinely knowledgeable, informed decisions. You may be faster or slower than your programmers, but however you rate your team's performance, factor it into the schedule. No one produces perfect code the first time.

Formula Checking

Programming formulas can be tricky and it takes time to compile the entire program before you can test it. A useful shortcut is to build and test the formula in a spreadsheet, fine-tune it until it is working perfectly, and then transpose it to your code. Check that the finished, compiled product is identical to the spreadsheet.

New Staff

Remember your first day at a new school? An existing pupil would take you under their wing and show you the ropes. The fastest way to bring new members up to speed is to pair them up with a suitable old hand. A few days buddying is normally sufficient to give newcomers time to meet people and learn to whom to look for guidance.

Infallible Introductions

When people first come on board, they need to be introduced. Names, roles, and memorable details should be exchanged. For example, "This is Sadie Brown. She looks after our databases and is a whiz at parasailing." "This is Chris White, our marketing guru. He did a great job on the Mars project." Associate each person with a memorable fact.

By the time you have walked them around all the departments (or the room) you will have given them an idea of the pace, who reports to whom, how they should behave when they hit a serious problem, what support they can expect, and so on.

Get to know your staff individually. Give them a lift or take them out for a meal. Find out what they've done, how they liked school, how things are at home, what they're proud of, what their aspirations are. And give them an insight into you. You can often do this without talking shop at all, but it will make your working environment more comfortable.

Before you allocate work or issue schedules, arrange a session to run through the minutiae. Explain how you intend the project to fit together, your management ethos, what you expect from each member, and what you are keen to avoid.

When the Clock Really Starts

Issues such as space, computers, and staff are straightforward: you've either got them or you don't. The biggest problem if you are starting up from scratch, have an agreed-upon project, and resources are signed off is a time delay between recruiting the right staff and waiting for their hardware to arrive, or for their offices to be completed. Make it clear to incoming staff that the clock starts when everything is ready and that budgets will be extended if delayed deliveries hold things up. Prevention, however, is the best cure. Make sure that the resource allocation and procurement is actioned as per your timetable and that the timetable includes a realistic provision for unexpected delays.

Know When to Take a Step Back

Painful though this is, it can sometimes be more productive to ditch a dud section of code and start again. The typical reasons and course of action are listed in Table 6-2.

Table 6-2 **Dealing with Dud Code**	
Reason	*Course of Action*
Programmer has written garbage	Assign work to another
Programmer progressing like slug	Assign work to another
Code works but seriously inefficient	Consider rewrite
Code works but programmer disgusted with their output	Rewrite if time permits
The program partially works	See if it can be corrected

If you find yourself in any of these situations, don't be afraid to appoint a new developer to tackle or rewrite the section. If the original programmer does the rewrite, it usually takes about a third less time than it took originally. If a developer is persistently coming unglued, consider seriously whether he or she is up to the job.

In academia, investigating something for three years and writing a thesis concluding that it doesn't work will almost always earn you a degree. In the commercial world, failure is the last thing that gets rewarded. Remember, though, that some of the world's most successful men and women faced failure before they found success. Indeed, they say failure doesn't deserve the social stigma with which it is generally credited. If you find yourself paddling uphill without even a canoe, call a meeting as soon as possible. If no one has a life-saving solution, try attacking the problem in a different way. A hard decision though it must be, there are times when it makes more sense to stop a project than struggle on.

Here are typical circumstances in which it's best to call all your senior managers together and get a consensus on whether or not to proceed:

+ The budget is unsustainable.

+ The schedule is going to miss the window of opportunity.

+ Key staff are no longer available and it's impossible to proceed without them.

+ A significant competitor appears.

+ Technology changes.

+ You hit bugs that no manner of head banging seems able to fix.

+ The backer loses faith in the project.

+ Marketing circumstances change radically.

Because you are regularly communicating with your senior people, the purpose of the meeting is unlikely to be a surprise. If a project has to be stopped, wind it down rather than bringing it to an immediate halt. It is important to find out what components of the project are reusable and document the lessons that can be learned. An aborted project may still justify itself by helping future projects.

Avoid Over-Stretching

Projects can have a habit of going really well until they are 90 percent complete; then they hit a snag and progress no further. Sometimes this is because the teams have been pushed hard all the way through the project and when the work is substantively over the hump, they give up. This pressured approach is unsustainable. It's just like running your car at full revs continuously—pretty quickly the engine will fail. The same is true of people.

It's a better management technique to relieve the pressure before the team is spent. As development hits the stage where documentation and beta testing kick in, relax the pace. By all means explain why, but allow them to recover their strength for the blitz of the final stage of development.

Know When the Project Is Finished

Developers, like any craftsmen, can polish and refine their work forever. Your project plan tells you the critical functionality that the software requires for marketing. Positive, clean tests will let you know when the bugs have been reduced to an inoperative level. As soon as these criteria are met, your software is ready for release. Even if you're sitting in a room tapping your way along on your own, you'll appreciate that you're doing more than just generating lines of code.

Checklist

Do not even think of beginning development until your project plan is complete. Here is a checklist for rounding out your project plan:

1. Employ the best people you can.
2. Pick people who know the end-user industry.
3. Find managers who have done it before.
4. Don't proceed until you have the right people.
5. Keep team sizes small.
6. Break the task down into easy pieces.
7. Make sure each person knows what he or she has to do.
8. Keep team members informed and enthusiastic.
9. Take the team into your confidence.
10. Protect developers from interruptions.
11. Veto inessential change.
12. Be available for staff.
13. Pace programmers every day.
14. Watch the clock.
15. Encourage programmers to help each other.
16. Set a good example.
17. Fire bad apples fast.
18. Carry potential customers with you stage by stage.
19. Test the software regularly.
20. Maintain a safety copy of your code.

Note A cautionary word about over-succeeding: Joe Tucci, who ran Wang for 6 years and brought it successfully out of Chapter 11, always used to tell his programming team each time we met that it takes at least three attempts to get software right. So don't be afraid of releasing a less than ideal product. The first version just has to have enough functionality to satisfy users, and with success and revenue you'll turn it into what you've always wanted it to be (which will probably be around the third release).

✦   ✦   ✦

CHAPTER 7

How Not to Reinvent the Wheel

What do the Volkswagen Golf and Beetle and Audi TT have in common?

They all share the same chassis. From the outside, they appear to be very different vehicles, but inside, their platforms are identical.

In the United States, the Chevrolet Venture, Pontiac Montana, and Oldsmobile Silhouette all use the same power train. Automobile manufacturers have learned over the last century that the capital required to develop a new product is more than even they can bear.

Mass production demands standardized parts, not just within the model, but across the entire industry. By standardizing production of spark plugs, automatic gears, door locks, electronics, and power trains, they have been able to lower production costs and cut development time dramatically, often eliminating testing for many items that have already proved themselves in widespread use.

Volkswagen has this down to such a fine art that they produce only four platforms as the basis for a spectrum of 30 models spanning four international brands. Now ask yourself what you might learn from this.

The automobile industry originally began standardization out of bicycle garages without any deliberate policy. They were using similar components, such as nuts, bolts, light bulbs, and tires. It took a long time before they realized that there were considerable benefits to using subcontractors and began consciously buying outside components. Initially, most of these components were small, low-cost items, such as spark plugs, tires, and starter motors. Standardization really took off when, after World War II, the Japanese had to kick-start their bombed-out manufacturing base. They had little other choice.

The Japanese soon realized that standardization reduced the call on capital, kept work forces to more manageable levels, and still gave them all the control they needed over suppliers.

This leanness became addictive. During the 1970s the Japanese started to standardize their major components such as engines and power trains (the combined engine/transmission component), not just within the brand, but throughout the Japanese automotive industry. They have even been known to sell some components to competitors, and entry-level vehicles are enjoying the same quality components as their top-of-the-range models.

The Goal

In the 1970s, firms wrote "Libraries," which were ready-packaged code written in languages such as Assembler, Fortran, or C. These provided a number of subroutines that programmers could stream into their software.

The popularity of Windows in the early 1990s saw the introduction of shared components in the Dynamic Link Libraries (DLL). As object-oriented languages became more commonplace, pre-written modules expanded into what were called *class libraries*. Class libraries were predominately written in C++.

Modern component software is often language-independent. You can bolt it on to your program in whatever language you have elected to use. Although you don't always get the source code, you don't actually need it; and if you're using ActiveX, Java, or COM components, you're already using it.

Componentware is the new name for these ready-made software modules. Componentware earns its place in the world by being attractive to the widest number of developers. This requirement also ensures that prefabricated routines have the longest possible life span.

Componentware doesn't dictate what it should be used for, how it should work, what language it should be used with, or even what standards should be applied. Componentware exists on the sole merit that it works and anyone can use it. This means that massive chunks of quite complex bug-free routines can be tacked onto your code overnight. Your programmers can then tune them to your precise specification. Componentware thus enables you to produce software far more efficiently.

Componentware is the smartest way to accelerate software development. Don't take our word for it, just look at the market. The sales of ActiveX Componentware alone grew over 12 times initial figures between 1996 and 2001. Add in today's Java and COM sales and their combined revenues are in excess of 5 billion dollars. Here's why:

✦ Programs take less time to develop.

✦ Production is simplified.

✦ There is less to test.

✦ Development overheads are proportionately reduced.

✦ The components have a higher quality than you may afford.

✦ Their reliability is proven.

✦ Purchased ready-mades can be reused on a range of products.

✦ Costs can be spread across development.

✦ Developers can focus on marketing with fewer distractions by development.

✦ Lower overall costs create a more advantageous break even (part of the development costs are taken off the balance sheet).

✦ Componentware can make your company more agile.

That said, it hasn't all been smooth sailing. Companies have been experimenting with component-based software production in a systematic way since the mid-1990s. The initial success rates were low. Fortunately, buyers and subcontractors both learned from their initial mistakes, and the lessons they learned could be helpful to you.

Think, Discuss, Agree

The effects of adopting Componentware are radical. Programmers spend less time writing bread-and-butter code. Production is partially accomplished by assemblage.

Radical use of Componentware does, however, mean that your people will be spending more time sourcing and vetting components, liaising with the manufacturers, and fine-tuning the bought-in functions. If you are going to turn the introduction of Componentware into an optimum advantage, don't impose it. You need everyone's cooperation.

In some teams there is a strong culture of the "not invented here/I'll build it myself." The programmers don't trust anything they haven't assembled themselves.

If your people are proudly self-sufficient, you should respect their sensibilities. Call everyone together and discuss the possibilities as an academic exercise. Emphasize your confidence in their ability to produce every item if necessary. Their abilities are not in question. But should you expect the chef to lay the egg?

Raise the question of whether the quality of items you might buy ready-made is compatible with the quality of the product you and your programmers intend to produce. Ask where ready-mades will and won't work. Discuss what opportunities buying-in might create. Remind them lightly that architects have long since given up baking their own bricks just as programmers have long since stopped writing their own compilers. Go through the list of modules required by your program and tentatively ask them to star which tasks might be subcontracted.

Point out that the software engineers will be able to devote more time to the super-structure of the software instead of its foundations.

Acknowledgment is vital. Your programmers are being asked to create many other important things that just can't be bought.

Explain how buying-in may tip the balance of the outcome of the project, particu-larly if you encounter unexpected snags. If the consensus is that Componentware has certain possibilities, don't let the negatives become a logjam. Get the ball rolling by setting up a small working party to look into some of the more promising possibilities.

Don't rush the outcome. Let the situation, not the personalities, make the case. Think, discuss, and come to a consensus. If the working party recommends that there are instances where it makes more sense to buy ready-made components, you will need to make the entire management aware of your plan to do so. For instance, the costing model charged by the vendor must be acceptable to them. Componenting has failed in the past when management hasn't appreciated its implications.

After you've checked into possible Componentware, step back and consider your software as a sequence of key components. See which ones make the best cases. Fundamentally, you will have to choose between an exclusively tailor-made product and a more quickly produced model, with purchased parts.

Don't fall into the common trap of expecting Componentware to get you out of a hole. Many people try out components for the first time only when they discover they are over budget or behind schedule. Using components has a big impact on the design of programs. They can't be dropped in without planning.

Which Are the Prime Targets?

Which areas of your project should you target for Componentware? The obvious suspects are parts of the code that you know will take a long time to write or that your organization doesn't have the skills to deal with in-house, such as an industry standard security routine or flexible reporting add-in. Items that will take time or cost significant amounts of money are ideal targets; these are the easiest to estimate for cost comparisons.

Sourcing Componentware

There are three sources of Componentware:

- ✦ Third-party vendors
- ✦ Components already written in-house
- ✦ Components that you already have a license to use

There is now considerable Componentware available from third parties. But where the software you are writing is specialized and no one has made the routines publicly available, you need not just write them as a one-off, but write them in such a way that they can be easily embodied in other projects.

The key difference here is that you are packaging the code as a separate module so that it can be reused instead of as an exclusive solution to current projects.

In-house Componentware still leaves you with the initial development, testing, and maintenance overheads, but there are no licensing or purchase complications.

Another source that is often overlooked is Componentware that has been legally purchased for some previous project and which you still have the right to use. The larger your outfit, the more likely it is that various goodies are sculling around.

The trick with all outside purchasing is to make sure you get what you want at a price you can afford. Take care when sourcing, especially if you are using new, relatively untested, and what you suspect might be immature components. Consider this checklist:

- ✦ Does the component match your project's requirements?
- ✦ Can you see it being used in other future projects?
- ✦ Does the producer have a laudable track record?
- ✦ Does it have the scope to cope with program developments?
- ✦ Can you try it before you have to commit yourself?
- ✦ Does it pass the prototype test? Choose something complex that will really challenge the component.
    - • How easy is it to embed/use?
    - • How do you rate the performance?
    - • How much time did you save by using it?

❖ Is the product well supported?

❖ Do upgrades/bug fixes appear regularly?

❖ Is the licensing agreement acceptable?

❖ In extreme circumstances, will you legally be able to get access to the source code? This shouldn't be necessary but what happens if they don't fix a bug in an acceptable period of time or they go bust (the source code should be held under ESCROW)?

❖ Does the business case for this component stack up?

❖ How ahead is the supplier of future developments?

The Wider the Use, the Greater the Benefits

If you adopt a component, you get the greatest advantage if you can use it on successive products. This spreads the investment and progressively reduces the induction time as you build up expertise on using it.

However, there's more to Componentware than this. Deciding to incorporate Componentware requires fundamental shifts in the way software is sourced and managed. There is something counterintuitive about buying products instead of writing every detail from scratch. Why pay for something that you can do yourself? It is sometimes said that if you write it yourself you will always have state-of-the-art code. Yet this is only true if you continually have state-of-the-art programmers.

Componentware will typically be upgraded and maintained like any other sold software because it is in the manufacturer's interest to do so.

Firms that are using Componentware successfully have a structured policy for buying components. This way, the knowledge acquired at certain pain and expense is rarely paid for twice.

❖ They build up a directory of sources.

❖ They mark preferred suppliers.

❖ They appoint a coordinator to marshal this knowledge.

❖ They write up notes on every component used.

❖ They sometimes rate them.

❖ They share their knowledge with new programmers in a structured way.

❖ They offer incentives for creating and using new components.

✦ They educate upwards so managers also know about component-based software.

✦ They indoctrinate new employees.

Be Aware, Things Are Changing

Even if you reject Componentware, be aware that your competitors may not.

Componentware enables latecomers to assemble major sections of a rival program with lightning speed. This gives their engineers time to concentrate on the heart of the project and to make sure it works more reliably, has sweeter interfaces, and so on.

Componentware is gradually changing the timescales of software development. Testing and maintenance will still have to be done but they will progressively be less of a deterrent to anyone who wants a share of your business.

Multi-platform Development

Producing software to work over a number of operating systems, such as Windows and Linux, is not straightforward. Some programming modules (as discussed in Chapter 3 on planning) generate code from the same signals (they invoke the relevant components at compile time to achieve this). This little monster is known as *cross development*.

Unless the program is a very minor affair, have separate product managers for each operating version. The issues and feedback from each system will vary, whatever the development environment claims.

Note If you were to implement just one chapter in this book as a means of speeding up and improving your software development, this should be the one. Componentware techniques are likely to give the most immediate and largest payback.

✦   ✦   ✦

Programming without Tears

People make things happen. So managing people has to be your top priority whatever your position on the team. It isn't about being bossy or manipulative. It's about creating circumstances in which everyone around you can succeed.

To know how to go about this you need to know one thing: structure follows strategy. Whether you are on your own or working with many, the techniques that you use to achieve this are fundamentally the same. However, managing the team is not the same as managing the business: At the top, management is essentially an intellectual activity—it requires thought. On the work floor it's about creating positive, useful circumstances by setting targets, recruiting the right people and helping them to bond, agreeing on objectives, sharing the work, helping others to succeed, and monitoring the overall progress. And the spirit is as important as the words.

Are You Experienced?

Most people who set up a project have never managed anyone before. Although almost all will have worked as a team, either in the family or a sports team at school or in a restaurant during holidays or weekends. Don't belittle such experiences. You can learn more about good management from the bottom than you ever will from the top. You'd be amazed how many well-known millionaires started life delivering the daily paper.

The key differences between newspaper delivery and information technology are ones of complexity and scale of responsibility. Deliver a newspaper late and an apologetic smile should get you off the hook. Miss your deadline on a $200,000 software project and you could soon be learning the meaning of the word "attorney."

In software production almost every member of the team is managing someone or something. There is an awful lot of delegated responsibility. Even new junior members of the team end up making decisions about how their bit of the program should work.

Management of the team begins with managing yourself. It is essentially about responsibility, and if you are working on your own, self-management is all the more important. So how do you manage yourself? Largely by applying the same principles that you would with a team. Assuming you get along with yourself, you passed your own interview, and you have no intention of firing yourself in the foreseeable future, you have to sort out three fundamental issues: doing the right things, doing them within the right time, and digging yourself out of your own problems.

In practice this means the following:

1. Write down your strategy. Talk it through with friends and current and former colleagues. When you are happy, it is effectively signed off.

2. Once you are clear about the order in which you are going to tackle your project and have worked out strategies to avoid getting bogged down, you are all set to schedule the work within your brief. Pin this timetable up in front of you so you see it every time you get up from your computer.

3. When you are alone it can be tough trying to resolve problems. However, just because you're working by yourself doesn't mean you have to solve all your own problems. Have a word with a colleague over lunch, e-mail a friend, or put up messages in news groups.

Whether you are a one-man-band or part of the largest programming team on the planet, we all have to self-manage. Own what you do and, when appropriate, own up. To the extent that you are a manager, you will be viewed as father, mother, therapist, counselor, hero, sacrificial lamb, and fixer. Little by little, you'll develop broad shoulders. As a manager, you are not the master but a servant and advocate for your team. The better servant you are, the better master you will be.

You are the one that points the way, that finds the hole in the fence, that helps others to get where they need to be, that listens to their problems, that eases them over the chasm when they get stuck; and you are the one that makes sure everyone gets paid at the end of the month.

Strategy

Your development plan dictates the strategy you adopt. You have a clear objective, some resources, and a certain amount of time. Strategy is the conundrum by which you work out how to fulfill your objective with the resources and time available.

There's absolutely no problem about the easy bits. That's like jogging downhill. Success hinges on your ability to bring those elephants over the Alps. It can be a fascinating challenge. The best way to start is to draft out your route. Once you have worked out how to tackle your task, you will know how many Sherpas, guides, and tent poles you will need.

Building the Team

Most teams evolve. People find themselves working together and they try to make it work as best they can. This is hardly a structured, scientific, or even a managed approach. It's much better to work out what you require for a team and choose the people accordingly.

The following are key criteria for team building:

✦ Putting together the right and complementary skill sets

✦ Choosing people who will have a positive effect on each other

✦ Separating responsibilities to avoid overlaps that could lead to territorial squabbles

✦ Ensuring redundancy on complex or critical parts

Choose the Right People

Managers complain about people like farmers complain about weather. In good times and bad, managers are heard to say, "It's terribly difficult to get good staff." Good people have never grown on trees so where do you find them? The fact is that most managers have never consciously worked out what is needed—like beauty they can recognize it but find it very hard to write a description.

Consider the people in your organization and work out who is making the real contributions and works well with the team. Work out why and write down their characteristic strengths. It is equally instructive to do the same exercise for features you don't like. You'll start building up four separate lists:

✦ The firm likes

✦ The firm dislikes

✦ Individuals' likes

✦ Individuals' dislikes

Update these as you go, build up better insights. Knowing what you need makes it a lot easier to write job descriptions. Whether you are employing headhunters or writing your own job advertisements, you still need to know what your company needs.

Recruiting

At the start, most firms find staff among friends, acquaintances, and people they have worked with before. It's a great way to begin because you usually know exactly what you are getting. However, you may soon run out of names from your little black book.

Sixty to 80 percent of computer jobs are filled without having to resort to outside recruitment organizations. Recruiting yourself will save you significant amounts of money, but it takes up a good deal of time. In writing your own ads and interviewing every likely applicant, you will very quickly learn the following:

+ A slight change in wording can make a great difference to the caliber of applicant you attract.

+ Interviewing, far from giving you any sense of power, is a tedious process.

+ You may not be as good a picker as you always assumed.

It's not actually that you are a bad picker, but people who want a job can be very clever about creating better impressions than they can live up to. Unduly smartly dressed people, for instance, can sometimes still be incompetent. The best applicant is often that person with the best motivation to do the job.

Whenever the job is a sensitive one, it is a good idea to have three interviewers present when you make your final selection. Someone else on the panel will usually pick up things you don't spot while you are concentrating on some other aspect. The ability of some people to pick up unconscious signals is phenomenal, but don't expect to uncover more than an interviewee is willing to reveal.

If possible, offer the applicant a day's working trial (perhaps on a Saturday). You will discover more in the first 10 minutes in the actual work environment than during the entire interview.

It is also good sense to maintain a file of near misses. The better applicants usually find other jobs within weeks, but you can sometimes come back to them a year or two later, and they are great to call on if you get let down almost immediately.

If the appointment is particularly critical or if you need a number of people at once, you may need to call in a headhunter or a recruitment agency. These external recruiters save time by providing you with a pre-screened short list of better people than you might find yourself because they can call on a greater selection. If they are unable to deliver on more than two above-average candidates, you're better off doing it yourself.

Headhunters

In prosperous times headhunters operate at the top of the market supplying CEOs, CFOs, CTOs, and other very senior people. In bad times they drop their sights further down the corporate ladder. They seek people proactively from known, screened clients. Good ones may be responsible for all the senior appointments in a client's career. Fees are typically 30 to 50 percent of first year's salary. Due to the caliber of staff they source and place, the screening process is rigorous. Good headhunters take the time to find out what you need.

Recruiting Agencies

Agencies that specialize in the area for which you have a vacancy are a better bet than those who operate as a general labor exchange. This is mainly because the specialists offer themselves up to those agencies. They then match applicants to vacancies. Recruiting agencies normally charge the equivalent of the first three months' wages. The fee is normally waved if the person doesn't last out his trial period. For bulk recruitment tapered fee structures are often negotiated. The quality of their screening varies with the interviewer and branch.

Online

The Internet rendition of the recruitment firm is the online job site. What they lack in personal attention they make up for in numbers. If you are able to write a sufficiently specific job description, they are worth considering.

Job Ads

The ideal job ad would attract just one applicant—the man or woman you really want. Help wanted ads don't need to be long. They just need to be interesting and pertinent. Read your competitors' ads and ask yourself, "If I read that would I be interested enough to give them a call?"

If you are advertising in a local paper that people read regularly, there is no need to repeat the advertisement, as the number of new readers each week is usually low. If the ad is going on the Internet or into a national publication, this is less of an issue.

Interviewing

> "Interviews are not about the best person for the job; interviews are about, and can only be about, who appears to be the best person for the job. From an interview we can only tell who interviews best."
>
> —Philip Garside – *The Secrets to Getting a Job*

The Right First Impression

Everyone wants to work for a good firm, so candidates are often willing to work for a little less at a good place. Interviewees know what leaves them with a poor impression of a firm, a general lack of purpose, no zing from the moment they step inside the door. Then there is the type of firm that seems to be ruled by martinets; where everyone is told what to do instead of being asked or invited; where management logic seems arbitrary, which leads potential employees to expect that the relationship between achievement and reward is going to be haphazard. Extreme attitudes and pettiness make a candidate's interest nosedive faster than a kamikaze.

Take care you do not give a misleading impression. Managers and programmers are generally intelligent, logical, self-motivated individuals. They respond warmly to firms with a clear sense of destiny, which can offer them a real career opportunity. They like firms that take them seriously and treat them as responsible adults. Like all of us, they are looking for a place where they can grow.

What Are You Looking For?

Most managers interview staff irregularly and are prone to forget the techniques they garnered the last time they conducted an interview. So make a list of your major requirements and rate each candidate accordingly. Major requirements generally include the following:

◆ Qualifications

◆ Achievements

◆ Experience

◆ Appearance

◆ Honesty

◆ Stability

Put People at Ease

There are at least half a dozen reasons people dislike interviews, including fear of failure, having to perform, trying too hard or not trying enough, and nerves. Putting people at ease overcomes most of these. Even formal, structured interviews can be relaxed. It is in everyone's best interest that the candidate performs well. No one likes to see people fail.

Opening Remarks

Good interviewers explain the company, the department, and the work at the beginning of the interview. The bad ones jump straight in with, "Why do you want the job?"

Put together a few paragraphs about the firm, how it started, what it does, its main objectives, and what the department with the vacancy is working on. Then begin to ask questions.

 Note   Be likeable. People like to work with people they like. Conversely, make sure you like the candidate for the same reasons.

Get the Candidate Talking

If you asked a candidate how he went about writing a program and he said, "gut reaction," you'd show him the door. You'd expect a structured answer to a structured problem. How many times do you hear people passing judgment on a group of candidates along the lines of "My gut reaction is to go for . . ."? All gut reaction says is that you haven't had enough experience to know how to calibrate one candidate against another. For high profile positions, many companies resort to psychometric testing, which is a quantitative way of evaluating their abilities, and these are correlated against the specific requirement for that job. For everyday use, have a set of questions that pose typical working dilemmas; then get each candidate to talk you through their answer or approach. Evaluate each of them accordingly. That way you've got some data that can be objectively compared.

Motivating Staff

It may come as a surprise that most surveys reveal that in information technology, money isn't the sole motivator. People in senior positions tend to take their remuneration and job security for granted and are motivated by challenges and opportunities.

Table 8-1 lists the motivating factors that are on most employees' minds, in order of importance.

Table 8-1 Motivating Factors for Employees		
Placing	*Primary Motivators*	*Secondary Motivators*
1	Good wages (including bonuses)	Pensions
2	Job security	Holiday
3	Promotion opportunities	Healthcare
4	Working environment	Maternity/Paternity
5	Appealing work	Long service (age balance)
6	Peer respect	Share ownership
7	Good management	Gym
8	Appreciation of colleagues	Charitable activities
9	Support	
10	Involvement	

Pay Structures

Playing games with people's salaries usually backfires. So if you pay someone significantly more or less than their peers, it will come out sooner or later. Someone has a bit too much to drink, they apply for a job at another firm and the person who catches sight of their job application tells a friend, or one of your maintenance staff is called in to mend some machines in Human Resources or accounts and gets sight of the payroll. There are so many ways private salaries can become public that it is best to structure them and behave as if they are already.

Inserting new clauses in employment contracts isn't workable either. In listed firms, the salaries and bonuses of board members are made public in the annual reports as a matter of law. These must be even-handed and transparent. Everyone will interpret sensible, self-evident salary structures as fair. This doesn't stop you from offering productivity-related bonuses for sales, programmers, and managers; it quantifies rewards with achievements. The golden rule is: Be consistent.

Equipment

It costs Ferrari around $20 million to give Michael Schumacher the equipment he needs to go out and win a Formula-1 race. Luckily, $2,000 to $5,000 will buy any programmer the state-of-the-art workstation that he or she needs to do their job.

In equipment, the following appeals to programmers:

+ High resolution, large screens
+ Fast processors
+ Sufficient memory
+ Reliable equipment
+ Good Internet connectivity
+ Up-to-date and licensed software
+ Automatic backup and version control

Large screens save time because all programs can be kept open and viewed simultaneously without having to open and close windows ad nauseam. They also put less strain on a programmer's eyes and reduce cross-checking errors. Fast processors reduce compiling time so programmers don't have to twiddle their thumbs while their computer completes this task. If a programmer compiles his program 12 times a day and the time shrinks from 7 to 2 minutes, he gains an extra hour's productivity available each day. Enough memory ensures that the computer doesn't run slow as it shuttles data between the RAM and the hard disk. If the developers are undertaking complicated operations, two machines can significantly increase productivity as it allows them to code on one machine and test on the other with the least possible disturbance.

Always use licensed software. Programmers by nature, apart from being highly logical, in my experience have a strong sense of fair play. They feel that it is wrong to write programs that people are expected to pay for while they themselves are forced to use unlicensed code. This comes out as a very strong, secondary reason for changing jobs during interviews.

Finally, programmers must have access to the software that they need (not to be confused with want). Make sure code is produced under version control and automatically backed up each night. This shouldn't be down to the individual programmer. Their equipment should take care of this automatically. In short, the better the equipment you give your staff the more productive they will be. The time you save should more than pay for the difference in cost.

Training

One of the great pleasures of running any firm is taking on young, inexperienced staff and over the years watching them grow in knowledge, ability, confidence, and overall professionalism. It's wonderful to know that you were part of that maturing. However, don't kid yourself—staff won't stay with you forever; you have them for but a portion of their working life. Training and promotion all play a part in keeping staff, but giving them advice, responsibility, and taking a healthy interest in their development all help. It is so much more rewarding to work with staff as people than to employ them as paid tools, and it goes without saying that this personal development isn't just one way.

Companies' approach to training is often polarized; either it is enlightened or it is selfish. Some firms only train staff when they have no other choice. Management sometimes fears that if they train staff they will be better qualified to get a job elsewhere or twist their arm for a raise. They are probably right. Other firms send staff for training regularly (often giving them an annual budget and leaving it to the staff and their line manager to decide which courses they should take). Enlightened firms actively promote training because they understand the value of knowledge. Studies demonstrate conclusively that training yields a very high return on the money invested.

Training is important and respected by staff. One technique that is particularly suited to firms starting up is to get staff to train each other. Once a week over lunch, you organize food and refreshments and one of the teams gives a talk to other members. A lunchtime doesn't sound like much, yet over a year it is amazing how much knowledge everyone acquires.

Planning and Delegating Work

In a pioneering industry where many of the rules are being worked out on the fly, the most important attribute of any IT manager is agility. To react correctly you have to know what is really going on.

Inspection and Communication

"You get from your staff what you inspect, not what you expect."

—John Barnes, marketing manager, Meto International, mid-1970s

The biggest cause of gaps between where a team has gotten to and where the managers feel it should be is the lack of regular communication. In the absence of information to the contrary, busy managers assume that the target is being achieved, but when they inspect the situation they often discover that everyone is behind schedule. The way to avoid such unpleasant surprises is to communicate with each member of your team daily.

You need to find out from each member where they are, if there are any problems, and what they plan next. Responsible programmers welcome communication and appreciate their boss's involvement and concern. You will normally get short but detailed replies. It is a good idea for team members to know when to expect you. If possible, make it a regular time. This way they can reflect on what they have achieved and are less likely to be thrown off track. There's no need to examine the code each day. However, it is a good idea once a week to look at what has been done.

Your team should be no larger than the number of people you can consistently check on in addition to your other duties. Otherwise, consider delegating this part of your responsibility to a progress manager.

Office Politics

In any firm discussion is healthy, gossip is slippery, and humor is appreciated. However, if communication degenerates into office politics, it diverts time away from what people are meant to be doing. People begin to question decisions and become consumed by hypothetical questions.

If certain people gossip endlessly rather than getting on with their work, warn them. If that fails, fire them. They not only waste their own time, they distract others. Most times, they'll be smart enough to take a hint and remember why you employed them. You could also try moving them to another room where there isn't such a willing audience. The only way to uncover disruptive traits in advance is to call their personal references about the applicant's attitudes before you take them on.

Severance

This section would be incomplete if we didn't go over the downsides of running a team. There are only two reasons for getting rid of staff: They are not up to the job or the business can no longer afford them. If you have to sack a person for any good reason, don't be shy about it. You owe it to them to have a direct, polite conversation in private. Address the subject frankly and honestly. This gives them a chance to review their behavior and make some changes in the future.

Be sure to make a record of the discussion, outline the steps that you have mutually agreed upon to terminate the relationship within the contracts of employment and local legislation. If they have lied, stolen, or committed a serious civil or corporate misdemeanor, you must take the appropriate action. In extreme cases this can involve the following:

✦ Immediate cessation of work (clearing desk/leaving building immediately)

✦ Informing police of perceived irregularities

✦ Withholding of references

✦ No payment beyond the day that they leave

✦ Taking legal advice and pursuing legal action if required

Inform the rest of the staff that the person has left. Explain that it would be unprofessional to discuss the circumstances in public. If the removal is politically complex or seems to be an unpopular decision, you may be wise to let one or two people know the background in private. Make sure that what you say doesn't contravene the employment legislation or compromise the firm. In general, don't say anything that you would not be prepared to say to the person's face.

Redundancy

I was made redundant from my first job after leaving college. I'd been computerizing an engineering firm that specialized in heavy-duty crushing equipment for coal fired power stations around the world. In the early 1980s the market collapsed and so did my job. I was only 22. The next week I started up my first computer firm.

Firms don't like making people redundant any more than the people who are being made redundant. If you have to make someone redundant, it is extremely important that you let them know how sorry you are and do everything you reasonably can to help them. Try to take into account other considerations, such as whether they are the sole breadwinner in the household, have children, or have taken on increased financial commitments. Make sure you take the following steps:

✦ Give them as much advance warning as possible.

✦ Have the conversation face to face—don't let them find out by note or hearsay.

✦ Write them the best reference you can.

◆ Phone your friends and peers to see if they have any vacancies. Make them aware of the person's abilities.

◆ Offer to screen their resume. Make sure that it is of the highest quality.

◆ Give them realistic severance pay to enable them time and support to get another job.

◆ Never do this during the holiday season at the end of the year. Forewarn them that tough decisions might have to be made in the New Year.

Caution Keep in mind that your remaining staff will find it very hard to stomach if you make three $40,000 staff members redundant claiming reduced sales when the next set of accounts shows that the CEO has voted himself a $500,000 increase or the rest of the firm is being flown to Las Vegas for a holiday party. Those who remain will probably say nothing to your face; they'll just start looking around for a more equitable employer. Injustice cannot be disguised.

Remote Workers

The advantages and disadvantages of employing remote workers are stark. They don't take up office space, drink your coffee, or eat up your overheads, but because you can't see them, you don't always know what they're up to. Just because a remote employee is not physically in the building doesn't mean you shouldn't maintain regular contact. Some managers believe that if employees are right under their nose it's only the smell and proximity of their own perspiration that keeps them working. That might have been the case with forced labor but it rarely applies to professional programmers. If you don't trust your telecommuters, you can always install a Web cam.

Careful selection is required for people working remotely both in temperament and maturity, as well of the type of tasks that they are given. Remote working is ideally suited for self-motivated, responsible, and highly competent individuals. Age doesn't matter. Some remote workers start coding for major firms while still in their teens.

It is very important that off-site workers have a quiet, dedicated space to work from. They must be guaranteed periods of uninterrupted time from wives, pets, and children. In my experience remote workers normally start earlier and stop later than their 9 to 5 office-bound peers. Because they typically work in quieter surroundings, they are sometimes better able to concentrate and can produce prolific and high-quality code.

Just because they aren't joined at the hip doesn't mean they can't be part of the team. Talk to them daily, and have them come to regular main office meetings (once a month). To function well, remote workers need to be considered with the same attention that you give your in-house staff.

Caution Make sure you are well informed of rules covering insurance for off-site workers. You could be liable if they have an accident while working.

Promotion

Everyone wants to succeed. Money isn't the only, or even the prime, consideration. The approval of their peers and experience that will stand employees in good stead later is key. However, promotion helps to justify their hours to their families who often have to forego a great deal. It is not my job to tell you how to promote staff, merely to point out that if you don't have a mechanism whereby people can earn promotion, you are operating your company on borrowed time. It is in your best interest, as much as your staff's, that the company be structured to allow its staff to grow with it.

Know Yourself, Know Your Team

Knowing what makes your staff tick provides you with the insights of how to get along with, communicate with, and motivate them. The only way to achieve this is to take the time to get to know the people with whom you are working. Similarly, you must know yourself; otherwise, you won't know how you'll behave when situations change, pressure increases, and so on.

Keeping Your Team

Comings and goings are disruptive and costly. Good firms have low staff turnovers. For example, Microsoft was rated the number one employer in the United Kingdom in 2003 (*The Sunday Times* "100 Best Companies to Work for" survey, March 2, 2003) and only had a 5 percent annual staff turnover.

One of the principal reasons why people in the IT industry change jobs is overwork. They may not mind it, but their family and children certainly will. Eventually, they cave in to outside pressure and start looking around. It doesn't make for good long-term productivity, and it denies you the ability to go into overdrive when you meet a real problem.

We can all name colleagues who continually work a 14-hour day. There's always some new panic owing to bad planning and indifferent supervision. The result is that the employee gets tired and irritable and starts making bad decisions. Their home life disintegrates because they don't have one. Boyfriends, girlfriends, wives, and husbands leave, and then they really do have a problem, and so do you.

A company that has gotten itself into this position finds it very hard to reward employees for exceptional work because the exception has become the rule. What do the employees do? They do the only thing they can; they leave.

Football team managers don't have hang-ups about keeping their players. They appreciate that their business is dynamic; so is yours. Good people are always in demand. Don't be surprised when a rival offers to pay big to attract your employees. Make sure you always have your eyes on replacements for all members of your team. Similarly, work out what their promotion prospects should be and what would be the best project or type of work for them to tackle next, not just from the company's point of view but from theirs as well.

✦   ✦   ✦

Squashing Bugs at the Source

What everyone had always suspected about bugs was set in stone in 1994 when Kaplan, Clark, and Tang published their findings on the comparative costs of tackling bugs (*Secrets of Software Quality: 40 Innovations from IBM,* McGraw-Hill, 1994*)*. Their findings are frightening, particularly as their research was conducted on the corporation that has more experience in programming than anyone, IBM. They found that resolving a bug once a program has been released may cost a thousand times more than squashing it at birth. In one case, programmers spent 7,053 hours inspecting 200,000 lines of code, preempting 3,112 potential defects at the design stage. Kaplan, Clark, and Tang calculated programmers' time at $40 per hour (1993 rates). The total expense amounted to $282,120, or $90.65 per defect. Compare this to their findings about putting things right after the product is shipped. Assume that the programmers have the incidence of bugs down to 1 per 1,000 lines of code (lower than average). Once bugs get into the field, the cost of rectification was calculated at $25,000 per fix. The bill, $5 million, was almost 18 times the cost of sorting the problems out during development.

Table 9-1 **What Bugs Cost to Fix**		
Stage	*Unit Cost*	*Multiplier*
Requirements	$	1
Design	$$$	3–6
Coding	$$$$$$$$$$	10
Development Test	$$$$$$$$$$$$$$$$$	15–40
Systems Test	$$$$$$$$$$$$$$$$$$$$$$$$$$$$$$	30–70
In Operation	$$$	18–1000

As you can see from looking at Table 9-1, you have *no* choice. If you want to get into business, let alone stay in it, bugs must be fixed at the earliest opportunity. Stark as this precept is, there is an even bigger lesson: Prevention is better than cure. However, as easy as it is for management to say that, it is notoriously difficult for programmers to deliver.

If some of the biggest, most experienced, most efficient names in the computer world have this sort of trouble, you can't expect to get off scot-free; but this doesn't mean you can't also be successful.

In computing, quality control is centered around the idea of making a program perfect. In practice this comes down to designing, constructing, detecting, measuring, and fixing methods that ensure that as many errors as possible can and will be removed at the earliest stage. It's not that bugs prevent programs from working in the end; it's the drain on resources. If you don't build quality gates into development from the outset, costs will skyrocket and the product will bomb.

How Bugs Became Bugs

Before looking at how you can optimize the process of creation, you should know why bugs in the computing world are called bugs. Not a lot of people know this.

When Harvard University was developing its Mark II Computer in late 1945, production ground to a halt. On inspection they discovered that a moth had flown between the relays of the valves that powered the early relays. The time was 15:45, the date September 9, 1945, and the person no other than Commodore Grace Hopper, who apart from being a stickler for program structure, is one of the pantheons of computer greats. She went on to help develop COBOL, the first compiler, and program Harvard's original M1 and MII computers.

The first computer bug really was a bug—nowadays they're all manmade.

Obsessed about Quality?

Computers are built on logic. To work satisfactorily, we logically presume they have to be flawless. So perhaps it isn't surprisingly that people seem to be quicker to seize on software defects than they are on the shortcomings of other, seemingly less logical products such as automobiles. Because customers are in constant contact with each other, reports of bad experiences spread like wildfire, often with dire consequences.

✦ Products get returned.

✦ More people have to man phone lines to deal with complaints.

✦ Corrective costs soar.

✦ Time is lost and there is a lot more work for everyone, including managers, salesmen, shippers, and accountants.

✦ Income plummets.

Whether the issue is major or minor, the consequences of any product not being entirely satisfactory when released are salutary. Even if you give your software away it must still be of merchantable quality.

How to Approach Quality

The approach a doctor takes to a patient differs according to whether he is dealing with a broken leg, post-natal depression, or a cholera epidemic. Managers and programmers similarly need to know the nature, scale, and prognosis of a program's defects. They also have to respond differently depending on whether the defect is an isolated glitch in a greenhouse watering control or part of a massive programming division working on a new national air traffic control system. In either case, the goals are identical: zero defects. Tolerances obviously differ.

How to Classify a Bug

As in the insect world, there are bugs and BUGS! In order to assign them a proper priority, it is essential to have some means of grading them. You have to know which bugs to squash first and how many resources to throw at it. A catastrophic bug requires very different attention from a cosmetic blip. Surprisingly, to my knowledge, there isn't a universal scale. However, Table 9-2 offers a four-point classification, marked from A to D in order of decreasing severity.

	Table 9-2 **Bug Classification**	
Classification	*Description*	*Example*
Class A: Catastrophic	Crashes the program, computer, deletes executables or data.	Erases data. Aborts the program.
Class B: Serious	Data is computed incorrectly. User may be seriously misled.	Erroneous arithmetic. Program doesn't do what it should.
Class C: Malfunction	Functional may skip or does not work as it should.	Feature in specification omitted.
Class D: Superficial	Proofreading error or visual blip.	Misspelled or missing, literals or visual issue.

So Class A bugs can destroy data, programs, crash the software, or even the hardware. Programs with catastrophic Class A bugs must NEVER be released. If one is found, take immediate action to correct it.

Class B bugs generate or save invalid data. These are serious bugs and should be dealt with expediently prior to release, although they are not as life threatening as the previous classification. In practice, if you can't resolve a Class B bug, you are better off removing the feature.

Most bugs fall into Class C. They cover everything from menu options never coming into play to data appearing in an inappropriate position. While these do not derail the program, they do affect user satisfaction. Treat or release these with circumspection.

Class D or cosmetic bugs are trivial by nature and are accordingly easy to fix. Although they don't jeopardize the viability of a program, they are no credit to any manufacturer. Obvious mistakes should be corrected as speedily as possible.

Classes B–D can be further broken down into two categories: Fix now or fix later. Any bug in the fix now category must be resolved prior to any outsider testing the program. Those classified as fix later may be left until the team has the time but should be resolved before the product is launched. So within a minute you've gone from a pile of bugs in your program to having a method for recognizing them and dealing with them sensibly.

How to Measure Quality

Fortunately for us, the problem of containing the impossible has addressed some very brilliant minds. They have broken down the problems of quality control into critical components that are as useful to managers monitoring the progress of technicians as they are to programmers themselves.

James McCall and colleagues identified 11 quality criteria back in 1977 (A. McCall, P. K. Richards, G. F. Walters, "Factors in Software Quality," RADC-TR-77-369, Vol I -III, November 1977). These were christened *Software Quality Factors* (*SQF*s) and are listed in Table 9-3. Although SQFs cover every aspect of quality across a program's entire life cycle and embrace every issue from maintenance to future porting to other operating systems, the 11 criteria do not necessarily bear a close resemblance to their dictionary meanings; so read on with care.

Table 9-3
Software Quality Factors

SQF	Requirement	Example
Correctness	Can the product work?	Matches specification and works accurately
Reliability	How long between failures?	Accuracy of operation
Efficiency	Will it work willingly at pressure?	Optimization
Integrity	Will the program thwart hacking and resist viruses?	Ability to weather attack
Usability	Can users benefit from the program easily?	Ease of use (understanding, learning, use)
Maintainability	Can the program be repaired speedily?	Ease of repair
Flexibility	Will it be fairly straightforward to adapt the program?	Effort required to modify program
Testability	Can the program be tested economically?	Effort required to test program
Portability	Can your program be readily adapted to a new operating system?	How easily it can move to other platforms (operating systems)
Reusability		Modularity of code
Interoperability		Ability to couple program in with another (for example, API)

Keep these in mind at all times when designing and coding programs.

Correctness

Correctness establishes the baseline by ensuring that the program matches its specification and does, within the design specs, what the user requires. This could involve something as simple as confirming that invoices are totalled correctly, or as complex as checking the correct computation of acceleration of a space rocket during launch. No "correct" program ever surpasses its specifications. Writing the right specifications is of paramount importance.

Reliability

Reliability assesses the statistical dependability of the program. Software should be 100 percent reliable. We are more familiar with reliability, or rather lack of it, in machinery.

Hard disk manufacturers rate the reliability of their drives as so many hours between failures, Mean Time Between Failures (MTBF). What they are saying is that it should work when you buy it for an average of X hours. Similarly, a CD duplication manufacturer might state their machine is 99.998 percent reliable. This means that on average, 1 in 50,000 CDs might be a dud.

Software reliability is compromised when it is receiving data from external hardware devices. If a sensor had 99.998 percent reliability and provided 50 readings a second, it would screen a dud software reading every 16 minutes 40 seconds. How reliable would you rate that software if it was monitoring heart readings during protracted surgery and you were the patient? Reliability needs to be brought up to a higher than acceptable level. What that level should be depends on the program's place and purpose.

Efficiency

Efficiency is the optimization of the program within the network of systems with which it is designed to work. Efficiency only normally becomes an issue when software is released into the real world and meets realistic loads. Some programs run slowly or grind to a halt. Although optimization is rarely achieved, most software works adequately. Programs can appear to be turbo charged when programmers are given time to optimize rather than add further features.

Integrity

Now that there are more frequent incidents of hacking and Denial of Service (DoS) attacks, programs need to be able to weather attacks and not form an easy breeding ground from which viruses can be passed on to other parts of a customer's system.

Usability

Usability can also be interpreted as user friendliness. Behind this portmanteau concept are five quantifiable concepts:

- ✦ Learnability
- ✦ Productivity
- ✦ Memorability
- ✦ Accuracy
- ✦ Satisfaction

These collectively boil down to the software being easy for users to learn and remember, not prone to errors, enjoyable to use, and efficient.

Maintainability

Good designers not only make sure their products work but remain operational for protracted periods. Look at a Formula-1 racing car during a pit stop. They have been designed so that all four tires can be changed and 50 liters of high-octane motor fuel injected all in under 7 seconds. That's maintenance. In the computer world Microsoft along with many other manufacturers now provide live updates for their programs and operating systems so that they are always up-to-date.

Flexibility

No one knows how your software will be used in the future or what other tasks it may be called on to perform when circumstances change. The spur for this may be a commercial opportunity or sheer desperation. Eidos, who is now known as the highly successful manufacturer of Lara Croft games, started out in 1990 producing video-editing software on the old Acorn Archimedes computer. This brilliant program was far ahead of its time. Sales never got off the ground. However, the company recognized the value of some of its key modules and adapted them for the high-speed video compression components required by modern computer games. If their premature program had not been flexible the corporation would have died. Flexibility is good business insurance.

Testability

Some great ideas are difficult to test. In the early days of flight the only way to test an aircraft was to fly it. As a result, several pioneers died. Engineers went on to develop less fatal alternatives than trial by gravity. Scale models, wind tunnels, and more recently computer simulations were gradually introduced. Have you thought out an economical way to test your program?

Portability

Portability is the ability of a program to work on a range of hardware with different operating systems. CPM was dominant from 1973–81. Then came DOS; it reigned until the mid 1990s. Then Windows took over. Statistically, it is only a question of time before Windows is superseded.

While computers are still in a stage of rapid evolution, software needs to be able to perform on an ever-emerging range of hardware and operating platforms. In the run up to Windows, several well-known software manufacturers came to grief when they postulated that the only way to produce a product for the new operating system was to write one from scratch. This took so long that competitors stole their opportunity. During this period, my company rewrote its e-mail software from DOS to Windows in less than a month, not because the programmers were related to Einstein, but because they had segregated the data-processing functions from the user interface. So they quickly learned how to write a Windows User Interface and were then able to latch the data-processing code behind it.

Even if you are tempted to think you only need to write your program for the current, dominant operating system, remember that they change every few years. Splitting the program so that user interface/operating system and data processing tasks are segregated makes it much easier to provide for such transitions. Never underestimate the business value of portability.

The Quality Movement

Mankind has been employing quality control from the day he began making things. Whether crafting an iron-age flint or prehistoric pot it's safe to assume that our forebears preferred to get it right, just like we do today. Henry Ford used quality control in his first automobile production lines to save costs and keep them rolling. Quality, as it is understood and practiced today, goes back to the seminal work of one man, W. Edwards Deming. Up until then, quality control was practiced sporadically. Deming advocated "Total Quality"—would anything less be acceptable in an age producing aircraft or submarines where the slightest mistake of the most insignificant item could cost everyone on board their lives?

At the end of World War II the Japanese economy was decimated. Their manufacturers had to make sure that every product unit worked. They latched onto Deming's work verbatim as a way of eliminating rejects. Deming's mantra was a comprehensive, systematic, systemic approach to the elimination of the root causes of defects. All subsequent quality regimes are built on this foundation.

In the intervening years many specialized quality standards have evolved from Deming's original platform. The most ubiquitous in current use are the International Organization for Standardization (ISO) 9001 requirements, which are now practiced in around 150 countries and takes three forms:

✦ ISO 9001 Quality Systems, Model for Quality Assurance in Design, Development, Production, Installation, and Servicing

✦ ISO 9000-3 Guidelines for the Application of ISO 9001 to the Development, Support, and Maintenance of Software

✦ ISO 9004-2 Quality Management and Quality System Elements (Part 2)

Your reasons for adhering to a standard might be pragmatic, statutory, strategic, or even political. Keep in mind that these standards are written in a generalized form so they apply to all products. It takes some time to translate them from their universalities to being specific to your software operation. You can speed up the process of implementing ISO standards by hiring someone or finding a friend who is familiar with them and knows how to apply them from their previous work.

Reusability

There is a pathological tendency among programmers to handcraft code from scratch every time they need something. However, this habit is beginning to falter now that the repertoire of off-the-shelf routines has become encyclopedic. A key factor when designing software is to consider which modules might be bought in or imported from earlier projects. This will seriously reduce the development and testing time. As you go, it is good to extend your repertoire and architect your programs with this in mind.

Interoperability

As programs get more sophisticated they are called upon more and more to communicate with other software. Interoperability is the measure of the effort required to achieve this. Coupling systems together is a key component of any software design. Developers who do not build this in from the outset, if required, typically use significant time and money to retrofit such a feature. You have been warned.

When designing and writing software, keep all these quality requirements constantly in mind.

Quantifiers of Quality Are Simply Indicators

Measurements simply give you a basis for comparison so you can appreciate the complexity of the program that you intend to produce. Give your specification to an idiot and you'll end up with coding chaos. Give it to an experienced genius and you'll wonder what all the fuss was about. These assessments provide the clearest indication of the caliber of programmer your project will need. If you plan to produce a complex, sophisticated product, you need a programmer who revels in marshalling complexity. However, even the best measurements will only take you so far. Most metrics, for instance, take no account of the language being used. While programs can theoretically be written in almost any language, you must consider which measuring system is most appropriate. There's a vast difference between the time it would take to write a word processing program in Assembler instead of a high-level language like C++ or C#.

How to Measure Quality

Managers need to be able to measure how much can go wrong to assess the size of the programmer's hurdles and get some idea of the man-hours and money required to bring the product to market. Programmers need to be able to measure it, too, to have some yardstick on their own progress.

In much the same way as there is no measure of darkness, there is no measure of quality. You actually measure the lack of these things—the amount of light or the volume of errors. When trying to quantify quality liability you should bear in mind that not all bugs are equal. If you have a colossal program with millions of lines of code and one Class A bug, the entire program is dead. The damage that can be done by releasing it doesn't bear thinking about (as you will discover in the sidebar on the story of the Ariane 5 rocket later in this chapter).

Software measurements polarize around two axes: characteristics and bugs. Characteristics analyze the specification and structure of a program and provide measurements that enable you to compare your program with others. To achieve this it measures such attributes as code length, code complexity, and function. Bugs measure the number and nature of defective parts and the rates at which they grow and dwindle. So characteristics cover both estimated indicators and physically measurable attributes, while bugs measure the dysfunctional results of the coding.

Characteristics such as the number of lines of code do nothing more than alert you to the size of the issue. They mean little in themselves. There is little you can do about them other than rewrite the entire program. You must be aware of them to put other characteristics in perspective. Hitting a sign that says "San Francisco 600 miles" is not much use to you unless you also know which way to go.

Complexity is a much trickier yardstick, though we all know that it means the number of opportunities there are within a program for things to go wrong. Complexity has been analyzed according to structures, algorithms, and cognitions. Characteristics such as these give you insights into how to structure and write programs in simpler, more direct ways so your coding is less prone to errors.

Functional Characteristics

Most of us would expect that the more complex a project is the harder it will be to realize, but how do you measure complexity? Complexity is, by definition, complex. There is no simple, single solution, though several hundred people have tried. The sections that follow provide a brief outline of the six most widely used systems. All of them alert you to the complexity of the project you are undertaking by enabling you to compare what you plan with what happened on other similar projects. This allows you to make better-grounded decisions about the number and quality of people you are likely to need and the controls you may need to put in place. Understanding them and applying these complexity measurement systems takes time and the calculations are sometimes highly mathematical.

- ✦ Albrecht's Function Points
- ✦ Mark II
- ✦ Feature Points
- ✦ 3-D Feature Points

✦ DeMarco's Bang Metric

✦ COnstructive COst MOdel (COCOMO)

Function Point Analysis

The most flexible, accurate, and widely used measuring tool for getting a feel for the size is Function Point Analysis. The five datums on which it is based are as follows:

✦ Inputs

✦ Outputs

✦ Inquiries

✦ Internal stores of data

✦ External references to data

Such information should be known at the planning stage. If the datum sizes aren't known, they can be assumed with from/to indications that can be estimated. Function Point thus gives you indications of the project's complexity before you start. The calculation is typically quick.

Mark II Method

Charles Symons' Mark II method focuses on the effort required to encode 20 parameters. It thus avoids using estimated number of functions. Mark II is predominantly used in the United Kingdom. It is similar to Function Point in the parameters it uses, but it works in a simpler way. The idea behind Mark II is to reduce subjectivity by using the same yardsticks regardless of the program's application. Mark II adds six more yardsticks to the 14 General System Characteristics.

✦ Data Communications

✦ Distributed Data Processing

✦ Performance

✦ Heavily Used Configuration

✦ Transaction Rate

✦ Online Data Entry

✦ End-User Efficiency

✦ Online Update

✦ Complex Processing

✦ Reusability

✦ Installation Ease

✦ Operational Ease

✦ Multiple Sites

✦ Facilitate Change

Feature Points

Devised by Capers Jones, Feature Points is another variant of Function Point. Feature Points reduces the values assigned to internal logical files and takes algorithms into account, which it weights according to susceptibility to error. This proved more useful for applications such as real-time, embedded, and mathematical optimization systems.

Bang Metric

Tom De Marco's Bang Metric is similar to Function Point. Bang has proven itself especially beneficial in real-time, telecommunications, and scientific software projects.

3D Feature Points

Made public by Boeing Computer Services Software Metrics Team in 1991, 3D is so called because it postulates that the complexity can be defined by measuring three features: data, function, and control.

COCOMO

Barry Boehm's COnstructive COst MOdel is concerned with the effects of complexity. As the name implies, COCOMO considers cost to estimate the amount of time required. Cost factors are weighted so they can be made appropriate for your project. This system is based on estimations of the number of lines of code likely to be generated.

Bugs

Measurement of the projected characteristics of your program may forewarn you of the scale of your task, but bugs are their inevitable manifestation. Code does not write itself peerlessly. Even the best programmers and managers are prone to error. There are three bug metrics to address:

✦ Damage potential (Class A, B, C, or D)

✦ Length and density (number of bugs for the lines of code)

✦ Rate of bug growth/decline

When you set up any type of measurement, including measuring bugs, pay attention to the accuracy and consistency of measurement data. Try to start measuring all features simultaneously. You can't know where you are (or were) unless you have kept a record. If few bugs come to light while you're coding, they are easy enough to deal with as and when they surface. Once their numbers go over 20, you need a record and some kind of disciplined procedure. Some people manage their bug logs in word processors, others in spreadsheets, ad-hoc databases, or purpose written software. Keep the following key things in mind when logging bugs:

✦ Where is it recorded?

✦ What is recorded?

✦ Who is going to manage the bug list? (Remember to have an understudy should the designated person fall ill.)

✦ Is the list accessible to all the relevant people including beta testers?

✦ Are the bugs classified so that people can identify bugs reported already and not enter them again?

✦ What is the remedial status? (People must know the bug status; that is, how many are reported, confirmed, being fixed (by whom and ETA), and confirmed fixed.)

Before you proceed, you need to consider the following:

✦ Who should have access to the list?

✦ Do you want one person in charge or one and a deputy?

✦ Should the person who created the bug fix the bug, or should someone take over this specialist function?

✦ How will you ensure that bugs that pose the greatest risk are dealt with first?

✦ How will you record the time it takes to fix each class of bug?

✦ Where will programmers find the fixit schedule?

✦ If a sufficiently serious bug rears its head, who will give the order to down tools, regroup the team, and attack the problem collectively until the problem is no more?

Version Control

In addition to recording the comings and goings of bugs, you also need to keep track of the succession of versions. Programs that go out to test come back for revamping and are subsequently reissued. Version control software keeps track of all changes that you have made to software during production. This allows you to roll the clock back to any point during development, if required. Version control software is mandatory.

Classification

If you are in control of a project you should know at any time how many bugs have currently been reported and remain unfixed and what their profile/classifications are.

Length

The longer the code, the longer bug purging is likely to take. Program length is the sum of all the lines of code in all the subsets in the program. It is not the number of lines generated by the compilers. The number of lines written simply tells you the extent of the product. You should always have an idea of the size of your program, but remember, it's nothing more than a milestone.

Number and Growth of Bugs

Knowing the number of bugs, total and in each class, is simple but highly instructive. It can be useful to chart the bugs' growth and decline so you can monitor the progress of eradication. Ideally, the graph is hill shaped, starting at 0, rising to a bump, and hopefully receding back to 0 reported bugs by the time of your first release.

Bug Density

Bug density is measured in bugs per thousand Lines of Code (KLOC). It is the easiest metric to calculate and a critical indicator. Simply divide the number of lines of code by the number of bugs and multiply by 1,000, as in the following example.

```
x = (n * 1,000)/L

x = KLOC
L = lines of code
n = number of bugs
```

The larger the x number, the bigger the problem on your hands. One bug per 1,000 is widely deemed acceptable. However, the problem with this is that it tells you nothing about the severity of the flaws. If you had a 100,000-line program with 23 bugs in it you'd be coming in with an apparently healthy KLOC of 0.23; but if they were all Class A bugs the program would be a disaster area. If, on the other hand, they were all Class C and D bugs, you might release it as it stands.

Discriminate Bug Density

If you intend to use the KLOC scale as a guide to when to launch your product and wind down your programming, you should monitor KLOCs by their severity:

KLOC-A = Class A Bugs per thousand lines.

KLOC-B = Class B Bugs per thousand lines.

KLOC-C = Class C Bugs per thousand lines.

KLOC-D = Class D Bugs per thousand lines.

These can sometimes be grouped as follows:

KLOC-AB = Class A+B Bugs per thousand lines.

KLOC-CD = Class C+D Bugs per thousand lines.

A Cautionary Tale

In June 1996, after 10 years' work and an investment of $7 billion, the European Space Agency proudly launched the Ariane 5 rocket carrying four uninsured commercial satellites. Ariane 5 lifted off perfectly for its first and last 39 seconds. Then, before the horrified eyes of space scientists, it self-destructed.

Clearly, quality checks didn't work. Why? Someone tried to cram a 64-bit number in a 16-bit space. The experts at the launch site in Guyana knew about this issue. However, they decided it was not an issue as the rocket couldn't go fast enough to generate this error. This was practicable but not perfect logic for Ariane's forebears. Unfortunately, everyone forgot that Ariane 5 was significantly faster than its predecessors.

What happened was this. The rocket's direction was controlled by built-in gyroscopes and accelerometers feeding the guidance computers. As the rocket picked up speed the Inertial Navigation System (INS) tried to stuff the 64-bit floating-point number into the 16-bit single integer space. This caused a runtime error. On receiving this, the INS decided to shut down in a fit of logic. Being smart, the designers had created a backup unit. The good news was that the backup system worked. The bad news was that it was identical, bug and all, to the main system, so it failed a few milliseconds later in exactly the same way. Both the primary and backup INS computers sent the same error message to the main computer. This interpreted the data as a massive but legal course correction and commanded a nozzle to deflect, forcing the rocket to flip sideways. This caused the booster to be ripped off the main frame. Ariane 5 lurched off course and self-destructed.

The irony is that the offending piece of code was only required to monitor the sideways motion of the rocket prior to launch, but was kept running for 40 seconds after the count-down in the event of a quick restart. The rocket malfunctioned 36.7 seconds into its flight. If it had been programmed to shut down 4 seconds sooner, it would have been the programmer's oversight that would have been buried.

This is where bug classification could have made the difference between failure and success. Simulations should have generated the problem. It would immediately have been classified as a Class A bug and the rocket would not have been allowed to launch until it had been fixed (and it would have cost a lot less).

Using KLOCs, the ideal release criteria are KLOC-AB is 0, KLOC-CD close to single figures. In this respect, it is much like the proof requirements for a book.

How to Minimize Bugs from the Outset

As previously mentioned, having your ducks in a row from the beginning is essential, especially when it comes to minimizing bugs.

Go Over Your Technical Plan with a Fine-Tooth Comb

Bugs start at the beginning. In 1993, a prominent U.S. consultancy discovered that 44 percent of all bugs start before the coding even begins. People write contradicting statements in their requirements and technical plans, which are faithfully coded up by the programmers. Ambiguities and errors in logic get built in from the outset. So inspect the technical plan with the same diligence that you are going to double-check code.

Split a Large Project Up into Components

Large projects are almost twice as likely to fail as smaller ones. They take longer, are more complex, and employ more people, so the chances of missing things that are going to go wrong compounds. Breaking them down into smaller modules gives greater manageability and vastly increases your chances of success.

Base Things on a Daily Build

The sooner you can start getting your program compilable, the sooner you can start testing it and the fewer bugs it is likely to have. If you are involved in a one-year project and the components only come together in the final month for testing, you are going to be faced with a swarm of bugs. There may be so many that the program can't even be tested as an entity. This is a recipe for disaster—different teams will blame others and you'll be lucky to get the code in on time.

Alternatively, get everyone to write their modules so they can all be compiled at an early stage. Admittedly, at the start the program is unlikely to do much, but you'll be able to produce a daily build and resolve issues on a day-by-day basis. By month 11 you'll have a development version that has already had 8 months of debugging done to it, which is an enormous help in completing on time.

Create a Good Communications Environment

Small programming teams produce disproportionately more code, and often better, pro rata than their larger counterparts, because they spend less time communicating information up and down a chain. If communication is an issue, consider arranging things so all your programmers can work in the same room or arrange for them all to share the same communal lunch facilities. Meal breaks are a wonderful time for them to discuss their problems and get their colleagues to listen in and propose fixes.

Testing for Bugs

If ever some pious programmer comes up with statements such as, "My code doesn't have any bugs in it," or "I've given it a quick test and it seems to be OK," consider this nothing more than a ruse to get you off their backs. Such statements are unrealistic and unprofessional. Ultimately, this is a sackable offense. Removal of bugs is key to you being able to release working, saleable programs.

Bugs don't unilaterally surrender themselves; you have to go in and route them out. Exhaustive testing of software is impossible, but the following sections present some practical ways to go about it, starting with internal testing both formally and informally, and then going on to public beta test scenarios and how to manage them.

Procedure

In air traffic control systems, safeguarding hundreds of thousands of people's lives per day requires a different level of testing from a word processor that sits tapping away on a person's desk. Yet all programs need to be consistently and comprehensively tested. To ensure this, write down the checklists that each product must pass before being considered as a release candidate. A checklist might look like this:

✦ New code scrutinized by development manager

✦ One hour of internal testing per day

✦ Passes test plan

✦ One week's public beta testing

✦ No reported Class A or B bugs remaining

Note A release candidate is a version of the software that you are prepared to make public. Test versions for beta testing are not surprisingly referred to as test candidates.

Test Plan

The test plan is nothing more than a list of tests that must be applied to a program prior to release. The testing may be done manually or automatically. With critical software, it is best that manual tests be done twice by different individuals and the results are compared. Discrepancies should be verified by a third party. Test plans and the test plan writers are best initiated and involved towards the start of your project.

Self-Testing

As you have seen, the sooner bugs are detected and fixed the sooner the product can enter the market. All responsible programmers analyze and test their code as they go along. They know that they have to do this from experience to make sure what they think they wrote and what they actually wrote are the same. Programmers who don't or aren't prepared to do this are behaving irresponsibly and you should seriously consider whether you want to have someone with such a low level of professional conduct working for you.

Self-testing squashes more bugs than any other method and significantly reduces the level of bugs from chaotic to manageable. If you are working an eight-hour day (an underestimate for most programmers), take a break every four hours and spend 15 minutes playing with what you have just produced. You'll be amazed at how many errors you find. By sorting out miskeying on the spot, you will find that you can plough on with the rest of your task much faster.

Equipment for Testing

When testing software it is vital that you install it on a clean computer with a standard operating system as shipped from the manufacturer and ensure that the software works the first time on such a unit. This is the situation that many of your users will find themselves in when they upgrade their PCs.

Internal Testing (Informal)

If you have been concentrating on producing the same portion of code for the past few weeks, chances are you are the worst person to test it. It's difficult to see the forest for the trees. When the product begins to take shape, allocate a period of time each day—say half an hour when all the programmers get the latest build and just play with the program (this makes a welcome respite from coding) and report any errors they find.

Buddy Coding (Informal Day-to-Day Inspection)

Not all parts of a program need to be buddy coded, but on complex parts it can be useful to have additional programmers to help do the work on the premise that two heads are better than one. Additionally, they can check each other's code, or the resultant product, as they go along. It is best practice to choose people with different personalities. Between them they are likely to spot more bugs.

Objective Inspection

British Aerospace used the inspection technique to good effect for the EuroFighter project reducing the number of errors per page from 20 to 1.5.

Inspection needs to be done by someone other than the person who wrote the code, so even if you are a one-man band try and get a programmer friend to look through what you have written. Inspection has two aims: detection and prevention. This approach might appear hierarchical but it's amazing how many bugs come to light when code is read through line-by-line by an experienced programmer.

The other advantage of close scrutiny by an outsider is that an experienced programmer can often point out areas that may lead to trouble in the future. Inspection thus gives you a double payback, and because inspection is done prior to release it's significantly more cost effective than subsequent repair.

Tip
If ever you want to test how alert your "inspectors" are, simply introduce some bugs into the code before you give it to them and see how many they spot. To really test them, use different styles of bug, grammatical, literal, logical, structural, and so on.

Consumer Trials

When the software has reached an approved level of functionality and stability it can be released for user trials. *Alpha testing* (the first trial) is performed by users under the supervision of the software developers. *Beta testing* (the second trial) is undertaken by users in their normal work environment.

If your software is sensitive or confidential, testers should sign Non Disclosure Agreements (NDAs) prior to being provided with your software. The form should make them aware of the benefits the software may confer (that is, it does x) and that after the Beta test is complete, they'll be presented with a free release copy. They should also be advised that there's always a chance that the test software might crash their system.

Selecting test groups is a sensitive business. You want them to be representative of your market, and they should fit the following criteria:

✦ Fall within your prospects' age range

✦ Have a suitable level of computer competence

✦ Be using the operating systems and hardware for which your program is designed

✦ Need your program

✦ Work in a firm of the target market size (the style of their organization, academic, commercial, informal, or tightly structured, may also be a factor)

Open Up the Beta Testing as Early as Possible

The sooner you activate the external testers the sooner real-world bugs will start to be reported. And you know by now that the sooner those bugs are attacked the better the product will be and the less it will cost.

Feature Logging

Software usage typically follows the 80/20 rule, whereby 20 percent of the functions account for 80 percent of people's usage. Your beta testers are unlikely to methodically try out every feature and check the software thoroughly for you. What they are prepared to do is use the latest development builds and report back anything they find unappealing.

What is very useful (you need to get the tester's explicit consent) is to write the software so when it is a test candidate it methodically logs which features were used. The software can then automatically e-mail you this log file. What you do when comparing tests is find out which functions are being used (and in which order). You might find that even with a couple hundred users trying out the product for two weeks certain features won't be used. The implicit message may be that these modules need to be checked to confirm that they are working. Alternatively, your target market may not need them at all.

Release Criteria

Software release doesn't benefit from uncertainty. Write in stone your release criteria that have been approved by marketing. This is surprisingly simple and may read something like this. Software is ready for release when:

+ It is deemed to have sufficient functionality to be saleable.

+ It has passed the internal test procedure satisfactorily.

+ There are no Class A bugs.

+ The incidence of Class B bugs falls within IT standards and is deemed to be trivial.

+ There are no other showstopper issues.

Should You Make the Bug Log Public?

There is no universal rule. If you are developing a product designed for technicians, it may build confidence if you publish a regular list of bug fixing progress. Technical users tend to like it. Users can look up issues and see exactly how much work the programmers have been doing between each build. On the other hand, publicizing bug fixes creates an impression that the software is under perpetual development, which any live software program is, but it just reinforces a "not finished" image in the customers' minds. This technique works to bond the program writers and testers during the early stages of product development.

A significant drawback is that by stating that a particular bug was fixed on a particular date you might expose yourself to people who might use this information against you. The purpose of qualifying your software is to allow you to establish standards.

Sign Off

When you arrive at a marketable version and the collective decision is to launch, it is important that you sign off on the product and make no further changes. The release candidate now needs to be transformed into the release product. To finalize the release version, take the following steps:

1. Install it on a clean machine and check that all current defects are fixed.
2. Change the version number to a release number.
3. Turn off all debugging code.
4. Compile the whole program.
5. Update readme.txt files and/or equivalents.
6. Insert matching help programs and documentation.
7. Apply a date stamp to release files.
8. Build the release set.
9. Check that all files are present and correct.
10. Produce a gold disk.
11. Virus test the gold disk.
12. Store the gold disk away from your work in a fireproof safe.
13. Compare on before/after installation Registry settings.
14. Make a master copy of the course code and seal it away (electronically rather than physically).
15. Distribute for press testing.

You, Quality, and the Law

No matter how airtight the waiver clauses are in your software licenses, if your product fails in such a way that it causes loss of life or hardship, it fails to fulfill the functions for which it was marketed, or it causes serious loss of earnings, don't be surprised if someone tries to sue you, however valid or limp their justification. Being able to demonstrate to a court that you undertake strong, consistent, and structured quality control will prove that you work professionally and have done all you can to behave responsibly and stop problems occurring at the source.

✦　　✦　　✦

Scoring with Words

Whenever the word "documentation" crops up, losers think, "boring;" winners think, "Profit!"

Documentation in its widest sense covers everything written in plain English that comes with your program. It takes two basic forms: obligatory necessities, which most developers cover well, and the supportive information on which few developers do themselves justice.

Copyright declarations, contractual details, warranties, and registration cards are familiar examples of obligatory documentation. Logon directions, help systems, manuals, training systems, Web sites, and coding notes are prime examples of support documentation, although not all of these are needed for all software.

Preparing the legal stuff is largely a matter of finding out the details required and the form they should take. Support matters call for much more reflection. Support documentation can be a huge asset or a serious internal hemorrhage. It all depends on how much real help the documentation provides.

Documentation is the first area that users look to for information. Genuinely helpful information (from the user's point of view, not yours) will tell your clients what they want to know in a way they can understand. This makes your product more enticing, raises satisfaction among purchasers, reduces the number of calls you have to answer from angry users, and generally strengthens your reputation. All of these things add up to money in as opposed to money out.

So documentation is something every program developer should view as a good investment. The effectiveness of supportive documentation determines the following:

✦ Whether sales spread through recommendations

✦ How much additional profit it delivers

Launching a program with set-up instructions that buyers cannot follow is like delivering a fireproof safe without a key. If buyers cannot get the program working easily they certainly won't recommend it to any one else, even if the developer is able to talk them through the installation.

In much the same way, selling a program with a Help system that doesn't offer real assistance turns what might have been a gold pan into a colander. You will be forever answering a barrage of questions and complaints. This not only makes support teams expensive to maintain, but every executive hour spent making up for a deficiency in documentation is an hour in which you cannot build your business.

It is therefore worth spending a little time to understand the difficulties buyers may have with setting up a program with which they are unfamiliar (the same difficulties you may have had yourself with other people's programs). A good way to begin to put yourself in your customers' shoes is to ask your colleagues to hand you a list of problems they've experienced. Here are some examples:

✦ "It's all there but the manual's too thick."

✦ "It's too sketchy."

✦ "There's no real intention to help."

✦ "There's too much computerese."

✦ "I've tried and tried the instructions but I just can't make them work."

✦ "I can never find the commands."

✦ "I can never remember what is where on the pull-down menus."

✦ "Program writers don't use the same terminology that we do."

How can you make sure that your support documentation won't repeat the same mistakes?

You will have to accept that preparing effective support documentation is a major task. If you are prepared to invest purposeful time and money on it you will save yourself far more costly retrievals later.

Crucial to all this is a strong intention to help your customers. Not even 3R programs can be totally self-evident. While your customer base may include a number of specialists who know more about computing than you do, such experts are rare. Most users will only have a smattering of computer expertise. Some may be new to computing, or if they have an expertise, it lies in another field.

Your users may be old. They may be young. They may not think the same way that you do. English may not be their native tongue. Therefore, your support documentation has to be pitched at a level that engages them all. It has to make sense readily to ordinary *and* extraordinary people.

Now that manuals have become a rarity, there's also a physiological problem. It's not always possible for users to consult the program and the Help section simultaneously, so there's no direct visual cross-referencing. Unfortunately, as Pavlov discovered, our ability to recall information in the wake of immediate physical movement is exceedingly poor. To be remembered across this scenery change, directions have to be in bites, each no more than a sentence long. Otherwise they won't be held in the human buffer memory while the user shuts down the Help section and reverts to your program.

In essence, this means reducing instructions to road direction terseness. The Help section equivalent of *"First left, second right, opposite McDonalds."*

Perhaps the biggest single complaint about Help sections is that they unnecessarily reinvent the wheel. Instead of using the terminology customers are used to, they introduce terms and concepts of their own.

Every specialist software program presents pitfalls to a pure technologist, sometimes because the users are diverse, but mostly because each calling has its own vocabulary of technical jargon and established ways of working.

Programmers who fly in the face of established usage can only alienate and confuse their readers. So do so at your peril.

Installation Directions

These really have to work. If you possibly can, make the installation of your program bulletproof. You'd be amazed how many fail at this first, most important hurdle.

Get the program to do almost all the work it can. Ask the users yes or no questions and nothing more challenging than filling in the storage locations, license agreement, e-mail address, and name. Explain what is happening as loading progresses and tell them how long each sequence usually takes.

Give them a contact number, in case they need help. If it is not practicable to automate initial program loading, make your log-on directions very simple. Break the task down into easy bites. Do not take the understanding of any technical expression for granted. Define each term before you use it. Explain what the program is doing as loading progresses. Show them exactly what the screen should look like at each stage. Explain anything tricky or novel in several ways so the user can get the hang of what you mean and check that his understanding is correct. As soon as loading is complete, tell the user precisely what he needs to begin using your program.

Once you have got a seemingly reasonable set of directions together, try them out on strangers. See if they can follow them. Watch their reactions where possible to establish at what point they are meeting difficulties. Embody their queries in a revised set of instructions. Then try the fuller and better version on another panel of strangers. Repeat these revisions until you get 100 percent comprehension.

Manuals and Help Systems

When it comes to manuals and Help systems, the better one holds up, the less you need the other.

The first question you need to ask yourself is *Do I need a manual?* Much depends on what your product needs. Computer languages, for instance, need printed manuals to explain their vocabulary and grammar while the Help program enables users to apply the syntax satisfactorily. This is particularly necessary with programs designed to be used by programmers. When their screens are crammed with the code they are writing, it is more convenient for them to work from printed text than constantly switching between windows on the screen.

Where a program commands a substantial price, customers may expect an impressive manual as a matter of course. It gives a tangible presence to a purchase that may otherwise appear to be extremely intangible for the money spent.

Alternatives to Print

A printed manual is a luxury item. It costs both time and money to write, illustrate, prepare, and print. Every hard copy also adds weight to your shipping bills. Furthermore, guessing a print run in advance can be tricky—even if you have prior experience. Then, if you update your software before you have sold the entire first edition, you will have a lot of expensive stock to write off.

Until the late 1990s developers were considered cheapskates if they didn't provide a printed manual. Since then, the increased market penetration of laser printers has made it practicable to provide manuals in Portable Document Format (PDF). This allows users to print their own manuals or sections of manuals when they need hard copies.

The PDF approach obviously does not work for devices such as modems, as users can't access the documentation via the Internet until their connection is working. However, for most other software, it's a far more efficient solution.

With millions of people using the Internet regularly, online manuals and help are becoming the most practical way to deliver support. The beauty of disseminating support via the Internet is that you can make advanced versions available to everyone at the same time as you launch your upgrades.

Perhaps because of this, it is even more important to appreciate the distinctions between manuals and Help systems.

Even developers whose livelihoods hinge on implementation don't always appreciate that the function of a manual and a Help system is not the same. For example, with the growth of broadband, people are beginning to interconnect their offices and homes. Most of the hardware support (for ADSL modems, routers, firewalls, and so on) is being supplied as files for the user to print out. The only problem is that in many cases these manuals turn out to be verbatim copies of the Help programs. So, if a satisfactory explanation cannot be found in the manual, there won't be one in the Help program either.

As previously mentioned, people latch onto ideas differently. Remember even the most intelligent users can find new concepts hard to grasp. So explaining something one way in the manual and another way in the Help system can dramatically increase the odds of comprehension.

When a user summons screen Help he mostly wants to know how to do something or get out of a spot. It's pressing and it's immediate. He's looking for crisp, clear directions that he can remember when he returns to his main screen.

When he consults a manual, he usually has a certain amount of leisure. He wants to learn more about the program, perhaps in the following ways:

✦ To clear up something he couldn't quite grasp in Help

✦ To find out how the program came to be written

✦ What it is designed to do

✦ How sequential functions work

✦ Whether there are any additional commands that would be handy

The complementary functions are not universally appreciated. If support is to be delivered via a single channel, all types of inquiry should be covered.

Manuals and Help systems are not like ordinary books. They don't tell a sequential story. Only a rival or a masochist would ever read either from beginning to end. Users consult them for guidance on specific needs. So each section needs to be coherent in itself and point the way to other useful sections. There are three popular approaches to support:

✦ **Alphabetical**—Easy to find if you use the search words your clients expect

✦ **Functional**—Useful where the functions are naturally separate

✦ **Task-oriented**—Where the entire activity aims at a specific result

Although each of these is laudable in its own right, all three ignore the initial task of orientation. Before they dive in, most users need an overview of the program. They need some sort of guide to know how to find their way about. They need to know which buttons to push to find all the commands, both crossways and downwards. They also need to be able to locate every embedded option and understand the program's purpose and functions.

The Alphabetical Approach

A lot of Help systems are little more than a dictionary, and some amount to even less. How often have you come across an entry such as the following?

Exit The Exit button

Most problems that users encounter when coming to grips with a new program stem from not understanding the program's terminology. So it is vital that each term used in a program be fully described. Expecting users to understand what special meaning you have given to an otherwise ordinary term is unrealistic. You need to explain each term before you use it.

You should also include all the alternative terms that users may have in mind when looking for specific guidance. Alphabetical Help systems and manuals are no easier than any other to produce. They only look as if they are.

The Function Approach

This explains each software function step-by-step. It's the obvious format to choose where the functions are self-contained, such as those in a graphic program. However, when more than one function has to be used to achieve a result, more comprehensive explanations are required.

The Task-Oriented Approach

Some Help programs and manuals are so uninformative that you can only understand them *after* you have worked out what the program actually does, when you no longer need the help.

Expecting a newcomer to second-guess which gate they should be going through to access a function displays a faith in human intuition limited to the famous paranormalist Uri Geller. However, if you explain features in the context of the tasks, it's easier for newcomers to get the hang of the program's geography.

Task-oriented descriptions allow you to talk users through activities that involve a sequence of actions, step by step. This can be particularly helpful when the task is essential, such as installing the software.

Good documentation often employs all three techniques in different places.

Have You Covered Everything?

As you have probably discovered, most low-ticket software has little or incomplete documentation. It isn't that that the manufacturer has left the manual out of the box; it's that the manual they packed is deficient. You might want to look up a particular problem and type in all the possible prompt words you can think of, but nothing appears. Then when you look down the topic list, you find that either the subject has been totally overlooked or is described in terms that users have never used before.

Some programmers invent their own vocabulary. If your program is at all serious, the best way to avoid ending up with a dysfunctional manual and Help system is to find a highly literate user to write them. This relieves the programmers of tasks they rarely relish and allows them to concentrate on what they can do best: get the software out on time. It also introduces an end user's point of view at an early enough stage to be constructive. An outsider is more likely to spot missing sections and steer programmers toward terms that minimize the educational burden and therefore the launch.

Don't Forget to Document the Program Itself

Programs don't document themselves. However, because the readership of the code itself is both self-selecting and restricted it is the most common form of documentation to be overlooked. Programmers believe that if their code works it should never need a second glance. Enhancements, maintenance, and bug fixing are all part and parcel of the process, so you need to document code to ensure its long life span. As a rule of thumb, document the code as you go and make sure your code is covered with enough helpful comments that a newcomer could read through them and together with the code itself work out what is going on. Most programmers include these only as an aid for themselves at particularly hairy parts of the program. If there are genuinely convoluted programming aspects these should be documented separately in an accompanying document. For large projects separate, full-scale documentation is mandatory. If this is changing frequently, try posting it on an intranet so everyone has instantaneous access to the changes.

A Few Tips about Writing in General

Writing isn't about impressing people. It's about sharing what you know via the spoken or printed word.

Technicalities and acronyms are a great way to telegraph ideas when you are talking to a peer, but rattling them off in blinding machine gun succession to outsiders just leaves the recipients stunned. Use unexplained, obscure, and complex words and you might as well be writing in Greek. Even when communicating to those who know a good deal about a subject, it is unwise to cram too many technical terms together. Indigestible passages invariably go in one ear and out the other.

Making a sentence interminable is another way to switch off readers. An average of 11 words per sentence is about as much as the average person can absorb. The best advice is to keep it simple. Write in Universal English. The best tips are those that experts have been giving for years:

- ✦ Keep sentences short.
- ✦ Favor short punchy Anglo-Saxon words.
- ✦ Select words that conjure up pictures.
- ✦ Throw out adjectives.
- ✦ Concentrate on verbs.
- ✦ Use technical words sparingly.
- ✦ Spell acronyms out the first time you use them.

Professional trainers recognize four principal modes in which we assimilate information:

- ✦ A few divine what the author will say from his or her opening sentence and run off immediately to try and test it.
- ✦ Most readers absorb information in small chunks and test things out in tentative steps.
- ✦ Some of them absorb whole subsections before they start to apply what's being said.
- ✦ One or two never make a move until the very last item of information drops into place.

Explaining software, however, is a linear activity. You can't do B until you have done A, and you won't understand B until A has been explained. So, if you don't explain everything clearly as you go and define every new term when you mention it first, your readers will get muddled and frustrated.

Successful documentation writers spend a lot of time thinking about their readers. Whenever they put finger to keyboard, they always have them in mind. *What do they want to know? Are they looking for a brief or full answer here? What is the best way to get this across? Will they all understand that word? Am I being too simple?* Trite as these examples may seem, they will give you an idea of the way you might create your own set of yardsticks. Also remember that every audience is composed of very different individuals. Not only do readers absorb information at different rates, but men think differently than women, adults think differently than children, and new users process differently than experienced hands.

For example, this book is aimed at computer professionals, business people, and students. So I have three imaginary friends looking over my shoulder as I write.

Before you start on any documentation, jot down the kinds of people you intend to address. Think about them in the following contexts:

+ Age range
+ Educational levels
+ Likely business experience
+ Computer knowledge
+ Energies and any special interests
+ Prejudices and limitations

Then ask yourself what level of complexity could appeal to them all.

How Should You Set Your Writing Out?

Have you ever noticed that some textbooks seem easier to follow than others? This is usually because of the way they are laid out.

The eye is a muscle and, just like your arms and legs, it gets tired. If a line of text is overly long, the eye tires more quickly. This is because the eye doesn't track a line of text in a straight line; it tackles the data in spans of about six characters and spaces, leaping from span to span in sections.

The longer a line, the more tired the eyes' rod and cone receptors become. They desperately need a microsecond's pause to recharge. And after every so many lines a slightly longer pause is needed. And after a few pauses an even more extended pause is required.

These pauses are provided naturally by line endings, paragraph breaks, and page turnings. Research shows that the optimum line length in English is between 30 and 65 characters (6–11 words). The optimum paragraph is about seven lines, and the ideal page setting extends to no more than 32 lines, though publishers sometimes push this up to 38 lines to save paper.

Type should be between 10 and 12 pt (there are 72 pts to an inch so 11pt is just under 1/6"), otherwise it will be hard to read. Anything smaller is difficult to read and impossible for the 4 percent of readers with impaired vision (American Foundation for the Blind – Survey 1994-5).

If the space between the lines of type is too tight, the eye has to work harder to avoid mixing up the lines (remember it arcs). If the lines are spaced too far apart, it becomes tiresome to maintain a regular reading rhythm. Aim for the following:

- ✦ Type size 10–12pt
- ✦ 65 characters per line
- ✦ Spacing between lines ½–2pt
- ✦ 32 lines per page

A Picture Paints a Thousand Words

The physiological explanation for this is that the brain processes images several times faster than words. Use pictures, images, diagrams, and flowcharts whenever possible and appropriate to speed up the assimilation of ideas. Pictures also provide an additional means of making a point. You can also employ tables, graphs, section titles, and bullets to break up your text and make it more digestible.

In software documentation, accurate representations of the screen readers should be viewing is the most reassuring way to keep the instructions in step.

Little Things Matter

Misspelled words rob documents of authority. With built-in spelling checkers on tap such mistakes are heinous. Readers will reason that if the author doesn't take the document seriously, why should they? The next thought that's likely to occur to them is that the program has probably been tested with the same lack of professionalism.

If the product is to be marketed in the United States, use American-English spellings; for other English-speaking markets, use world English-English. The differences are subtle and few. The American spellings were created for phonetic consistency by Noah Webster in 1783 (*The American Spelling Book 260 impressions from 1783-1843*). In the intervening 200 years, we have grown to recognize both spellings. If you can't run to two print runs, use the localization for which you believe most of the product will be sold.

And Once You Have Written It?

Believe it or not, a lot of companies lock their documentation away in a cupboard. Unless there are legal or financial issues for doing this, there's nothing more useful to clients than up-to-date manuals to match their software. Documents are meant to be published, so do so.

✦   ✦   ✦

Before You Say "Go!"—The Release Process

Even if you have never been involved in a software release before, you have certainly seen something very similar—a NASA space launch. Basically, it's the culmination of years of preparation, testing, and vigorous checking. At last you are ready to go. You have checked the systems, trained the astronauts, invited the press, and so on. There's nothing more to it than someone pressing a button, or is there?

If you are wondering why an entire chapter is devoted to "the release process," it's simply because it is this important. If you have had a brilliant idea, researched it diligently, developed it impeccably, and then you mess up the release process, you will have wasted everything.

Now, after that stark warning, take comfort from the fact that the release process, like this chapter, is straightforward and short.

The release process covers everything from bringing out a new product to uploading a minor bug fix—the process for each of these is essentially the same. And, surprisingly, it's the same whether you are releasing millions of boxed product to be sold in every computer store in the world or running a Web site requiring an upload of a single copy of the latest cut. At its heart, release is about distribution and communication: making new product available and making sure that clients, future clients, and staff all know about it.

Given the simplicity of the goals, it's amazing how often elementary mistakes happen. Haven't we all had the following experiences?

- ✦ Software being announced that isn't ready
- ✦ Software released but sales/support not informed (they normally find out when customers call in)
- ✦ Forgetting to write the documentation
- ✦ Not synchronizing the advertising, marketing, and public relations (PR) with the actual release

The best way to get a handle on this is to plan and draw up a watertight checklist.

It is not uncommon in software organizations for release to be tacked on to the end of the quality control process. I don't advise this. First, it isn't just a software operation and there are logistical and marketing operations that need to be integrated. Second, by treating release as an extension you increase the chances of turning the whole thing into a fiasco.

Software Release Covers Everything

If all you are thinking of doing for your software release is uploading some files to the Internet, you are missing great opportunities to promote your product and gather new users, often at near-zero cost. Release in its entirety covers the following:

- ✦ Advertising
- ✦ Communication
- ✦ Crisis management
- ✦ Distribution
- ✦ Documentation
- ✦ Logistics
- ✦ Marketing
- ✦ Legal approval
- ✦ PR
- ✦ Training

The activities you undertake are dependent on the product itself and the nature of the actual release.

- ✦ Marketing
  - • Preparation of advertising/marketing/PR material (in advance)
  - • PR and software samples to journalists

✦ Logistics

- Duplication of software

- Printing of manuals

- Delivery to distributors

- Uploading of software

✦ People

- Train support staff about the new product

- Inform sales staff of new features and reasons for purchasing/upgrading

- Update training program

The Chronological Countdown

Ideally, if you had a magic wand the entire release process would happen simultaneously. The developers would hand you over a finished product and simultaneously manuals would be printed, CDs duplicated, press contacted, files uploaded, and so on. However, in the real world there are inevitable delays and you must consider the sequencing. Here's the helicopter view of how to approach it.

A new product or release is about to come out. A date has been set. What do you do? First you work out how likely that date is to be met. Does the development team have a good track record? How much work and bug fixing has yet to be done? Do you need to build your schedule around factors that have fixed components, such as synchronizing with a major computer exhibition? If you have any worries, build in an appropriate contingency.

Then, long before QC sign-off on the product, you need to initiate a number of other tasks to ensure they happen in time for the launch.

✦ Write/update manuals and Help systems

✦ Commission printers

✦ Draft press releases

✦ Set training in place

✦ Contact the press

✦ Create the marketing materials

✦ Reserve advertising time and space

✦ Plan launch events, and so on

By specifying the program properly, the manual, Help system, and training writers will be able to compose the relevant parts of the manual even if those bits are as yet unfinished when they start writing.

Public relations, as you will see in Chapter 14, is wonderful not just because it can often be gained at zero cost, but because independent magazine and newspaper articles command an integrity of review over any self-penned and funded advertisement. Make the most of this opportunity. It only comes once in every product's life.

If appropriate, try to get journalists to cover your product in the general and trade press. The press typically require twice their media production cycle's notice, so a monthly magazine likes around two months' notice to slot your details in, and weekly publications need two weeks. The odd one out is newspapers. Although they come out daily, most have weekly computer sections, so again, they need two weeks' notice. Unlike magazines that have lots of space to fill, newspapers don't and are highly selective, so you have to have an interesting story and coincide with their topics.

Advertising has long production lead times, especially if artwork (TV, pictures, drawings, and so on) is required. Media space has to be purchased (page in magazines, television/radio slots) in advance. Whoever is in charge of marketing will take a view how far in advance, if at all, they want to start product awareness to build up interest before the actual launch.

If your release is backed up by advertising it is vital that you don't overshoot your deadlines. If you are undertaking this, I advise adding in a contingency period, at *least* a week, after the expected delivery date so that you have time if the software fractionally overruns.

If your product is a Web site, a lot of the logistics that are about to be described are irrelevant. You only have to copy the software onto the Web servers and away you go. However, if you were Microsoft bringing out a new version of Word, you'd have a lot of physical components to produce and distribute in time for the launch.

Print times depend on the complexity of the document, and availability and capacity of the printer (a 300-page manual can be printed, dried, and bound in under a week). Disk and CD duplication is relatively fast but book your slots in advance. Unless you are going to overwhelm the local haulers (Microsoft hired 300 refrigerated trucks for the launch of NT), shipment can be ordered as required. Allow a day or two's margin for shipments being delayed and so on.

In the midst all of this logistical and marketing work, the penultimate part of release is communicating. Distributors need to be informed of the new product and versions and your own sales and support staff must be informed. Sales need to know what the product does, the benefits, why (and why not) customers should purchase and upgrade, and have clear pricing policy to work off. Support need to know the new features, bugs that have been fixed, and an overview of the types of problems the developers feel the new versions will generate. It is effective for senior developers and marketing staff to explain this to both the sales and support staff. This underwrites the importance of release.

It is frightening how many companies let their customers tell their staff that a new release has been put out. Imagine how that makes your employees feel—are they part of the team or are they irrelevant?

> **Note** It is smart to have a general programmer on hand for the support staff during the early days of release who can help go through calls and monitor if anything irregular is going on. This is a good way for the programmer to see what they are inflicting on the support teams and for support to feel part of the development process.

By now the software has been duplicated, manuals printed, and advertising and PR are created and in place. What's left now is the actual launch. This covers the uploading and publishing of software online, activating online versions (games, Web sites, Web services), and PR launch activities such as launch parties. Remember to include the development and support teams; they've been doing all the work. Nothing is more undermining for developers than being shown corporate videos of senior executives swigging champagne at a launch party and knowing they're just expected to get on with work as if nothing has happened. Release is the culmination and celebration of many months' work and is your opportunity to recognize and thank everyone who has helped to create the product.

Types of Release and the Appropriate Actions

There are fundamentally four types of release:

✦ New product

✦ New version

✦ Interim update

✦ Minor release

New Products

When you are releasing a new product you will end up using or considering all aspects of release. This category also includes programs for new operating systems. This doesn't happen often, as Windows and Linux seem to have been with us forever. However, during the early 1990s people were releasing the Windows and OS/2 versions of their DOS workhorses. Such changes are rare and demand a massive cultural change in training, support, and selling. It requires users to be effectively bilingual during the changeover period, which normally lasts several years.

New products can set a new price.

New Versions

New versions contain serious new features and the inevitable fixes. New versions are typified by a new version number (such as Windows Server 2003) or even a new name.

New versions normally command an upgrade price rather than forcing the user to repurchase.

Interim Updates

Interim updates often contain bug fixes and features that were intended to appear in the original release but had to be postponed.

It is not common practice to charge for interim updates.

Minor Releases

These cover minor bug fixes or cosmetic enhancements. It is common for firms to release them simply because there have been no new updates and they want to stay in contact with their customers.

Minor releases are not charged for.

Table 11-1 shows a comparison of the aspects involved in each type of release.

Table 11-1
Comparison of Release Types

Department	New Product	New Version	Interim Update	Minor Release
Support	✓	✓	✓	✓
Marketing	✓	✓		
Advertising	✓	✓		
PR	✓	✓	✓	
Sales	✓	✓	✓	✓
Charge	✓	✓	?	

Release Issues

As with any part of the software development process, issues come up when it comes time to plan for your software release.

Strategic Planning of Release Dates

Deciding the release date often gets turned into a control issue rather than a functional one. Don't let this happen. The right date is an agreement between the members of the technical team, who know when the product will be ready, and the marketing side, who know when the world can receive it. Releases go wrong when ill prepared software is forced out. Conversely, programmers aren't allowed to look towards infinity and beyond for the time that they guarantee the product will be both perfect and bug free (it will also be extinct). For new products, Release is more a strategic decision than a technical one. WordPerfect, the world's most bought DOS word processor, made a serious tactical error during the early 1990s when they put their graphical user interface (GUI) developments in the OS/2 version of their product and looked upon Windows as the number two. The Windows versions of WordPerfect came out 16 months after its Microsoft competitor and was badly bugged. That was bad strategic planning. WordPerfect was relegated from the greatest name in word processing to a footnote in under three years. Remember, dates aren't just practical considerations—if you mistake an opportunity you can jeopardize the entire firm.

Which Day?

Weekends, national holidays, or even the day before are bad news because if there is an unforeseen glitch few or none of your support or programming staff will be around to fix it. However, the week before a long weekend is an excellent time to release software, as people have spare time and often use it to upgrade and install new software.

One Author's Experience

In the 1990s, I used to develop Internet e-mail software and one version was running about a month late. It had been used unmodified for almost six weeks by a large, diverse, and capable beta test crew, with no negative feedback. It was released on a Friday evening and 2,000 people downloaded it the first day. The result was tepid anarchy. No one had taken into account new users on the original Windows 3.1 release (most people were on 3.11 by then) and using certain products where the manufacturers overwrote an official Microsoft Control Dynamic Link Library (DLL, a set of programs that can be called by other programs to perform common tasks) with their own variant.

The programmers located the problem within a few minutes. The solution was to do a version test at installation, and if a bastardized DLL was running, the install program would copy over the official one. If this had been done earlier in the week, only a few users would have had the problem. Fortunately, customers were impressed with the fix rate, but that problem should have been spotted earlier—in short, everyone had egg on their face, albeit a quail-sized egg.

Experience strongly suggests that it is wise to allow a good week after clearing quality control for problems such as version third-party conflicts to surface. Then, on the Monday of the following week, double-check your results (builds, bug reports, fresh installs, and so on) and at the same time brief support and sales before releasing your program first thing on Tuesday.

Table 11-2 shows an ideal release schedule.

Table 11-2	
Release Schedule	
Day	*Action*
Week before	Finalize testing
Monday	Final checks, brief sales, support, and so on
Tuesday	Release
Wednesday	Support in high state of readiness

Aren't Gold Disks Just for Pop Stars?

Gold disks in software production refer back to the original writable CDs for PCs that appeared in the mid 1990s, which were gold plated. Today most software firms use CDs or DVDs to master their releases for archiving purposes.

Web Site Uploads

Following is a checklist of actions that you must take for every Web/FTP shareware site your software is available from.

1. Issue message/update Web page saying that new versions are about to be uploaded.
2. Upload files to site with new names.
3. Put new page in.
4. Download files to new machine.
5. File compare what went up and came down are identical.

This is a separate list from other release duties and you should work methodically through it.

Who's in Control?

Remove the fear, uncertainty, and doubt (FUD) factor from software release by nominating a single person as your release master. It is their job to inform people of the release dates, manage the launch schedules, and, in the worst case scenario, be responsible for halting the process completely.

Stopping the Release Process

If you ever have to pause or postpone the release process, you have to act quickly and assuredly. The only way you can do this efficiently is to have a prepared checklist available of tasks that you need to invoke. Typically, they cover the following:

1. Draft explanation—be honest.
2. Inform staff (make the confidentiality of the information clear, if appropriate).
3. Contact printers/duplicators to skip or halt production.
4. Contact all journalists. Ask them to pull copy and explain the situation.
5. If advertising has been placed, try to cancel it. Failing that, run a previously prepared standby ad. Don't just pay for advertising space and then not use it.
6. If the release has been made public, issue an explanation on your Web site.

What to Do if a Release Goes Seriously Wrong

You've released a product, it's uploaded all over the world, and all of a sudden you find out that there's a serious problem that either stops the program from working or can corrupt data. What do you do? Panic isn't an option. Simply keep a cool head and work through your release schedule. First you have to quantify the problem and work out very quickly whether it is a problem you can easily work around, a problem that will take time to fix, or if the situation is irrevocable.

Workaround

Check the workaround works—it might be as simple as altering a setting or doing something in a slightly different order.

1. Upload the fix.
2. Document it prominently on your Web site.
3. Contact and advise all users that have the original version.

You'll be amazed at the warm response you will get from customers when you take quick, proactive action to rectify problems. Behaving professionally earns respect.

Fixable, but Not Immediately

You'll have to make a call on how fast you can really sort this out but remember there's nothing worse than making a bad situation abysmal. So always err on the side of caution and allow more time for safety in these circumstances. What you are doing is postponing the release.

1. Contact everyone who has the software.

2. Remove the offending files from Web/FTP sites.

3. Replace with previous version.

4. Upload statements explaining the situation.

5. Treat the fix upload as a quality control and release operation.

The Situation Is Irrevocable

The sooner you pull the release the less indecisive your organization will appear. Customers who have paid for upgrades should be refunded immediately.

Apportioning Blame Helps No One

When a release goes wrong don't be negative. Use the energy to do the following:

1. Quantify the problem.

2. Work out the solution.

3. Take the remedial action.

4. Pacify your customers.

5. Log the cause of the problem and write it into your company's annals to make sure that it never happens again.

When you have resolved the problem and the dust has settled sufficiently for you to get the problem into perspective, you can assess the scale of the damage and the corporate response.

✦   ✦   ✦

Setting Up a Company

Why do companies exist?

During the Middle Ages, kings and their enterprising subjects collided. Kings started granting licenses to people to discover countries, pursue trade, and so on. This was a clever ruse to make sure the king got a cut without having to put up any real money. The money was normally raised by enticing several wealthy subjects to invest in the enterprise (remind you of modern investment methods?). These missions were highly speculative (just think of the number of trips to "discover" America before Columbus succeeded).

To protect themselves and the king from subsequent loss they devised the concept of the corporation (from the Latin *corpus* for *body*) or company.

The company is a legal body in its own right, just like you or I. It can be sued, taxed, rewarded, and is made liable to the law in just the same way as an individual. We take companies for granted nowadays, but whoever encapsulated the idea originally was a genius. Then came a slight but enormously important refinement: The *limited* company.

Limited companies limited the liability of the investors, so they were prepared to take risk. Legally, they could lose what they invested but no more.

A Universal Solution?

Companies as we know them today originate from the English/ Low Countries/Dutch style of companies set up around 1650 onwards. These include the concepts of shareholding, share trading, corporate accountability, transparency (at first this was rather opaque), and profit.

Note   London's first dedicated stock exchange was opened in 1773. New York brokers were dealing under a sycamore tree on Wall Street in 1791 until their first proper Exchange was opened the following year. The first stock exchange, or Bourse, is believed to have started in Bruges in Flanders (now part of Belgium) and is named after the Van der Beurze family who owned the house where the activity began.

Companies by their very nature are very similar the world over, whether you are in Seattle or Singapore, Moscow or Madrid. But always check to find out how they are interpreted locally.

Why a Company?

Who is going to sell your product? This is not a trick question. You personally? The firm that you work for? A software publisher? Someone else?

Most private developers the world over set up a company for the reduced risks and tax advantages it often brings.

Setting up a company is surprisingly straightforward (otherwise companies wouldn't be so popular). In return for all the advantages that go with companies, there are responsibilities and procedures as well as some terminology with which you should be familiar.

The Plusses

The five core reasons that software developers cite for using a company as the vehicle to sell their software are as follows:

- ✦ **Presence**—Companies are perceived to be professional.
- ✦ **Security**—Legal protection from creditors.
- ✦ **Tax benefits**—Companies give you more tax options. (In some jurisdictions there are also other financial advantages.)
- ✦ **Shareholdings**—Gives key players a slice of the action as well as a means of raising money.
- ✦ **Public accountability**—Suppliers and clients' companies are reluctant to trade with anything less. Taking the step to become a company shows you are prepared to accept the responsibilities and obligations of formal trading.

Companies are set up under the jurisdiction (laws) of the country in which they are incorporated. They have to behave in accordance with the law and tax codes of that country. This does not stop them being able to trade abroad.

The Minuses

Incorporation requires you to make regular statutory returns that provide general and accounting information to the public. This information is pedestrian and compulsory. You still have to submit similar figures to the taxman each year even if you are trading privately. There are costs associated with preparing and sending these returns, which are obviously higher than if you aren't incorporated.

You need to ask yourself two key questions:

✦ Can I even operate without being incorporated?

✦ If I do, do the pros outweigh the cons?

To make life easier, most countries operate a tiered system making the costs and complexity of the annual returns lower for smaller traders.

Before You Jump

If you receive money in return for your software, there are only three legal mechanisms under which you may trade:

✦ Private individual

✦ Partnership

✦ Company

Trading as a Private Individual

As a private individual, you can trade either under your own name (for example, Bill Smith) or as yourself trading as a wholly owned entity (such as Bill Smith trading as Bill Smith Software).

Whereas your name is legally considered unique to you, you should ensure that when you use it to trade with, it is not being used by anyone else. Otherwise, you could be accused of trying to pass yourself off as another firm. This is why you often see trading names qualified in various ways such as "Bill Smith trading as Bill Smith Software" or "Smith Software (London)."

This is often referred to as *sole proprietorship* or a *sole trader*. One person runs the entire business—with or without hired help.

Sole proprietorship will give you no legal protection against creditors if you go bust. This can literally mean selling your house and almost everything in it to pay off your debts. However, you can usually set off your private gains against your trading losses.

For small operations, where turnover is low and there are no liabilities, trading as a private individual is a real option. If you choose this route, there is nothing to stop you from incorporating later.

Trading as a Partnership

Partnerships are shared businesses with a legal status between that of an individual and a company. The arrangement is common among professions such as law, architecture, and medicine. Indeed, in some countries, it is these professions' only allowable form.

In ordinary commercial operations a partnership rarely lasts longer than it takes for one partner to realize that he can fare just as well without the other. Partnerships are rarely found in established software houses.

However, some people just drift into them. What often happens is that one person has an idea and works on it until he hits a snag. Then a very useful helper appears. Without any formal discussion they gradually begin to collaborate. In the United States this is sufficient for them to be classed as partners and jointly be legally accountable. After a while the project may prosper sufficiently for the partners to enter a formal agreement. If things go even better, they may elect to turn their partnership into a jointly owned company with limited personal liability.

Trading between Limited Liability Companies

Limited liability companies come in two forms: private and listed. Listed companies can issue shares that are tradable on a major stock exchange. Private companies cannot.

Publicly listed companies have to disclose regular financial information to the public such as their sales, expenses, profits, assets, liabilities, as well as more sensitive issues such as management remuneration packages.

Private companies have the same legal protections and tax advantages as public ones, but the returns they complete are usually less stringent.

In the United States, private companies represent about 99 percent of the 15 million organizations existing. In the United Kingdom, there is a private company for every 15 people.

In the United States, a subsidiary firm can be called an "affiliated company," which is classified as a separate company type. Affiliates occur when an incorporated company (a corporation) buys another firm (the firm becomes an affiliate). Alternatively, they set up a new division, which they can classify as the affiliate.

The Corporate Vocabulary

As you might expect, company speak comes with its own vocabulary. Here's a breakdown of the key words you are likely to hear:

✦ **Articles of Incorporation (often called the Articles of Association in other countries)**—These are the company bylaws by which your operation is to be run.

✦ **Audits**—An audit is the inspection and preparation of your company's accounts. The books are assembled for a regular, specified period, normally 12 months, and presented according to your jurisdiction's accounting standards and principles. The audit will contain a statement of your financial position (the balance sheet) as well as financial activity (income statement) and cash flows. It is common to show comparisons between the current and previous year's performance so shareholders can appreciate the main trends.

Typically, firms, or their accountants, prepare the accounts and then an external auditor (can be the accountants) will pick a sample of the transactions (for example, 10 percent) to test the figure work for verification.

The auditor is required to provide a cover letter for the audit expressing their estimation of the financial state of the company and their satisfaction with its compliance to current legislation and practice.

Be aware that until you get into the swing, audits take up a lot of management time in both the preparation and signing off. It is advisable to have a senior director, preferably one who deals with the financial matters on hand throughout an audit to answer any questions.

If your jurisdiction requires audited figures to be submitted, make sure you get them in by the deadline, as there are normally penalties for late submissions. If you fail to submit your returns at all, the firm will be barred from trading.

✦ **Corporate administrator**—(a.k.a., the company secretary) The role of this position is to ensure all statutory paperwork concerning directors, registered offices, shares, annual returns, audits, and so on is completed correctly and promptly.

✦ **Dividends**—Payments made to each shareholder. Dividends can only be made from monies left in the firm after it has paid corporation or company tax. A dividend is paid against each and every share. (So if you own 100 shares your dividend payment would be 100 times higher than a person owning a single share.)

Note

Tax law often provides for separate rates of taxation for earned and unearned income. Receiving money as dividends rather than income can affect how much you pay.

✦ **Directors**—The directors (often vice presidents in the United States) are the people who run the company. They are responsible for making sure it adheres to its legal obligations. The directors of the company constitute the main board.

In the United States, directors are managers of the shareholder's board. Vice presidents manage day-to-day development, manufacturing, and trading.

✦ **Dormancy**—Strange though it might sound, in some countries there is nothing to stop you setting up a firm and not letting it trade. You might maintain a dormant company because you want to reserve a particular trading name or get the paperwork out of the way. In such circumstances, annual returns still have to be submitted but legal requirements of annual accounts are not required providing your tax office is satisfied that the firm has not traded during the financial year.

✦ **Articles of incorporation and memoranda of association**—These are actually two separate documents and go by different names depending on where you live, sometimes they are unified to include the rules of association.

  • **Articles of incorporation**—Set out the company's rules for running its affairs, including issuance and transfers of shares and directorial powers.

  • **Memoranda of association**—These set out the factual information of the company: its name and registered office (must be within the jurisdiction, meaning no Swiss companies with registered offices in Reykjavik, for example) together with the objectives of the company.

✦ **Incorporation**—The act of creating the company or corporate body.

✦ **Liabilities**—What you owe your suppliers, normally money (see Chapter 17).

✦ **Local jurisdiction**—The local laws by which a company is bound.

✦ **Registered office**—An incorporated firm is a contactable firm. To ensure this, incorporation requires that every firm have a registered office to which all statutory correspondence is addressed. This does not have to be your office or home. If you choose anywhere else, such as your accountant's address, it is your responsibility to make sure you receive and deal with all company correspondence. To be efficient, registered offices should be near the main operation.

✦ **Shareholders**—The people who own the company. Shares are the mechanism by which their part of the ownership is determined.

What It Costs to Set Up a Company with Limited Liability

Table 12-1 shows the worldwide variety in cost and set-up time. Times are estimates given by firms who specialize in company registration. When available, they are considerably shorter than those using lawyers. Setup costs are the government fees. Always find out what is involved.

Table 12-1
Cost Comparison

Country	Company Classification	Setup Time	Share Capital	Ready Mades	Setup Costs
Australia	Proprietary	4 weeks	Optional		
Austria	GesmbH/AG	2–4 weeks	From 0		500–3,000€
Belgium	SPRL	2 weeks	18,600€		
China					
Denmark			16,800€		
France	SARL, S.A.	2 weeks	7,500, 37,000€ (Only 20 percent of SARLs has to be paid at incorporation. The remainder must be paid within five years, For SAs 50 percent share capital has to be paid up.)		700€
Germany	GmbH	4–6 weeks	25,000€		
India	Limited				
Italy	SRL, SpA	4 weeks	10,000, 100,000€		2,000–2,500€
Japan					
Netherlands	B.V.	2 weeks	18,000€	Yes	
New Zealand	Proprietary	2–4 weeks	0		
Portugal	Lda	4 weeks	5,000€		
Russia	Variety	3 months	$350–$3,500		$300+
Singapore	Ltd	2–3 weeks	S$100,000		
Spain	SA	2–4 weeks	60,102€		Min 300€ (% levied on share capital in addition)

Continued

Table 12-1 *(continued)*					
Country	*Company Classification*	*Setup Time*	*Share Capital*	*Ready Mades*	*Setup Costs*
Sweden	AB	4 weeks	100,000SEK	Yes	3,500SEK
Switzerland	AG/GmbH	2–3 weeks	20–100,000 SFr		1,500–2,000SFr small co
UK	Ltd	1–7days	0	Yes	£20 (Add £60 for same day incorporation)
USA (California used for this example)	LLP, LLCs	1–2 days	0		$70–100

Doing all searches and paperwork yourself is invariably cheaper, but it often takes longer, especially if this is the first time that you have done the paperwork.

Corporate legislation is updated periodically. Always check with your government body or professional advisor for the current status.

Professional Advisors

Unless you are fully trained, several aspects of running a company require specialist advice, particularly accounting, legal, and intellectual property issues. Many of them you will only need from time to time. It is a good idea to build up a shortlist of lawyers and accountants you can call upon at short notice.

Depending on country and turnover, you may need to submit a formal set of audited accounts. These need to be signed off as correct by a qualified accountant who knows the regulations and mechanisms by which the annual audit must be completed. An accountant's role is to make sure you conform to the current financial legislation, to advise you on how to reduce your tax charge, and to avoid costly mistakes. One of their first tasks will be to advise you as to when your tax year should run from to give you the maximum tax advantage and reduce the amount of necessary paperwork. This is because in most countries your first tax year can be longer than a year. Subsequently, the start of your tax year can be changed in many countries.

There is no need to have a legal advisor (retain an attorney) unless there is a pressing legal issue.

The Basics of Setting Up a Company

All companies might appear to be the same but there are several different types. Choosing the most appropriate setup is essential from the outset.

✦ **Private unlimited company**—The shareholders/members liability is limited to the value of all debts and claims against the company. The most notable example is "Lloyds of London" insurance syndicate.

✦ **Private limited company**—Liability is limited to the face value of the shares, whether issued or not.

✦ **Private company limited by guarantee**—The extent of the directors' liability is limited to the value or not of the irrevocable undertaking to cover a specified amount. This only has to be paid up if the company goes into liquidation.

✦ **Public limited company (Listed)**—The shares can be offered to the public through the major stock exchanges. Shareholders' liability, like a private company, is limited to the amount of unpaid shares held.

Unless you are able to go public immediately, you will probably want to form a private company.

Who Can Form a Company?

Almost anyone can form a company. However, most countries disallow people who are certified mad or, in some cases, those who have criminal records. There are no minimal educational requirements. However, some countries do have minimum and maximum age restrictions. While some of you will feel that these are the strongest requirements for being a successful company director, it's also best if the directorial candidate hasn't been previously disqualified by a court from being a company director. Nationality can also be an issue. If you are not a national or resident of the country in which you wish to be a director of a company, check the local requirements to make sure you can hold office.

Share Capital

Countries use the cash level of entry as a political instrument according to whether they want to encourage enterprise or minimize unproductive paperwork. For example, in the United Kingdom you can set up a firm with an initial share capital of just £1 ($1.5). In Switzerland you must put up SFr 20,000 ($15,000) for a GmbH limited company, while in Austria you need €40,000 ($42,000) for a GesmbH, their equivalent.

Most countries charge a stamp duty (% tax) when shares are created.

Companies are allowed to issue shares up to their formal limits by the act of incorporation. Shares allow you to parcel out the firm among financial backers and key personnel. Significantly, they can be used to raise capital by giving the public or investors a share in the firm in return for money.

Shares can be classified. You can offer holders the rights to a vote and/or share in dividends.

Directors do not technically have to be shareholders although they normally are.

To Form a Company

There are three ways to form your company:

- ✦ Get a solicitor/attorney/notary to set it up for you.
- ✦ Buy a ready-made entity. Ready-mades are firms that set up companies in advance. They specialize in corporate registration.
- ✦ Do it yourself. (Again, depending on the national view of companies, this restricts your options.)

In many European countries where the local law dictates that you have to go the legal route the cost increases considerably, especially if the articles are hand drafted.

 Note   In The Netherlands they reissue dissolved companies that have been cleaned up— a novel form of recycling.

Some countries, including the United States and United Kingdom, make it very easy to download the paperwork and forms from their registration body via the Internet so you can set up your firm by yourself.

If you are having a problem drafting suitable articles of association, go down to the offices of your state or country's business governing body and consult some of your rivals' information (remember, these are publicly available).

The registration body is not there to give you legal or corporate advice but to make sure you have the right forms and to answer questions in that regard.

Whichever way you decide to go about setting up your firm, you will need to choose and agree on the following:

- ✦ Directors
- ✦ Corporate administrator/company secretary
- ✦ Registered office
- ✦ Memoranda and articles of association

Details required on the forms include full names, addresses, dates of birth, occupations, and details of other directorships held within the last five years. They also require those companies' registered offices. Although some of these details are held in the memoranda of association, the official forms are the ones entered into the databases, so you must complete the forms as well.

If you subsequently elect a new director, or they change their name (in getting married or divorced), retire, die, switch their nationality, or alter their primary address, you must notify the registration body, within 14 days. It goes without saying that the same requirements apply to changes of the corporate administrator/company secretary.

The company's articles delivered to the registrar must be signed by the initial subscribers and witnessed by independent persons to verify the signatures.

Note It is best to fill out company paperwork using black ink, as blue ink (especially light blue) can photocopy badly due to the light frequencies used in many photocopiers and microfiche cameras. If your documents can't be legibly copied correctly, they will be rejected. The registration authority must always receive originals. Make copies of everything you send, and use recorded delivery for all important documents.

Statutory Declaration of Compliance

This goes by many names. It is the document that states that the officers of the company will obey the law and honor their corporate, directorate, or company secretarial offices relating to the incorporation of the company. The declaration is invariably signed by a notary and/or one of the founding directors. In some countries the corporate administrator/company secretary is allowed to do this. Finally, a validation must be signed in the presence of a justice of the peace, notary public, or a commissioner for oaths.

What Happens Next?

When all the documents have been completed they should be sent by registered mail to the company registrar at your country's registration body (Securities & Exchange Commission (SEC)/federal registration body; Companies House in the United Kingdom).

The registrar's department will then scrutinize the documents and, if valid, issue their authorization. Some countries have a fast track system for company formation to speed up the verification. In the United Kingdom this can be done on a same-day basis providing the documents are received before 3pm.

The company can start trading from the day it receives certified authorization from the registration body.

How Many Company Officers Do I Need?

The statutory number of directors required varies from country to country and on the type of firm you are setting up. In some countries, if you want to have one director, this must be stipulated in the articles of incorporation. Having said that, you cannot be the only director *and* the corporate administrator/company secretary. Providing there is more than one director, either may be the company secretary.

Shares and Shareholdings

This is the vital area. Whoever owns over 50 percent of the shares legally controls the firm. However, decisive control can be affected (depending on how the remaining shares are allotted) from a much smaller holding. Releasing shares is the most economic way to bring investment revenue into the company.

A share is part ownership of a company. The company can issue any number of shares when it is created. They don't have to be purchased on day one. Shares that are purchased are called *issued* and the remainder *unissued* stock. Shares have a nominal price (initial price set against them), which the founders of the firm will dictate; this is called the par price.

About Going Public

Public companies can not only solicit public investment, but they can also advertise for it. Furthermore, they can raise shares on their national stock exchange that can be traded internationally.

Public companies are bound by much more stringent regulations than private ones. They need more directors, more share capital (a significant proportion of which must be paid up front), stricter auditing, and face tougher penalties for non-compliance.

If you are big enough to be considering this route, you will, of course, have been informed about the details by your lawyers, accountants, and city advisors.

Can I Switch from a Private to a Public Firm?

Yes, providing it has share capital. The process isn't simple, but it is surprisingly straightforward. The process may be reversed and set in motion by passing a special resolution.

Declaring the Company Status

Requirements vary from country to country but it is normally mandatory for the company status to be listed on all stationery and official publications. All of the following issued on behalf of the company must also display the company status:

- ✦ Letters
- ✦ Invoices
- ✦ Pro-forma invoices
- ✦ Quotes
- ✦ Statements

- ✦ Receipts
- ✦ Bills
- ✦ Promissory notes
- ✦ Endorsements
- ✦ Checks
- ✦ Orders for money or goods

The company number and place of incorporation must appear listed on all business letters.

On important business correspondence, the address of the registered office, if it isn't the same as the trading address, should also appear.

Ironically, directors' names don't have to be shown. However, if you show any, you must show all. If you are worried about the order in which to display these, list them alphabetically; that way none can take offense.

Corporate Responsibility

The moment you incorporate, you have signed up for corporate responsibility. This embodies statutory obligations as well as behaving in a way that is socially acceptable.

Directorial Responsibilities

The most common responsibilities include the following:

- ✦ Administrative duties:
  - Accounts
  - Annual returns
  - Notice of change of directors
  - Notice of change of the registered office
- ✦ Financial:
  - Director's report (signed by director or corporate administrator/company secretary)
  - Balance sheet (signed by a director)
  - Profit and loss account
  - Auditors report signed by the auditor
  - Notes to the accountants

If you are late you will be fined. If you are overdue you may be shut down. Don't blame the accountant; they'll sue you.

Money is an enormous responsibility in running a firm and in making sure you have the money to meet your financial liabilities.

Corporate Administrator/Company Secretary Responsibilities

This is an administrative role and while it handles several corporate duties, it embodies limited powers. The bulk of the work is filling out forms and ensuring that statutory paperwork is filled in correctly and dispatched promptly.

In some countries a director can be a corporate administrator/company secretary; in others it is a separate role. It is their role to transmit any changes to the legal makeup of the company to the governing body promptly.

The role of notifying company members (this can include shareholders) of changes is normally the responsibility of the company secretary. There are legal time limits that are deemed to be adequate notice. In the United Kingdom you must give them a minimum of 14 days' notice for a normal meeting and 21 days for the annual general meetings (AGMs). Note that for unlimited companies the notice period is typically seven days. The rules and regulations vary depending on the type of firm, and from country to country.

The corporate administrator/company secretary duties also entail sending the registrar of companies copies of special or extraordinary resolutions within 15 days of them being passed, and providing copies of the audited accounts to every member of the company, shareholders, and anyone else who has legally requested a copy. In the United Kingdom, these must be sent out at least 21 days in advance of the AGM to ensure people have ample time to digest them.

The company secretary is also responsible for recording the minutes of all board meetings. They must also make the company records available for inspection, if requested. Finally, they keep custody of the company seal. This is used to endorse share certificates and other legal documents.

Record of Accounts

A company's accounts should start from their date of incorporation. The first financial year will end seven days either side of this date. However, in the first year it can be altered. The accounting reference date is typically the last date of the month for the month your firm was incorporated. So, if your firm was incorporated on March 19th, the reference date would be March 31st (last day of that month).

The accounting reference date can be altered. You might want to coincide your year-end with other members of a consortium. I often like year-ends to be December 31st so all audited figures and statistics reflect the calendar year.

Make sure you know when you must have your accounts in. You will pay if they are late. There are strict deadlines that must be met. Make sure you are aware of these before you start trading. They vary radically from country to country.

Annual Returns

The annual return is a synopsis of the company's directors, secretary, shareholders, and share capital information. Most countries require that you submit a nominal fee with this submission each year to ensure your company remains registered.

Change of the Registered Office

All correspondence from the governing body goes to your registered office. This includes important correspondence and reminders. If you change your official address for whatever reason, you must notify the governing body promptly (within 14 days).

Informing Your Registration Body

You are normally required to inform your state's company registration body if anything has changed within the company, using the correct forms and within the allotted timescales. Such changes might include the following:

- ✦ New directors being appointed.
- ✦ Directors resigning or dying.
- ✦ New corporate administrator/company secretary or change in status of the current position occupant.
- ✦ New shares being allotted (within a month).
- ✦ When you pass any special or extraordinary resolutions (within 15 days).
- ✦ If any mortgage charge/loan is put on the company (within 21 days).
- ✦ A change of the registered office must be informed (within 14 days).
- ✦ Copies of special and extraordinary resolutions and specific categories of ordinary resolutions need to be filed.

Once filed, most of this paperwork is checked to ensure that it has been completed correctly. If so, the data is entered into their systems and made publicly available to anyone wanting to see it.

Annual General Meetings

Companies must have an annual general meeting (AGM) once a year where the accounts are presented and any questions as to the direction and running of the company can be raised. Generally, only directors, shareholders, and invited guests can attend AGMs.

Health and Safety

The major change in corporate and directorial responsibility in recent years has been on the issue of health and safety legislation.

Fundamentally, these codes require that all types of organizations accept and ensure that all health and safety risks are properly managed and are in line with current legislation. This is a responsibility of all directors and key managers and affects not only staff, but also anyone else who may be onsite or involved in your company's activities (such as customers). Key areas to consider are maximizing the well-being of your staff and taking steps to make sure people don't suffer accidents or fatalities. This ultimately leads to a better place to work, increased productivity, and lessens prosecution and penalties as a result of on-the-job accidents.

Caution It is impossible to take health and safety too seriously. Directors must always take a proactive approach. In some countries, corporate manslaughter is now a recognized offense.

Insolvency

A key concept of incorporated companies is that they limit the liability of the shareholders and directors in the sense that they are not liable for any debts. There is one caveat: If a director has given personnel guarantees, these are excluded from liability exemption; otherwise, this would be considered fraudulent trading.

The most common mistake people make is to trade insolvently, whereby they continue running the business when it does not have enough money to meet its creditors (people to whom it owes money).

Note Directors may become liable personally for company debts even if they believe they have acted honestly and in good faith. See Chapter 18 for more information.

Resignation

Any director or corporate administrator/company secretary can resign their post at any time. It is not uncommon to announce this at directorial meetings or the AGM. Otherwise, putting it in writing to the managing director or company secretary will do. If this is done by e-mail or fax, a formal, signed letter should be sent by mail. Remember, for the registration to be official the relevant paperwork must be submitted to your country's registration body.

✦   ✦   ✦

Pitching the Price

Pricing is notionally the most powerful of all marketing tools.

In practice, marketeers rarely get much say in the launch price. *Marketers* are people who bring goods to market. *Marketeers* are people who plan how those goods should be brought to market. By the time they come on the scene, competition, development costs, and distribution limits have already boxed in the retail price.

If the take up is disappointing, there is very little the marketing team can do apart from introducing a special edition, either an enhanced program at a premium price or a stripped-down version at a discount. The response to these will provide hard information to enable management to judge in which direction prices need to move to optimize profits. However, these are tactical not strategic tools. With software, unit production costs start at next to nothing and grow to negligible. Almost all the costs stem from development. These have a way of shooting up from extremely expensive to more than the firm can afford. So the idealism that starts the entire project off needs to be reined in at a very early stage.

Pricing Theory

The theory of price is that if you pitch the price sky high, only one person will want it. If you give it away, everyone will want one. Neither is actually true. In general terms, the higher the price, the scarcer the sales. Conversely, the lower the price, the more numerous sales are likely to be. The trick is to pick a price where numbers sold at X unit profit generates the largest payback. It's simple, but it isn't easy.

Set the price too high and sales will trickle in. Set it too low and you might be flooded with orders yet generate little profit. On the other hand, you might not sell at all. Cheap goods are often perceived to be worthless.

Gauging the Correct Price

Pricing a product is a two-part exercise. First, you must take into account external factors over which you have little or no control. These establish the ballpark within which your product must to be sold. Second, you must narrow the box by weighing those factors over which you do exercise some influence.

Five external factors define the space you have for maneuvering:

1. The cost of developing the product and bringing it to market
2. The market's size
3. What that population is able and willing to pay
4. Direct competition
5. Prices set for similar products

Four factors determine the extent to which you can narrow price:

1. The perceived value of benefits conferred on the user
2. The profit target you set
3. The positive effects of salesmanship, advertising, and PR
4. The effect of spin-offs

The following sections consider these in turn.

What Is the Real Cost of Development?

Real costs encompass everything you need to spend from the day you start until the product enters the market, *plus* the on-going cost of remaining in business. So, if you spend $100,000 developing your program and calculate the running costs at $50,000 per quarter, to break even your sales in the first year must be at least $300,000.

You may find it less painful to put down everything if you imagine you are listing all items you can claim as tax deductions. This includes but is not limited to the following:

+ Salaries
+ Materials
+ Insurance

✦ Rent

✦ Heat

✦ Electricity

✦ Water

✦ Legal costs

✦ Accountant fees

✦ Stationery

✦ Telephones

✦ Travel

It has probably occurred to you that it is a good idea to keep these outgoings low.

Market Size

You cannot sell programs to more customers than there actually are.

So first define the market at which you are aiming. It is estimated that as few as one percent of the bombs dropped in World War II actually hit their target. It is only recently, in the Iraq War, that this problem has been solved. You, too, need to define your target market with similar precision.

When you have done so, go down to your public library and consult the professional directories. If, for instance, you are writing a program for Houston lawyers specializing in intellectual property, you might narrow them down with the categories of information displayed in Table 13-1.

Table 13-1 **Target Research on Houston Attorneys**		
Category	*Number of People*	*Percentage*
Population of the United States	282,798,000	100.0000
Working population	115,061,184	40.6867
Total number of practicing attorneys	1,058,662	0.3743
Attorneys practicing in Texas	64,593	0.0228
Attorneys practicing in Houston	>5,000	0.0018
Attorneys in Houston specializing in intellectual property	399	0.0001

Sources: U.S. Census Bureau/American Bar Association/www.martindale.com

If there are too few customers to repay the costs you know will be incurred, either abandon your project, gather the necessary quorum from other countries, or redefine your target on a broader base and adapt your program.

For example, you might add features that will enable your product to match some standard educational syllabus. This would immediately enable you to sell to academic as well as lay users.

What Is the Market Able and Willing to Pay?

The short answer is, more or less what they have been paying already, if indeed there are precedents. People's expectations are conditioned by how they perceive their own needs.

- ✦ What they can afford.
- ✦ Whether they have the money.
- ✦ Whether they think it is worth stretching to get.
- ✦ Whether their peers expect them to have one.

No one knows the exact mix of these factors. For one thing, there's a big difference between what people say and what people do. Chains of logic only carry them along so far before they get swept away by some emotional crosscurrent. A girl does not need an engagement ring as much as she needs breakfast. Yet, emotionally, she wants it much more and will move heaven and earth to push her prospective groom to the jewellers past McDonald's.

Direct Competition

Through the revenue it received from every DOS and Windows operating system sold, Microsoft has been able to fund other software development in a way everyone else can only dream of (wonderful for Microsoft, but death to competition).

Very few competitors could begin to compete on price, let alone quality. Yet many program writers thought they could emulate Microsoft's marketing. Some of them developed fine programs, but on a scale set by Microsoft, could they sell them at a profit? Sadly, no. In the end, they could only sell their companies to other greenhorns who thought themselves smarter.

With the eclipse of the 21st century, this era is coming to a close. Software and software companies are growing up. So don't compare your product with Microsoft unless you are really in their league. Don't be pressured to price your goods to align cost-wise with theirs. Think about your own situation, what you are offering, and what your customers should be paying for your product. Price your product accordingly. Then figure out how to sell it at that price. Otherwise, it's back to the drawing board.

On the other hand, if you are entering a market sector where customers think your competitors are pricing their software realistically, you have got to be able to put your product on a shelf alongside them.

Directly competitive prices need to be judged with precision, quantified very carefully. Whose features are the telling ones? Whose company is better known? Whose brand is strongest? Whose reputation stands higher? People always pay a premium for features they deem to be plusses.

Don't be tempted to copy earlier entrants slavishly. No developer becomes a market leader by following in a competitor's footsteps.

Prices Set for Similar Products

The range in price between various brands of supermarket butter may be less than 35 percent. Yet the difference in price of cars between various models might be 1,200 percent.

This difference can only be established if the customer is actually prepared to play ball and pay. Why are they prepared to delve so deeply into their pockets? Is it the manufacturer who produces it or the buyer who fancies it?

One way or another, end users are adept at distinguishing between good and bad offers. Most times, you will want to offer good market value. If you must run against the grain and charge more, you need an extra factor (which need not be material) to make up the value.

The Value of Benefits Conferred on the User

Until you know what your program is worth to buyers, you cannot know whether you are addressing a viable market. Unless yours is a custom-made program, you will rarely be able to assess your income potential down to the nearest 1,000 dollars. The real question is whether the ballpark is the size of the Pacific or a skating rink.

The ballpark figure is a combination of quantity and quality. How many potential buyers are there? How much are they willing to pay? This is an area where you must be guided solely by the facts you are able to uncover through research and asking questions.

Fairly obviously, the more potential users there are, the easier it is to amortize the gear-up cost and the rosier your prospects of profit. The qualitative question, however, needs interpretation. Consider how potential buyers might justify your program. For example, if your product is designed to enable intellectual property lawyers to accelerate searches, draft patents, and check documents, your market research should tell you how much time it is likely to save them. Suppose respondents put time saved for these tasks at a minimum of an hour a week. That's 52 weeks each year. If there are 10 attorneys to a practice and each charges $250 per hour, the annual saving is $130,000.

With the program, they could offer a prompter, better-vetted service as well as having more working time to bill. They *could* pay you over $100,000 for the program and still be better off. You could reasonably assume then that they might willingly invest one year's time saving to enjoy that saving for many years after.

If you put your mind to it, the worth of a program can usually be quantified, either in terms of increased productivity, time saving, or capital economy. Furthermore, your software might help buyers hold on to existing customers or win new ones.

Every benefit that the customer sets a value on enables you to make your product an essential as opposed to a discretionary purchase.

What Profit Do You Want?

Because profit is what's left after you have paid everyone else, many who are new to program development think profit comes last. Not at all; profit comes first! If you haven't got a profit for yourself, you haven't provided the wherewithal to cover the inevitable unexpected. And if you haven't earned a profit, your creditors won't want you to be in business for long.

Be selfish for a second. Look yourself in the mirror, tell yourself you are worth it, and name your price.

The Positive Effects of Advertising and PR

Advertisers (as opposed to advertising agents) can tell you that advertising often works better as an accelerator and brake than as an ignition button. It's easier to speed up or slow down sales. The hard part is getting them started in the first place. With software, of course, you haven't got a fixed assembly plant that limits production. Your least likely problem is being unable to keep abreast of demand.

The most costly advertising and PR task is the product launch, not just because launches need bigger and more frequent spaces to get noticed, but also because they need to get across the program's new benefits. Furthermore, launches can go wrong. The neatest, most effective exposition of a product is rarely developed on day one.

The truth is that software has a much more complex educational task than supermarket products. With hindsight, you may be delighted with what advertising and PR have done for you. However, the most you should bank on in advance is that if advertising and PR are effectively employed, they will firm up realistic estimates.

How Associated Products Can Increase Your Income

One of the golden rules is to take your profit where you can. If you are new to software development, it may come as a pleasant surprise that most software products can provide not one but eight revenue streams. Unless you have deliberately constricted your product, you can derive income from all of the following:

✦ Core products (standard product)

✦ Upgrades (when new functionality is added)

✦ Maintenance contracts (support)

✦ Add-ons (extension products either written in house or by third parties)

✦ Lateral developments (modifying the product for new markets)

✦ Custom-made developments (specialist developments)

✦ Consultancy

✦ Bulk/original equipment manufacturer (OEM) licensing deals (technically, this is the large version of 1 but has to be handled differently)

The wider your income stream the greater the revenue you will generate and the longer your product's life cycle is likely to be. The opportunities that arise from these streams need to be taken into account when you are modelling the core product.

Upgrades, incidentally, are typically charged at 60 percent of the recommended retail price (RRP). Maintenance is rarely more than 30 percent.

Add-on prices are dependent on the extra value they offer, yet it's hard psychologically for them to achieve RRP prices in excess of 50 percent of the mother product. If you price the mother product too low, it may not be worthwhile for anyone to create add-ons, no matter how badly they are needed.

Lateral and custom-made development together with consultancy rarely happen with under-priced programs, mainly because of perception. If you're selling a product for $25 you're clearly running a manufacturing operation. Servicing is just unrealistic. If, on the other hand, your product sells for $2,500, clients will assume that you do custom work for it all the time.

Bulk OEM licenses are a law unto themselves. Each one needs to be negotiated to maximize profit without compromising your future. For deals of 10,000+ units or $500,000+ (the discounted price, not the RRP!) initial, guaranteed order, you are typically looking at sealing the contracts at a 75–80 percent discount off RRP. It's yet another reason to set your core price as high as the market will bear.

Price Bands

It isn't just different brands that sell at various prices; it's groups of products as well. You wouldn't expect a grand piano to sell in the same price bracket as a penny whistle. Study your own market sector. See if you can work out why prices are of the order they are. Then see if you can work out why your potential competitors have settled on different prices within the main grouping.

The breakdowns shown in Table 13-2 are typical. Actual prices tend to be of the $99.95 ilk, just below the perceived price break.

Table 13-2 Price Grouping Breakdown	
RRP Band	*Typical Products*
$500,000+	Medium-large custom implementations, departmental-enterprise solutions
From $25,000 to $249,999	Custom-made accounts packages, serious application server, high-end enterprise databases, corporate AV solutions
From $10,000 to $24,999	Clustered O/S, high-end accounts, E-commerce Web server
From $2,500 to $9,999	Basic enterprise databases
From $1,000 to $2,499	Network O/S
From $600 to $999	Reporting software
From $300 to $599	Graphics packages, project, complete office solutions
From $100 to $299	Window O/S, RAD programming tools, word processor or spreadsheets purchased separately
From $50 to $99	Branded Linux O/S, basic account packages
From $0 to $49	Shareware, Freeware, utilities
Free	Linuxware, Star Office

These are indicative raw software costs. Consultancy costs can vary depending on the caliber of staff and the man-hours used as well as the true cost to compensate for pulling staff off other work.

Never Undersell Yourself

As previously explained, software prices tend to be lower for historical reasons than strict arithmetic justifies. Entrepreneurs tend to try to amortize development over too long a period or share costs among more customers than ever materialize. They omit the unavoidable on-going costs of product maintenance and development.

When people are scared that their product won't sell, they tend to convince themselves that if they make it cheap it will walk out the door. In this case, keep your market research in mind. Good market research should give you some indication of the real thresholds.

If you set the price of your software too high at the start, it should at least have a quality image. If you have to, you can always lower the price later. You have only to rationalize the reduction on grounds that it's "owing to heavy demand and the economies of scale." No one ever complains. However, try it the other way around and there will be grumbles, complaints, withdrawals, and you will soon realize that the only thing you can do is enhance the product and re-launch it under another name. This is a very expensive process and hardly anyone does it.

Remember, unless you are selling direct, you only receive a fraction of the retail price. Suppose you are selling a product for $100. If you end up halving the price you must sell more than twice as many units to net the same profit because you encounter increased freight, accounting, and support costs. Distributors and dealers might give up on the product or renegotiate a tougher deal to compensate them for their additional work. Table 13-3 demonstrates the profit differential if you reduce the product price by half.

| | Table 13-3 | |
| | **Profit Comparison** | |
Components	**$100 product**	**$50 product**
List Price	$100.00	$50.00
Freight per unit	−$2.00	−$2.00
Insurance	−$0.20	−$0.10
Distributor Discount	−$60.00 @ 60%	−$30.00 @ 60%
You receive	$37.80 or 37.8% of RRP	$17.90 or 35.8% of RRP

Note   Remember, a high price signals to potential competition that this is a lucrative market; set a lower price point and you might ward some of them off—this is a hard call but you have got to get it as right as you can.

Other Ways to Win Revenue

As the saying goes, there's more than one way to skin a cat. This is certainly true of extracting your price. For example, instead of selling the software, you might give the software away and charge for training, installation, and maintenance. At trade shows charging for software and giving free talks rarely works. Swapping the costs and charging for a lecture in return for $100 of free software is much more successful.

Another technique used by David Harris's long established Pegasus e-mail software is to get the software free but pay for the support and manuals.

Critical Mass

Certain products require you to pass a particular critical mass before they will work. Imagine trying to sell e-mail or a fax machine to the first customer. The benefits are theoretically the same, but with whom could your customer communicate? Lotus got around this when they released their Notes groupware product by selling a minimum of 200 licenses per company. This ensured that users had someone to talk to. It also ensured that only larger companies adopted it initially because only they could afford the initial cost ($62,000). The strategy also gave Lotus prestigious user names such as Price Waterhouse from the outset to use as references.

Closely Related to Price Is Market Share

Your ability to determine the price you can charge boils down to statistics. Assume you make the world's most staple product—bread. Assume that you are the only person in the world who can bake it. Can you name your own price?

Of course you can. Nevertheless, how many loaves you sell will depend on your policy. Price them high enough and only the richest of men may be able to afford them. What proportion of the world population will you sell to if you price it within the reach of all? Still not 100 percent, not just because some people will prefer rice, pasta, or manioc, but because others are allergic to grains. There is always some reason.

Even without competition, you will never achieve 100 percent penetration in an open market. Eighty-five percent is usually tops. Where there's competition, 20 percent is generally regarded as a dominant share. Your prices can affect the price of your competitors, but you are probably not strong enough to force others to raise or lower their prices in harmony with yours. You need at least a 30 percent share of the market to stand a chance of doing that. Even then you will need to be astute.

You can only be blithe about prices if your market share is an effective monopoly, in other words over 50 percent. Such monopolies can be created not only by being first and keeping the pole position, but also by setting standards that everyone else would like to follow. Notable examples include Microsoft's Windows, PKZip, and Adobe's Acrobat.

Note Manufacturers may have their own dream definitions of monopoly. Sometimes these are worldwide, other times making them a big fish in a small pond. Ultimately it's the customer's definition that counts, and it's still a genuine achievement.

The Crux

When sails gave way to steam in the early 1800s, captains asked about engineers used to grunt, "Oil and water never mix." Any engineer who overheard agreed. This was a telling way of expressing mutual reservations that both sides are still trotting out two centuries later, though with mutual smiles and hollow intentions. They have long since arrived at a successful and respectful modus vivendi.

Those in the software industry are now going through a similar experience. Let's face it, the disciplines of computer programming and marketing are different, and the temperaments involved in these disciplines don't always dovetail.

IT people (the developers) find marketing daunting, both as a concept and an activity. They perceive that marketing people always think they are running the show and have a plausible explanation for everything. They cease to be logical when it doesn't suit them. They spend money on intangible activities that could be used to buy hardware or develop vital new features. They are not always successful and what they do is most perplexing.

Marketing people find programming equally daunting: Both as a concept and an activity. Programmers always act as if they are the kingpins. They always have some catch-22 to explain everything. Whenever pressed, programmers talk in a language all their own. They spend time wrapped up in problems of their own making instead of simplifying their task and giving marketing a chance. Moreover, the IT people don't always come up with the goods. What they do is arcane.

Each side often pretends the other doesn't exist and steers a wide berth. Like the ostrich with its head firmly planted in the sand, the feet (in this case both departments) only go around in circles.

Get-nowhere postures aren't restricted to new or even small firms, but for any enterprise to take off, each side needs to get the best out of each other. It's the only way to create a prosperous business from an arid screen of zeros and ones, whether you are dealing in digits or dollars.

One of the main factors in interdepartmental strife is simple ignorance of what the other has to do, and from ignorance grows fear. This book's task is to form a bridge over the fear and link the two disciplines together, a situation that will be strengthened by success. There isn't a successful software house that hasn't somehow fused the two energies into something very strong.

✦   ✦   ✦

Promoting Your Product

How do you win the wager of marketing? Essentially, people know what marketing is. They know what it is meant to achieve, but their experiences rarely match up with the promises. Most hard-strapped software developers resent the marketing budgets they are expected to sign off on (often dwarfing the entire development budget several times over) that is being spent on a flutter.

Marketing

Almost everyone in business has their own definition of marketing. Economists describe it as the "strategic use of resources to complete the cycle from production through to resale." Marketing people, who are particularly keen on repeat purchases, describe marketing as "the efficient creation of customers." Computer people describe marketing as "the umbrella name for all promotional activities that enable a copy of the master program to get from the company's computer to the customers' computer so both parties profit." These definitions are all true.

Marketing people, when they are letting their hair down, describe marketing as "an intellectual activity." Businesspeople retort that it is about the acquisition of money. Again, both are right.

Marketing is such a respected and institutionalized activity now that it is hard to get an interview for a management job in any blue chip corporation without an MBA. Yet marketing only climbed out of the Jack and Beanstalk era when Harry Henry at McCann-Erickson in London wrote a book on the subjects as a client-winning ploy. That was as recently as 1962. To put this in computing terms, this was the year before DEC sold their first Mini Computer.

The difference marketing makes boils down simply to this: At every nodal point in his career, the businessman fundamentally has to make a bet with himself. He has to bet that he can sell at least so many units at such and such a unit profit before such and such a time. The marketing man asks a slightly different question. He asks, "What is the best way to make such and such a profit by selling such and such a product before such and such a time?" In other words, he reduces the chances he has to take by narrowing his risk. The way he does this is by taking a leaf out of the professional gamblers who go to Las Vegas. He notes the performance of the wheel.

There are only two ways to bring any product to market: the Jack and the Beanstalk way and the marketing way. Jack set out to sell his widowed mother's cow and ended up with a row of beans. The marketing way remembers all of the Jack and the Beanstalk case histories, draws practical lessons from them, and systematically employs all the winning strategies. It is not an infallible system, but it is the nearest legal thing you will ever get to loaded dice.

Bringing a product to market hinges on the single conundrum: "How am I going to go about selling my product at a viable profit?" This begs some very basic questions:

+ Who would want to buy my product?
+ Why would they want to buy it?
+ What is particular about these people?
+ Where do they live?
+ What job do they do?
+ How old are they?
+ How well educated are they likely to be?
+ What's their spending power?
+ Would a woman be more susceptible than a man?
+ How can I contact them?
+ What price will they pay?
+ How can I explain the benefits in a way that they'll appreciate?
+ Does it do what they need?
+ How long will it take to sell it to them?
+ How can I generate fresh orders from appreciative customers?
+ Can I glean repeat sales?
+ How many sales might this generate?

If you appreciate these questions, you're already on your way to understanding the thinking behind marketing. You can't know the answers if you haven't asked the questions.

When people first started to develop software, they only thought about selling and marketing around the time their test subjects began to give the program their thumbs up. Only then did the inventors have sufficient confidence to believe they might actually sell it. However, by the time they arrived at this point, they had spent 90 cents of every dollar only to find that there was almost no market for the product; or, if they were to break even, it had to be sold at a higher price than the market would bear; or that there was no economic way to contact would-be buyers; or the benefits they offered were not the ones the market wanted.

Fortunately, you know that it is suicide to leave the fundamental marketing questions unanswered this late. You would be gambling with your money, time, and career without lifting a finger to lower the odds.

Before you formulate any plan, you need to know not just what must be done, but how much notice to take of each of the factors as well. Before you draft a plan you will need to seek out the most reliable answers you can get to the following seven questions:

1. What are the product's real advantages?
2. Who potentially are the core buyers?
3. How do you get in touch with them?
4. What is the optimum market price range?
5. How should the product be branded?
6. Is the product marketable?
7. What is everyone else in this area of the market doing?

Write a Marketing Plan

The best way to put your thoughts coherently together and check that you have considered everything you should is to write yourself a marketing plan. Imagine you need heavy funding and you go to a backer who recognizes that you have a great idea but wants to know how you are going to make money out of it before investing any of his own. What do you tell him?

Ideally, you tell him what you have already told yourself. Explain the product briefly. State the benefits it offers. Pinpoint who will use it. Produce evidence of how many potential users there are. Define how many you expect to convert. Set down what they appear willing to pay. State how you plan to get your goods to them. Outline everything you will be doing to speed sales along. Then do the sums.

List all your costs. Provide a working timetable. Calculate your net income. Subtract outgoing monies from incoming monies and anticipate your profit. Note any special risks and opportunities. Where in doubt, use from-to figures. Summarize the best and worst possible outcomes. There's no need to go into great detail. In fact, a management summary is usually more useful. This way the critical bits stick out.

As you write your plan, you will begin to see how all the pieces fit together. You may even be able to add bits you have overlooked and generally sweeten your plan. When you are satisfied, show your plan to friends who you trust and whose judgment you value. Then lock it away somewhere safe. As circumstances inevitably alter your prospects, revise your plan accordingly.

Keep your investors, supporters, and staff informed so that everyone knows what is happening and keeps pulling in the same direction.

What's in a Name?

The bottom line answer is money. Choosing a suitable company name is the first test a firm has to pass when outsiders (who have nothing else to judge it by) come to size it up. It costs you the same amount to register a bad name as a good one. So you might as well choose a name that will make the product easier to sell, perhaps by explaining what it does, by adding credibility, or by making the product at home in other tongues.

For example, Microsoft is a carefully considered and created company name. When the company was founded in 1975 the name explained what the company did—they wrote software for microcomputers (the name PC didn't exist until IBM launched their Personal Computer six years later). This saved them valuable time explaining to customers what they did (there were only three employees when they started). It was also a good name by other yardsticks: It's short (three syllables is often considered tops), understandable, and acceptable internationally. There are no negative connotations and it's unique.

It is not uncommon for firms to take their founders surnames, such as Boeing, Norton, or Siebel to name three. Occasionally, it also works with two founders, such as Hewlett-Packard, but never more. This may assuage the vanity of the founder and reappraise him in the eyes of his or her mother-in-law, but it only works in marketing where the name of the founder is so inextricably associated with the product that the two are synonymous, such as Christian Dior and Ford.

Unless you are pioneering a program so unique that no competitor will dare copy you for years, or your name is unusually memorable, it's unlikely to bestow any distinctive advantage. It may even be a limitation when you want to diversify. The classic theory used to be that one used one's own name for the holding company and another name (or range of names) for one's products. Where the fiscal problems of administering the company are greater than the problems of selling its products, this division has practical advantages. For most software houses, however, it simply doubles the cost of education. First you have to explain who you are. Then you have to explain what your brand is. You are far better off making the name of the product the name of the company and exploiting it for all you and your backers are worth.

Branding

In crowded markets, branding is the one mechanism that can make your product stand out. It is easy for consumers to understand, as they know the rules. Yet branding only makes any searing impression on buyers over time. With this evaluation go strong implications of repeat purchases.

Brands matter. Good brands can be phenomenally valuable in their own right. At the start of the second millennium, Interbrand valued the Coca-Cola brand at no less than $84 billion. Brands, regardless of who (within reason) administers them, are a door opener to market share. Nestlé was prepared to pay nine times the book value of the long-established English confectioner, Rowntrees, to gain control of their brands like Kit-Kat.

Brands also allow you to charge more. General Motors and Toyota share a production plant in Europe, where they ran off almost identical cars—the Toyota Corolla and the Geo Prizm. The Toyota Corolla sold for $2,000 more than the Geo Prizm. Yet even with this premium, the Toyota Corolla outsold the Prizm by 200 percent, because the Toyota brand name has greater brand value.

The concept of a brand covers many possibilities. It wraps up everything that competition, trade, and customers associate with your product.

+ What it is
+ What it does
+ How your market feels about it

Chosen thoughtfully, a brand name can enable you to model the impression buyers will form in their minds. Like love at first sight, it can be a very quick process. To get a brand off to a good start, find a name that encapsulates your product and catches your public's imagination. Choose one from the final list that makes an immediate mark yet has potential to develop. The concept of your brand name needs to be supported by a complete suite of visual furniture. So think logo. Think symbol. Think typography. Think color. Think style. Think music. Think everything that can support your brand by association or mood. Think!

A strong branding culture endows new products with an immediate identity and enables developers to exploit consumer recognition. Because the concepts of branding are more ambitious than simply naming, good brand names need to meet more criteria. A good brand name meets as many of the following as possible:

+ Is not yet used—Singer, Hoover, Guinness
+ Is easy to pronounce—Omo, Mars, Ford
+ Evokes a suitable mood—Nike, Hyatt, Smarties
+ Is reasonably short—Rawplug, Birds Eye, Oracle

+ Suggests the product area—Band-Aid, Oxo, Pepsi Cola, Microsoft

+ Evokes a strong visual association—Shell, Orange

+ Is internationally acceptable—Rolex

+ Is free from negative associations—Sony

The more the brand captures the public imagination the more immediate its acceptance and the less you have to invest on pumping information. Whenever the brand is a desirable one, people naturally pay more attention. Not unsurprisingly, successful software houses spend around 80 percent of their advertising on promoting the brand and only 20 percent disseminating information.

Where a name is too long or means nothing to a foreign buyer, initials almost always take over (IBM instead of International Business Machines, BMW in lieu of Bayrische Motorenwerke, or SAP instead of Systeme, Anwendungen, Produkte in der Datenverarbeitung).

Brands are a complex subject, but there are two aspects on which you might concentrate:

+ The name you choose is likely to be much more useful if, like an ice cream cone, it is able to carry all the flavors of the product that you foresee.

+ You need to single out the most useful single attribute that could be associated with your brand.

Begin by whittling down a shortlist of advantages. These might include reliability, integrity, speed, time saving, and prestige. Set up a list and work out a pecking order by consensus. Then put all your imagination into finding a name that lives up to the expectations you have for your product.

To arrive at a professional exposition of your logo, use a consultancy that specializes in branding, if possible. Alternatively, consult your friends in the business.

Establishing Your Corporate Image

There is no point in a software company putting forward one public face while its brand managers or dealers behave in another. You need good consistent policies all the way through. If and when the time comes to differentiate the company from some of its diversifications, you will probably have the money to explain the reasons and the differences to your shareholders and your public.

Don't Take it Upon Yourself to Educate the Market

Some products are so novel that the buyer must have it explained to them why they need the products before there is a chance of sales taking off. With hindsight, both the fax machine and e-mail are blindingly obvious innovations, as you will see later on. The first took over 130 years to take off and the second around 20.

Double Check That Name

Image how thrilled I was to be invited to the launch of a new computer at London's prestigious Dorchester Hotel in the late 1980s. Apricot (which later became part of Mitsubishi in 1990) then was the main U.K. microcomputer manufacturer and was on a roll; sales had never been better. The evening started well with cocktails in the famous foyer and a three-course meal in the colossal ballroom (where the U.K. version of the Oscars normally take place). After dinner the lights dimmed, a drum rolled, and a spotlight picked out Apricot's CEO who took to the stage to much applause. He started to tell us how the latest computer with the new Micro Channel Architecture was going to make all our fortunes and trail blaze the standard for computers from here to eternity. And its name was the Apricot Chi. How could we go wrong with a computer named after everyone's favorite panda at London's Regent's Park Zoo?

The applause continued unabated. Then I saw a friend, a fellow dealer, with a funny look on his face. Patrick was French but had lived in the United Kingdom for the last 10 years. I went over to him to ask what was wrong. Patrick whispered in my ear, "Chi is French slang for crap."

This major firm had spent millions designing the product, choosing the name, printing the literature, running the initial machines off the production lines and no one had remembered to check the name in the major languages.

Two months later, the machine entered the market retagged as the *Apricot Qi* without so much as a blush.

Table 14-1 lists some notable damp starts; these form some of the best-known names in their fields.

Table 14-1
Notable Slow Starts

Year	Product	First Year's Result
1874	Remington Typewriter	Only eight purchased
1883	Coca-Cola	Income $50, Costs $70
1948	Scrabble	532 sets sold
1956	Liquid Paper	1,200 bottles sold
1975	Microsoft	Turnover $20,000

Some very well-known products experienced slow starts. It was a smart move on Bill's part not to give up.

Are You Ahead of Your Time?

Benjamin Franklin used to say that if a man built a better mousetrap the world would beat a passage to his door. It's a lovely statement but it oversimplifies. In the pre-industrial world, where the greatest concern was being overrun by mice and the most sophisticated agricultural defense was a man armed with a hoe, the mechanization that the trap offered to solve the most pressing problem must have been nirvana. However, in a progressively highly developed society it isn't always as easy to see the mice for the cheese.

Some products fail because the world isn't ready for them. The fax machine, believe it or not, was developed before the American Civil War. Alexander Bain, a Scotsman living in England, actually patented the invention in 1843. A stylus at one end generated differing electrical signals as it was moved. These were sent down a telegraph wire and reproduced by another stylus at the other end. It worked, so why didn't it catch on? Well, nine years later, Giovanni Caselli built a variation called the Pantelegraph. The French Post and Telegraph agency actually used the Pantelegraph to transmit documents between Paris and Marseille from 1856 to 1870.

Then in 1888, Professor Elisha Gray (the man who received his patent for the telephone three hours after Alexander Graham Bell) patented another variation called the Telautograph.

Fifteen years later Dr. Arthur Korn demonstrated photoelectric telephotography using selenium cells. This enabled words to be accompanied by half-toned pictures (pixels in shades of grey).

Ten years later Edouard Belin's Belinograph employed telephototransmission, which made possible the direct capture of documents.

Then, finally, in 1966 Xerox put huge marketing effort behind their Magafax telecopier. This was the precursor of the modern fax machine.

The fax machine finally took off in Japan (because it was easier to send their symbolic language by fax than the other means available at the time—telex, telegram, and so on).

In the United Kingdom, the fax only became ubiquitous as a way of getting around the 1977–78 postal strike.

Why did such a useful invention have to undergo five major iterations before it became a worldwide success? The idea was brilliant and recognized as such from the outset. The marketing reasons are fascinating and highly instructive. To begin with, few people in 1843 wrote and read regularly. So the fast message market was infinitely smaller; and the message market that did exist was mainly centered along the new railway lines. Morse telegraphy monopolized these installations.

It is noticeable that the two who followed Bain basically repackaged the concept under their own fancy names, but they didn't have the resources to educate and create sufficient customers and met with no more success.

International communications, which might have opened up the pioneers' markets had to wait for transoceanic cables to be laid. It was only when Marconi demonstrated the transmission of signals by wireless telegraphy (from Cornwall to Newfoundland) in 1901 that inventors began to think sideways. Out came two vital product improvements: the ability to incorporate pictures and the elimination of manual encoding. By the close of World War II, international communications had mushroomed to such an extent that would-be users began for the first time to look for quicker, easier, cheaper modes of transmission.

One corporation finally introduced electrostatic replication and invested enormous intelligence and capital to promote it. Their educational efforts slowly began to make headway.

Two special classes of potential end users recognized the fax's value. In one instance because the complex forms of the script could be more easily transmitted to Europe and the United States by fax than by telex, which is better suited to alphanumeric symbols.

Understanding Your Product

What you are doing is not always what you think you are doing. What failed deaf aid was used to establish the first and only true corporate monopoly that the United States has known? That would be AT&T, initially founded on February 28, 1885. Alexander Graham Bell's father taught deaf people sign language. His son, Alexander, was trying to devise a machine to enable partially deaf people to hear when he inadvertently developed the telephone.

The Teflon on the upper side of a frying pan was actually discovered while trying to make a replacement for Freon 114 used as the cooling agent in Frigidaire refrigerators back in 1938. Coca-Cola was concocted by its inventor, John Pemberton, as a "brain and nerve tonic" in 1886.

These examples demonstrate that what you start out to produce, what you think you have produced, what the public want, what the public actually think you have produced, and what they are prepared to pay for are not always the same thing.

During the market research phase listen to what people are saying they really want. During the pre-release, beta testing period ask people openly if they can think of any other users for your product. Have brainstorming sessions with your development marketing team and see what you come up with.

Before you can market your product you have to understand all its options. Options give you choices. You need to know these at the outset so you can prioritize them. There's no point in spending your entire marketing budget on election prediction software whose peak demand is once every four years only to find out that it's also an invaluable everyday statistical marketing tool for market research, advertising agencies, and brand corporations. Your product could be significantly more valuable than you believe it to be. Consumers often see a product differently from its creators. They will have worked out how they can use it and are prepared to pay for it. When you know this, you begin to understand your product.

Are You Sure You Are in the Business You Think You Are?

People are not always in the business they think they are. A tights manufacturer might consider that they are in hosiery. Yet women don't buy hosiery. They buy allure. And allure is a much more valuable market. In one sense the difference is semantic. In another it's dollars.

Kodak thought it was in the paper processing business and diversified into cigarette papers. While it seemed not a bad move at the time it was made, the philosophy, attitudes, and priorities that went with it led Kodak to miss the chance of going into digital cameras. If only they'd realized their real business was information storage.

If, for example, you are writing a program to design forms, think for a moment. Which would an international corporation be willing to pay more for, a program that simply prints forms, or a program that gives them outgoing communications control of their empire? The first definition restricts usage to forms. The second makes possible central control of corporate policy documents, map directions, training courses, instruction manuals, and more.

Your product may be significantly more valuable than you ever conceived it to be. By the time consumers realize its possibilities, some competitor may already be working on a more cleverly positioned rival. Don't give them the pearl in your oyster. Listen carefully to what colleagues and contacts suggest. Ask program testers openly and early on if they can think of any other use for your product. Organize that brainstorming session to see if your team can place you in a smarter position. It could transform your entire strategy and future.

Firms that don't know what business they are in will flounder. Coca-Cola sales only skyrocketed when someone realized that a pick me up can be more than a health drink. Similarly, AT&T isn't about telephones; it's about communication. The definition that centers on the physical product usually misses the point. People don't buy products; they buy benefits. Good definitions are inspiring, incited, and open vistas. Firms that define their business incisively rarely fail. So if you think you're only in the IT business, think again. You are also in your customer's and your potential customer's business.

The Best Strategy of All

The most successful launch strategy is to reduce your risk to nearly nothing. Instead of doing everything yourself, pre-sell the program. Microsoft got itself commissioned by IBM to write DOS and never looked back. See what you can do to persuade a corporation or interested organization to commission you to produce the program you want to write. Then write your basic program of which theirs is a variant. This way, your client covers your overheads, pays for the development, acts as first-class testers, and carries you while you get it all running smoothly. Your client gets what they pay for: a program exclusive to them, exclusive for a certain specified period, or a program denied to their direct competition (that's up to the lawyers). You get a deal you can live with and a huge kick-start.

A Digression about the U.S. Market

More opinion is expressed about the U.S. market than any other. To an outsider, America must appear to be one massive, rich, and homogenous market. Everyone seems to be successful. It still draws outsiders to it with the same Klondike-itis that lured the forty-niners to California from gold fields as far away as Australia and Peru 150 years ago.

To this day, even large European firms with long established reputations attack the U.S. market with the understanding of a five-year-old playing Monopoly. They believe that a healthy share of this lucrative market will be the salvation to all their problems. Sales will skyrocket. Profits will multiply. The managing director will bask in fame. Global domination is only a short step away. Sadly, the number of latter day Columbus's that foul up the launch of their products continues. The capital they pour in to get their venture on an even footing frequently comes dangerously close to capsizing the entire organization. They drool over the potential prize yet have no strategy for achieving it.

What they fail to realize is that by the time a successful U.S. company brings its products and services to Britain, they (and its corporation's executives) have been refined by progressive distillation in many submarkets, some as big or bigger than any nation in Europe. Americans' engaging combination of confidence and humility stems not from insecurity but from a business environment that only yields to the flexible and persistent. The United States is not a single homogenous market. There are at least five major markets:

✦ Pacific coast

✦ Midwest

✦ South

✦ New York

✦ The Eastern seaboard

Their histories, ethnic composition, industries, temperament, demographics, and legal requirements all differ.

To succeed in such a vast concourse, you have to continue narrowing your sights until you reach an objective you can handle. So discover where the softer, richer markets are and where the greatest concentration of potential buyers live and work. If your software only applies to legal firms doing high-tech cases, your market will gravitate towards the centers of software and hardware development on the Western and Eastern seaboards. All of a sudden you have pulled focus from a hypothetical 283 million targets to several tens of thousands concentrated in a few key cities. This reduces the potential market size considerably and the figures now are real.

The on-going advantage to the client is that they will almost certainly be able to acquire updates and enhancements at less than they'd pay if they were shouldering the whole of the on-going cost.

The ripcord rule of this strategy is that you must not relax on cloud nine. However much support you are given, you will run out of altitude eventually. You must be in control.

The Second Best Strategy

If you can't get a key sale before you start, get a key sale before you go public. Most successful software has a cherished key player, such as Price Coopers' early endorsement of Lotus Notes. Success at an early stage is like drawing an ace out of the pack. The initial success not only lifts morale internally, it also lifts the product ahead of competition.

The importance of these sales can be significantly greater than the nominal value of the software. The adoption of Lotus Notes by a litmus buyer brought greater press coverage than Lotus could ever afford, and guaranteed a substantial income to Lotus for years. This underwrote Notes' future development.

How to Find a Marketing Advisor

IT specialists often say that the best marketing people are normally to be found within the industry. It's true, but by the time our industry finds them they are immensely successful and rich and out of reach. Whether you intend to hire a freelancer from time to time or have your own marketing advisor full time, you are looking for a man or a woman with a particular set of skills and abilities.

Small ads for freelance consultants can be found in the trade press and via the Web. The fact that they need to advertise for work is no real ad for them. So speak to all your contacts who have had good experiences. Ask who they'd recommend. Another way is to call up the manufacturers of products that you feel have been well marketed (good marketing that sticks in your mind). Unless they are a direct competitor, they are usually delighted to give you tips. Your interest is a sincere compliment to their judgment.

One way or another you are likely to assemble a formidable list. In practice, marketing consultants tend to specialize, sometimes in particular media (television), at other times in product areas (pharmaceuticals). So your list can be rapidly whittled down.

Exceptional people are rare by definition and hard to come by. Yet good professional exponents have three qualities in abundance: penetrating powers of analysis, ability to synthesize in unfettered ways, and an exceptional ability to communicate. The first two are not surprising, as marketing is both a science and an art. Good marketers will have swathes of relevant figures at their disposal that guide them as to what is likely to be the most propitious solution for you. An ability to develop new patterns of solution is the rarest of these key qualities, yet it may also be the most critical when you need a David to beat Goliath, someone who can solve the problem without burying it under money.

You should look out for the following points:

✦ Excellent communicators. Make sure that their best spiel isn't the one they use to sell themselves.

✦ Ability to make insightful sense of statistics. They need to be respectful of facts and have intellectual integrity.

✦ Understand the concepts of your technology.

✦ Are at home with end users.

✦ Are deft at translating functions into end-user benefits.

✦ Can seize on market segments that fit the functionality proposed.

✦ Can add value to a product.

✦ Track record is useful but the past doesn't always predict the future. Note the quality of their training and experience. Check always with previous employees and clients.

First, Clear the Decks

The ideal product introduces just one new idea that people want. Salesmen may get bored with it. The boardroom may get tired of it. Yet one new idea at a time is as much as the general public can handle, or at least as much as any entrepreneur can sow effectively.

As soon as you put this concept to a computer person, you are likely to get shot down for genuine, special pleading reasons. The industry has reinvented how people write, count, and draw, without pencil or paper. What took printing over 100 years to get from Mainz to Moscow, took micro-computing less than a January to June. In the scramble to get there first, what started as plenty of room for all quickly intensified into a vehement struggle to preserve one's territory. Everyone, it seems, had legal claims to structures, subroutines, and screen arrangements. This meant that instead of freely coming to a consensus of the most advantageous program forms, programmers were forever having to re-design the wheel and their customers were forever jumping through hoops in their attempts to dominate the form. Now with shareware and ready-made modules, things are slowly beginning to look hopeful.

Yet all such protestation merely makes a diversionary argument instead of addressing the point. The less your customers have to learn, the more readily they are likely to use it. If you feel diffident about the amount of fresh information that users have to take on board, consider how much training your own staff needed. Try and recall what friends and family found hardest to grasp.

When software was in its desktop infancy, it was essential to teach people about the computer as well as the software. Now that everyone learns computing at school, nearly everything you have to explain should be about your program. If not, you are probably setting up unnecessary hurdles for yourself.

So how can you make your program largely self-explanatory? The secret is to keep it simple. Reduce the number of new ideas that users have to take on board and present them as far as possible in terms that users will already understand. One strategy is to concentrate on the most important new feature and set aside the others for future updates. While you can present much in ways customers haven't seen before, you have to ask yourself whether doing so is at the expense of your customers . . . and ultimately of yourself.

It is usually best to place things on the screen where people expect them and arrange the menu order according to the users' own priorities. Above all, explain things concretely and clearly. Streamlining a program to minimize your educational task isn't dumbing down the product. It is simply an act of courtesy to your customers to make them feel good about their purchase.

Build in Something Special

One of advertising's greatest philosophies is the unique selling proposition (USP) invented by Ted Bates of Hobson Bates, the then U.S. advertising giant. For advertising to work it has to have something worthwhile to tell people. That something has to be *unique* (exclusive to the product), something no competitor can currently offer. It has to *be selling*, in other words, something for which customers are ready and willing to pay. And you have to be able to express what you are offering in the form of a *proposition*.

Note   That desirable exclusive something need not be a product. It can be a feeling of well-being, additional energy, peer recognition, or even the price—anything you can tell people about which they can't get elsewhere.

Ted Bates, who had enough confidence to fill the Metropolitan Opera, undersold himself. The USP is not merely an advertising technique. It is a concept at the very heart of marketing, and for a very simple reason: You can't say it if it is not true (at least not for long), and if it is true, it has to be true about the product (or service).

The Sony Walkman, the Palm Pilot, Doom, a *Harry Potter* novel, the latest Coldplay CD—these are all products with mega-sized USPs. What are you going to add to your product to give it that "Je ne sais quoi?" Unlike the French saying, you must know and be able to express what makes your software a must-have proposition. In car manufacturing it centers around engineering excellence. In IT it's all about technology leadership. Yet when you analyze these USPs, they often amount to little more than taking a trivial idea further than anyone else has dared to and fine-tuning it.

Just after Word War I, when cars were coming in, my grandfather had a literally dying business. He made horses' nose bags. Seeing the writing on the wall, he decided to go into overalls. To find out how, he took himself to evening classes and became so skilled a cutter he was soon running the class. To simplify the pattern cutting for overalls, he standardized armholes and made three lengths of sleeve (long, medium, and short) and two lengths of back with three widths of front. He then talked the proprietors of newspapers and cookie manufacturers into having overalls made to measure for their workforce. Offering tailor-made overalls was seen as only one step away from a designer suit. He then got a deal and a healthy advance.

The following week, armed with an assistant, a tape measure, and a sheaf of forms, he measured everyone (he once did 300 in a day). As he called out "Sleeve 18 and a half," his assistant jotted "M" for medium in the sleeve box. When they got back to the plant, his machinists simply stitched up the right assembly of pre-cut pieces. It's what's called *chart tailoring* today.

Michael Dell had a similar idea. In 1984, he went into business assembling PCs. Nothing new in that; people had been doing it for a decade before him. Michael, however, married the production line process galvanized by Henry Ford to the Japanese just-in-time production techniques. At the same time, he dramatically reduced the number of parts while still allowing the purchaser to configure any machine within reason. These he produced to order. In essence, this is a high-tech application of the chart tailoring process. It attracts sizeable orders, keeps inventories low, and produces a positive cash flow (you get the money in before you have to give it out).

Could you apply a similar, minute yet seismic, shift to your software development?

Create a New Buzzword or Phrase

Creating a new phrase or acronym not only guarantees uniqueness but also gives you a decided advantage if it catches on. To do this the new word or phrase has to be memorable, relevant, and center on a fresh idea. It also has to make abundant sense in universal English.

It is important any word or phrase you invent is firmly tied to your product, even though at times it may feel like a stone around your neck. Otherwise, if it has any merit, it will be adopted lock, stock, and barrel by the competition. That's especially galling after you have spent so much time and effort educating the public.

Above all else, try to ensure that any buzzword you introduce spreads understanding. Too many computer acronyms are not immediately obvious, such as *DDT*, which stands for *dynamic debugging tool*. Too many computer phrases are not correct; freeware isn't free and desktop publishing when it was first described was only desktop printing. This isn't the time to muddy the waters in the hope that others will think you are clever. This is the time to put on your thinking cap and make a contribution.

Another way to achieve a unique advantage is to introduce an industry standard. Examples of firms who have pulled this off include Ethernet (3Com), Zip (PKZip, Inc.), and Acrobat (Adobe). The fact that so few firms are able to do this shows how rarely an opportunity arises. Nevertheless, if you have a ground-breaking product that will help a wide swathe of computer users, there may be a golden opportunity within your grasp. The trick is to make it open enough that it becomes freely adopted, yet protected in such a way you are able to exploit it profitably. Register and trademark the name.

On Being First (First Mover Advantage)

Another way of expressing the USP is as the downside of being first. The margins in software are so competitive that it doesn't pay to be a runner up. The only way you can get into the top spot is by outspending your competitor. Even then, you will be sharing a bone. If you are Procter & Gamble, you might risk this on occasion. However, you might end up spending more on marketing than you recoup in sales. At the moment, it is only in the largest, most lucrative software niches that there is room for a strong number two.

However, you don't always have to be black and white different. You just have to make sure your product has something worthwhile that sets it apart. Although there are gaps at all levels, most program developers in the 21st century may be wiser using their insight to locate a submarket where a program is sorely wanted. This would enable you to build up from a smaller base and give you a greater chance of controlling that section. Dollar for dollar, there may also be room for greater added value.

Communicating with Your Public

For 70 years Unilever never pioneered an innovative product. They'd watch and wait until someone else had done the spearheading work. When they thought the time was right (and the potential profits promising) they would either offer to buy them out or start a rival, using heavy advertising to buy their market share. For example, for nearly seven years they watched Vesty, the giant chilled meat importer with the largest cold stores in the country and its own fleet of modern refrigerated ships. Vesty had as a sideline decided to enter the domestic frozen food market under its own brand, Fropax.

Fropax had an excellent range. It used quality ingredients and, after an indifferent start, introduced the most pick-upable packages with wraparound photography. Initially, sales were small. There were just not enough domestic refrigerators in British homes. Vesty rented their spare cold storage to the timorous Unilever. When fish fingers became the latest rage, Vesty made sounds to evict their cold store tenants.

Unilever, meanwhile, had acquired the Birds Eye franchise. They now commissioned a huge cod-slicing factory in Lowestoft and built an even larger cold store than their rivals and a modern office complex complete with fountains and an alligator at Walton-on-Thames, just outside London. These snappy moves alerted grocers to the strength of Unilever's intentions.

This strategy was typical of the way Unilever moved at the time, and by and large it worked. Everyone knows Birds Eye. You never hear of Fropax now. In the mid '60s someone asked why. There were a lot of astute observations and lots of talk about instinct, but no one could tell the board why.

So they decided to tackle the question another way and investigate why new product ventures fail. They knew that about a third of all launches plunged within three years, and not always because the product was inadequate or unreasonably priced or even badly managed. By the time Unilever had examined several hundred failed products in considerable detail, a definite, common sense yet quite unexpected explanation began to emerge. All the failures had one thing in common: They all underestimated the cost of educating the market. With the money they allocated, the market developed more slowly than they needed. Unilever simply stepped in, picked up the pieces, and took it from there, which is why marketing is about the efficient creation of customers.

Advertising

Advertising is the public face of marketing. Everyday we read ads in papers and magazines and see them on television. They are the means that allow manufacturers to communicate their news to the public. Advertising is your carte blanche to inform the public on your terms. However, advertising comes at a price. At the time of writing, a quarter page in the Technology section of the *New York Times* costs $41,520, not including the costs of producing the ad. A typical 30-second advertising slot on television for prime time will set you back $200,000 ($1.6 million during the Super Bowl). Mainstream campaigns require deep pockets. Microsoft spent $250 million worldwide just on the launch of XP.

Most software developers don't have nine figures to spend on ads. Even the big IT players are small potatoes compared with the heavy year-in, year-out users. Heavy software advertisers (seven digits) can't do much more than promote new releases in bursts. Software houses have learned over 20 years of trial and error that the most they can get across is one thought about their new program and one feeling about the brand. The image-building element (more to do with the way that they do it) ensures that the investment in previous releases is remembered.

A Few Words of Advice

If you have a large budget, shop around for two or three advertising agencies where most of the clients have a similar expenditure. Assure yourself that the agency's philosophy fits comfortably with your own and you can work productively with them. Give each agency an identical brief. Tell them where you are, where you want to be, and how much money you have to get you there. Then ask them to make a presentation (normally free). If their presentation makes good business sense, satisfy yourself that your account will be important to them and that you have their commitment to your stated aims. Negotiate hard but leave enough on the table to ensure you get good service. Once you appoint them, within normal limits, trust them. Nothing turns a working relationship into a friendship like joint success.

Tip Losers choose those they find most compatible. Winners have the courage to pick the best solution.

If You'd Like to but Can't

If you don't have big advertising dollars you are in the same boat as thousands of others. Nevertheless, there is a lot of common sense to advertising that you can adapt to your advantage. The shorthand for the process of conversion is generally known by the acronym AIDA.

1. **A**ttention—The product is brought to your prospect's notice pertinently.

2. **I**nterest—The prospect begins to think this might be useful.

3. **D**esire—Longing replaces logic as interest deepens.

4. **A**ction—Finally the prospect decides to make the purchase.

David Ogilvy said that 90 percent of this work had to be done in a 16-word headline. Try hard, but remember, most copywriters in a lifetime never get the reader beyond the **D** for **D**esire.

Advertising Is Extremely Versatile

Even though your budget may only run initially to isolated ear spaces on either side of a magazine title, be aware that advertising can say almost anything on your behalf.

Advertising is a very flexible tool. It can announce that your product is now on the market. It can do all of the following:

+ Supply details

+ Correct misimpressions

+ Spread the news of updates

+ Give dealers confidence out of all proportion to the business it may bring

+ Earn you better and fuller display positions

Advertisements can also be used for promotions, seeing off the competition, building new markets, extending a product's life, and reminding the market that your product is there.

With advertising you usually only have one shot. The prospect sees the ad, scans the headline, and maybe reads on but probably only for a little bit. So be aware that you have to hold the reader's interest for as long as possible after you have captured it. Most times you will only capture a fraction of the readers who open your page.

It used to be said that informative advertising (as opposed to ads aimed at a continuous roll of repeat impulse business) had to be repeated three or four times to reinforce the message so that people believe it. However, the real problem is that it takes this number of exposures to harvest most of the interested readers. Each time the ad appears, you gather in a swathe. After three or four tries you get stymied by diminishing returns. The ad costs more than the business it brings.

Choice of Media

Whatever the ad's purpose, it either works or is wasted. For advertising to work you have to know where to contact your customers. Indeed, the selection of suitable media can be as relevant to returns as any creative approach. Banks, for instance, often target college students. They don't expect to make an immediate fortune, other than on overdrafts, but people are reluctant to switch banks often, so the banks are in there for the long haul. They'll make the real money in selling their customers mortgages for their homes, helping with stocks and savings, arranging their pensions, and finally executing their wills.

Similarly, Pepsi and Coca-Cola aim at young children in the belief that once smitten with their taste, they'll be repeat purchasers for the rest of their lives. The average American consumes 600 cans of soft drinks each year.

Anything that allows you to target your market precisely will make it possible to use insightful media and lift your sales figures.

Working with Lower Budgets

Having close to a zero budget doesn't mean you're restricted from all promotional activities. It simply means that your options can't include expensive space and time. Advertising without using paid spaces in papers and magazines or slots on commercial radio or TV is known as *below the line* advertising. To get the best from it, you will have to engage the brain to compensate for lack of money in the bank. Your largest investment will be the value of your time.

Below the line promotions do not have to be expensive. They can only be used to contact a limited number of people. However, you can do more to ensure that the people you do contact are genuine prospects, and you will have better opportunities to explain the advantages of your product in reasonable detail. So what you lack in numbers you can make up in quality. The secret of success lies in providing genuine help by having an accurate knowledge of the target's situation and needs and behaving with courtesy. There are eight particularly useful below the line tools that you can deploy:

✦ Specification sheets

✦ Sales leaflets

✦ Press releases

✦ Newsgroup activity

✦ PowerPoint presentations

+ Your Web site

+ Personal letters

+ Exhibitions

Specification Sheets

Specification (spec) sheets are primarily aimed at convincing the technical advisors in a client company that the advertised product is worth recommending to management. Spec sheets usually run to one or two sides of paper. They are the one area where technical jargon (within reason) has a place. They describe the main features to build confidence in a product of which the potential buyer may have little or no direct experience.

Spec sheets are aimed at those who consider themselves immune to sales pressure, so they never try to sell the product off the page. Instead, they allow a physical description of the product to speak for itself. They explain its weight and dimensions, describe its features and the full installation requirements, and give the reader a point of contact for further inquiry. Pack and screen illustrations are often included to show details and scale. As a rule, these technical descriptions are distributed in advance of a sale, although they sometimes accompany the product as well. The responsibility for producing spec sheets is often delegated to the developers or project managers.

Caution   Do not let your developers or project managers volunteer more information than you need in the spec sheet. It is easy, out of sheer pride, to offer such a wealth of details that they would save any competitor reading them thousands in research and development.

Sales Leaflets

These are the selling counterparts of the spec sheet, but they tend to have colorful illustrations and attention grabbing headlines and speak in terms of benefits rather than features to urge the reader to contact his dealer. Most have a single sheet format but some, according to prestige or need, run to four pages.

Sales leaflets can be one of the hardest documents to write in-house because everything has to be condensed and made simple. The chairman of my Internet software company was a quiet and thoughtful man who among other enterprises had set up one of the original X-vision firms in the late 1980s. We didn't always share the same point of view but we were usually able to talk things through and work out a stronger result. The only time we ever raised our voices was when we tried to write our own sales sheets and clashed over the use of terms, what ought to have priority, and the trickiness of separating functionality from benefits. If you experience difficulty in putting your sales leaflets together, perhaps you should consider talking to a professional copywriter and designer who are used to producing these items.

Remember to put the spec sheets and sales leaflets in Acrobat PDF format on your Web site for clients to download and print off. Check the print quality yourself when you do this. If your distribution channels don't include dealers and printed spec sheets, you can use your in-house color laser printer to run off hard copies, as required. At this stage, these items of print *are* the product. If you have a quality product, use quality paper; and they need to be ready for distribution well in advance of any countdown to the launch.

Press Releases

It is possible to get masses of magazine reviews of products and even half-page articles in major broadsheets for products with no marketing budget. Having something interesting to say, clearing the idea with the journalists in advance, and sending the press releases (and occasionally following up with telephone or face-to-face interviews) pays off. Use them. They cost only your time and a few phone calls and stamps.

Build in Credibility before You Start

If your product has anything really new about it, people will quickly realize that it's a good idea. Even so, most will not be able to make the final and logical leap to purchase until they can see that someone has landed safely on the other side first. Unless personal belief is converted into credibility, there are very few sales, especially where people are buying on behalf of their boss.

Good case studies are gold dust. The Dymo range of handheld labelers were first promoted to the public in Britain and very nearly failed. Dymo then decided to switch their thrust towards business users. On the back of four case studies, within 18 months they were trading strongly and expanding into Europe. Within another four years they had sown up the entire European professional market and were powerful enough to go again for domestic sales. This time they succeeded. Dymo is now part of Esselte, which is one of the top 100 U.S. corporations.

The secret of effective endorsements is to get good ones—believable statements from believable people. A.N.Other from Wisconsin or Joe Bloggs from Tonbridge Wells isn't good enough for you. (Dymo got user case histories the caliber of Ford.) Endorsees need to be people who you would take notice of yourself. Each endorsee need cover only one aspect of your product's benefits and should speak at a person-to-person level. Never use any endorsement without the author's permission.

Incidentally, it is inadvisable to give software away to gain an endorsement. It makes the recommendation hollow. In any case, people who don't pay for software rarely use it or value it properly. If endorsees don't use your product, they cannot be used. It's wiser, however tempting it is to take shortcuts, to sell your product at the standard price and then find some other way to express a personal "Thank you."

How to Write a Press Release

Many of us have been on the receiving end of clumsy press releases that are passed on as received, complete with excessive, superfluous statements. So when it is your turn, you will want to provide an interesting story and give your journalists some worthwhile lines to quote. It should also include all the bread and butter facts:

✦ Your name (or who to contact)

✦ Company name, address, e-mail, and telephone numbers

✦ A headline (to sum up the story engagingly)

✦ The story itself

✦ Release date (or embargoed until)

Most journalists will tell you they do not want an article from you. Writing the article is their job. Your job is supplying the facts. Yet, when you follow this advice, you can often be dismayed to find your notes reprinted verbatim. At other times you may find your release notes transformed beyond all expectations. My advice is to write your release in factual note form but organize the items, paying particular attention to their order, so they are interesting to read anyway. Then if your journalists are in a rush and your piece is well written, they will occasionally run it almost unaltered.

Facts are the building blocks that journalists need to write any piece, so include as many as possible. This way individual journalists are more likely to come up with quite different pieces, giving the avid reader a useful spectrum of views of your product. So compare your product with others, if it has new features explain their benefits, and cite well-known users if you can. Include a few quotes only if they are strong and memorable.

Journalists typically require two months' notification for monthly publications and two weeks' weeklies. Dailies rarely review software unless they are mass-market products or there is some human interest such as the help it offers to the disabled. Because of these lead times, press releases are usually one of the first items that need to be tackled when you prepare a launch. It can also be useful to put PDFs of press releases on your Web site under the Press section for journalists to download. You'll be amazed how many articles can appear from this without you having to do anything more.

Many releases offer headlines that say little more than "XYZ Inc. launches new product"—that's really going to have them digging for their wallets! On the other hand, a line like "XYZ Inc. launches mobile Internet GPS Terminal, helps first blind climbers to top of Everest" may set journalists scrambling in several directions. It also provides a readymade headline for hard-pressed journalists.

Always keep a record of which press release went to which journalists and what coverage resulted. If certain journalists aren't touching your stuff, just phone them and ask them why. They'll be very candid. If it's a no-go, find another contributor to the publication who is sympathetic.

Ideally, press releases should be no longer than two pages. Three is pushing it. Accompany them with photographs whenever possible, preferably in the electronic format JPEG (for publishing quality definition).

PowerPoint Presentations

These are now getting a bit old hat. Part of the trouble is that the program hasn't progressed with the times, and part of the trouble is that few firms have the time and skills to develop a presentation beyond bullet points and subtitles. This said, nothing significantly better short of an audiovisual program has been devised in their place. As you'll see in the next chapter, software can be successfully sold without having to demonstrate the product.

PowerPoint presentations exist to focus everyone's minds on a series of pre-defined benefits and sales points. They are an ideal prompt to prevent sales staff from omitting any crucial point. They usually work best when there is only one key point to a page. Pages can then be flipped slowly or quickly according to the client's interest. No page should need to be on the screen for longer than 9 seconds. Any presentation over 10 minutes is usually more than enough for most audiences.

Making Use of Newsgroups

Newsgroups where people post and reply to messages about particular topics are one of the hidden treasures of the Internet. You can exploit them in two ways: by having your own to support your product (dealt with in Chapter 17 on support) and by posting messages about your product in relevant public groups. Be circumspect about this though.

✦ Select newsgroups relevant to your product.

✦ Ignore newsgroups for competitive products. It is unprofessional to advertise in someone else's group.

✦ Gauge the etiquette of each group. If they appear receptive, put a tentative oar in the water. If borderline, e-mail one of the brighter contributors and ask his or her opinion. If it seems acceptable, post a short statement explaining your product, bullet point the benefits, and supply a Web address where they can get further information, if relevant. Try to restrict this to 10 lines or 100 words.

✦ Replying to messages in a newsgroup and subtly saying how your product solves the problem that a user has posed is acceptable. Replies, however, carry more weight when they come from disinterested third parties who have no connection with the developers.

✦ If appropriate, you can send a follow up e-mail to any member of the news-group personally who appears to have a requirement for the product you are offering. Try starting with something along the lines of, "I saw the message you posted last night. I had the same problem so many months ago and decided to do something about it . . . "

Your Web Site

Your Web site is your foremost item of promotion. Using the Web enables you to produce the electronic equivalent of a full color brochure and update it at your leisure. Despite this, it is not a universal open sesame to sales. It needs backing up with other channels of communication (see preceding and following). Traffic at the site also depends on the efficiency of the search engine, referrals from other sites, and your ability to draw people in once they've clicked on.

As with print, the impression created by the first page is of paramount importance. You have to grab, hold, and develop attention within 30 words; and the end of each page needs a hook that pulls the browser further in.

Where a limited budget precludes you from getting professional copywriting and art direction, it is inevitable that fewer people will visit it. Nevertheless, it is amazing what the power of intention can enable you to achieve, so keep a close check on the leads your Web site develops and, by intelligent use of all feedback, make sure it builds into a real selling site.

Web sites as a critical information and selling tool are covered in detail in Chapter 16.

Personal Letters

Think long and hard about what you have created and who would benefit the most from it. Set your targets very high. Let's say you invented an add-on that doubled the speed of Microsoft XP—write to Bill Gates. You've written software that allows you to track down international terrorists by cleverly filtering mobile phone calls—write to the president and the head of the CIA. You've developed a cheap method of analyzing water purity for the third world—write to the head of the United Nations. Get the idea?

These letters need to be personal, completely written, and focused for that individual. They need to make the point in the headline or opening sentence, for example, "I've found a way to speed up XP by 200 percent," "I can pinpoint a terrorist phone call in under a minute of it being made," or "I have found a way of saving several million lives of those who die from cholera each year at almost no cost."

You need to explain what the product is, the benefits, and how it works. I'd also be inclined to put a short explanation of how you came to create your tool, such as, "My school was about to ditch all our Windows computers in favor of Linux because

Windows was running too slow," "I lost a close friend as a result of September 11th," or "I saw a program on disease in Africa and realized I could do something about it." Give them a short history that they will never forget. Remember to put your contact details in. Try not to go over two pages. Check the document carefully to make sure all spelling is correct, it's professionally laid out, and test it on some friends to find out if it works.

Typically such letters are screened for senior executives by a phalanx of top-notch personal assistants. If you have something interesting to say they will forward it to the boss or the relevant person.

Try and send one letter out a day. The material you build up can be used in future marketing activities.

 Caution Tempting though mass e-mailing is, due to the ease of gathering thousands of e-mail addresses and bulk e-mailing them, it normally backfires. If enough recipients complain they can have your Web site taken off the air. To reinforce this, at the time of writing this book legislation is being prepared in several western countries to make spam illegal. In short, don't spam—it rarely works and at best it could completely backfire.

Exhibitions

Everyone knows that exhibitions are the places to go when you want to find out the latest about cars, furnishings, or fly-fishing. Computer exhibitions are one of the biggest of these draws. Choosing the right one, if indeed there is a choice, is the easy part. Don't worry if you can only afford a small stand in some corner at the back. Most visitors make a point of walking every inch of the venue. Exhibitions need more planning than you may anticipate when you courageously sign up for your space months in advance. Check whether backdrops and stand signs are provided. If you have to find your own, organize things so that they are inexpensive, reusable, easy to erect and strike, and will look good. This last is most important. Next you will need ample supplies of the following:

✦ All your literature

✦ Blow-ups of your proposition and your program's main points

✦ Desks, chairs, and computer equipment for full demonstrations

✦ Whatever else your ingenuity and purse can devise

Make sure the impression of your stand will give your visitors confidence. Being clever with limited resources is smart. Cutting obvious corners isn't. You will also need at least two competent people to man the stand who know the product inside out, who are good with people, and who will allow you to sneak around and see what everyone else is doing. It's great fun and it's exhausting.

Public Relations

The best kind of praise goes by word of mouth. If you have something interesting to say, professional journalists will be eager to listen. The moment you start thinking about your software, start making notes of journalists who cover your area, similarly magazines, both consumer and trade. Find the best person to send the Press Release to, when they need it by, and most importantly whether they are interested and when they are next doing something covering your field. Bear in mind that a "Yes" can turn into a "No" later on if they run out of space. Note:

+ Their magazine
+ Name and title
+ Address
+ E-mail address
+ Direct telephone number

Naturally, there is a limit to what you can achieve compared with a professional who has spent his or her life courting the press. So if you have money after covering other promotional items yet not enough over to sustain a full-blooded advertising campaign, consider professional public relations (PR).

PR is the least used tool of marketing, yet it could be the most important. PR's role is to bring you to the favorable attention of your various publics, such as journalists, distributors, educational authorities, and so on. Used well, its effect can be quite disproportionate to the number of people introduced to your product. A good PR man will also know when the trade press is running special theme editions of pertinence. If you are unknown, it's a good idea to make contact with them before you issue any press release.

PR is essentially about liaising with those who form opinions in their field and providing them with information about people, products, and services so they will speak about them favorably. The work ranges from getting journalists to write reviews to getting key industry figures to be aware of you, your company, your vision, and your products. This is a job you shouldn't expect from advertising. Advertising is a scattergun tool that hits many lightly. PR is a sniper's tool. It aims particularly at that key minority who can really influence your market—the men and women who dictate what happens to your product next.

The effect of PR is to bring your product to the attention of a wider market by liaising with influencers and journalists, arranging trade, correcting misinformation, and organizing socially useful events. The crucial thing is to make sure you hire the man who will do the work. This isn't always the man who sells you on his PR consultancy. You should also be aware that it is easier to promise PR than to deliver it and that the cost of using these professionals is not cheap. PR consultants who deliver "free" column inches typically command incomes 50 percent higher than their peers in advertising.

What you should look for is someone who gets a kick out of helping others succeed, someone who has a genuine interest and knowledge of your product area, and who has a naturally high energy level. The right person will have good relationships with the trade press and be friends with many of the individuals who can help you. He or she can use these relationships to obtain magazine reviews and editorial in publications that you cannot tap yourself and add to the credibility of your product by initiating articles that originate from parties without any obvious axe to grind. It goes without saying that such a person should also have a good grip on business and be professional. They aren't easy to find, but they are out there.

Social Events

Social events are better suited to keeping clients than gaining them. Go to any sporting event and most of the best seats are taken by corporates entertaining their clients. This is seen as an excellent way of bonding outside weekday working hours when no one's under pressure. The events chosen normally reflect the team or sport that the managing director is interested in. This isn't as egocentric or one sided as it seems. There's no point in inviting people to an ice hockey match if you know nothing about it; you'll be in danger of making a fool of yourself. Stay on safe ground where you have knowledge and passion.

Social events have been extended over the years to include the following:

- ✦ Opera
- ✦ Sport
- ✦ Theater
- ✦ Cooking demonstrations
- ✦ Art galleries

You don't have to take over the Museum of Modern Art. You could consider a small local gallery or bakery.

Evaluation Software for Journalists

The press and TV people need full versions of the product and all the standard supporting print items. Only with a complete kit can they can test your software like a buyer. All items supplied to journalists should be clearly stamped "NOT FOR RESALE." Journalists respect this.

Identify Your Program's Principal Strength

As an exercise, open a newspaper or turn on the television and note what the principal advertisers consider works best. Most of them only make one point. The main feature of your program might not be easily found, and even when you do figure it out, it isn't always easy to explain in terms that make instant sense to a buyer. Your main point can sometimes be obscured by other colorful features. The principal benefit almost certainly separates your product in customers' minds from the alternatives. It is also usually the main reason for their purchase.

The market research you undertook initially should be checked to confirm that the consumers' reactions to the finished, or nearly finished, product matches. Don't be surprised if respondents bring up a spectrum of benefits. The main problem is to concentrate them into a simple, single sentence appeal.

When Land Rover brought out the latest version of their Discovery family 4x4, they were very proud of the 700 odd new features they'd added to its predecessor (which was already the best in its class). They didn't want people saying, "Ah yes, 700 economies without one real advantage," so they didn't push them individually. They didn't even promote the vehicle's obvious ruggedness, versatility, and security. They simply sold an aspirational lifestyle. So listen particularly to the way those questioned phrase their answers. Although their replies may be varied and inexact, reflect on them. There is often a single form of words that unites them.

The prime attribute and its benefit occasionally differ from one market to the next. For example, a supermarket has a different set of priorities according to whether it is located in Vancouver or Miami. If you find yourself in such a situation, you may need to accommodate both.

Selecting Your Market?

Why water an entire desert if it only has 10 trees? Sandals and a watering can would save you a fortune, but first you have to find the trees. Fortunately, the world's market breaks down into national, regional, and local submarkets. Some are so small that marketing people describe them as niches.

As every market is composed of many small units, much hinges on your ability to know what you are looking for. The juiciest prospects rarely huddle in a forest together. So you need to be able to identify them individually, to consider their peculiar needs and then formulate a single widely popular product. A popular product, however, does not give you a green light for worldwide sales. That's very hard to achieve. There are hardly any products apart from codeine, two colas, and McDonalds that are marketed universally.

Obtaining facts and figures on these submarkets is largely a process of combing the Web, though you may find it quicker to visit a local reference. Specialized trade libraries, industrial associations, and top newspapers and trade publications also maintain useful information services. Together they enable you to hone in on the prospects with the best matching profile. Promoting your product with rifle accuracy is obviously less expensive than peppering everyone. For instance, if I want to test market a specialized intellectual property program in Houston, Texas, I might begin by discovering that there are around 283 million people in the United States, and that 155 million work, of which just over 1 million are in the legal profession. Further reference would establish that almost 65,000 of these are in Texas and more than 5,000 Texan lawyers work outside the state. By consulting local registers, I discover that 399 of these Houston-based lawyers claim to be experienced in Information Technology. I then obtain the address of every single one courtesy of the Internet. From soup to nuts, this search takes about 10 minutes. Now that I know I have under 400 people to contact, it gives me an accurate appreciation of that market's size and significantly more focused opportunities to make a sale. The odds are infinitely better than approaching 283 million people on the off chance of striking it lucky.

Establishing your market's real size can change an airy hypothesis into a heck of a sensible start.

Positioning Yourself in a Way People Can Grasp

You can only buy two things: goods (cars or computers) or services (legal and financial advice). People tend to give priority to goods and only buy services in the face of a pressing need, such as having a legal document drawn up when selling a house. When you purchase gas, for instance, do you buy mileage, or do you buy gallons?

The more you position your software in words that conjure up a physical picture in your customers' minds, the more likely they are to open their purses. Perhaps they are more accustomed to buying goods from visits to a supermarket every week while telephone and electricity bills only come in once a month. Intangibles are almost impossible to quantify and nearly impossible to describe except by simile, which buyers instinctively distrust. Because of the uncertainty, people tend to spend a lot more time justifying services because they buy them less often. So if you are developing a program to accelerate the booting up of other programs, you would probably be wiser to describe it as a "Fast key" than a "Speed starter."

When you talk about goods you conjure up a picture that's three-dimensional. When you talk about services, the impression you suggest is abstract. There's an irony here. The benefit that people buy with chocolate is taste and pleasure. Yet does Nestlé sell taste and pleasure? No: They sell it by the bar.

There's also another way to position your product to advantage. Do you remember how Arm & Hammer's baking powder suddenly reappeared as a toothpaste? The creative team represented a dull white powder that hadn't seen great days since Becky Crocker as an efficient new health product. But the public knew and trusted Armour and supported the change.

Some of the most successful and least expensive marketing comes about when a product is given a fresh marketing twist.

Harness Your Strengths

Whether you are designing software or an automobile, new features take time to develop and incorporate. Why waste an enhancement just because it's ready? If you know a competitor is bringing out a new product, plan your release to coincide with his. It torpedoes your competitor's presumptions. He was aiming at overtaking the old product. Because of this, a product enhancement can be a very powerful tactical tool. One major innovation is all that's required to make the tactic work. Table 14-2 provides examples from both the software and automobile worlds.

<table>
<tr><td colspan="2" align="center">Table 14-2
Enhancement Rollout Examples</td></tr>
<tr><td>*Software*</td><td>*Automobiles*</td></tr>
<tr><td>Works with XP</td><td>Now with driver air bags</td></tr>
<tr><td>Imports all major file formats</td><td>Now with passenger air bags</td></tr>
<tr><td>Internet Ready</td><td>Now with side air bags</td></tr>
</table>

Consider Some Variations on the Standard Sale

IT has invented more variants on selling in the last 30 years than have been dreamt up in the previous three thousand. Fortunately, you don't always have to part with hard-earned cash to kick off a software sale.

Shareware

This typically involves a free 30-day trial before the software locks until the bill is paid. One big advantage with this style of sale is that there is normally no need to reinstall software, as a valid licence key will activate the full version. However, this kind of trial doesn't suit everyone. Much like free food samples in supermarkets, many nibble but few buy. Even so, some prospects, having used your program, may feel lost without it.

The most successful shareware sellers restrict functionality during the evaluation period. This gives prospects an additional motive to buy. Their developers have made millions. However, a quick look at popular shareware sites such as Tucows shows that every category just teems with competition. If you are a newcomer with no known name behind you, prospects may be hesitant about trying any product whose quality and provenance are unfamiliar.

Note Contrary to what the names imply, most shareware or freeware is restricted or time-limited in some way until you pay up.

Adware

This is just the thing for corporations who want to use software incentives in their promotions. It's a particularly good technique for low-cost, fun products aimed at teenagers. Ads of every description adorn the product but the recipients get the program free for a designated run time. The downside is that these promotions each have a very short life, so the only way you can ride the adware roller coaster is by having a highly specialized, highly motivated sales force so that one advertiser comes in as another pulls out.

Upgrade Ware

This is really a teaser. The customer gets limited access free but gets billed when he wants to access full functionality. On the basis that 10–20 percent of the functionality delivers 80–90 percent of the users' requirements, it's a close call between giving them a useable product for free or annoying them by inviting them to try an unusable product (for example, printing facilities disarmed).

Third-Party Certification

These are spin-offs of your program developed by others and marketed with your approval. Provided third parties don't intend to develop anything you have in mind, it is usually a good idea to encourage them. Make sure you retain sensible control through quality screening regimes and certification. The more people that have a vested interest in variations of your product, the more it will be publicized and sell. On the principle that where there's trade, there's life, third-party programs tend to extend the life of their parent.

Free Software

Free software isn't always the market spoiler that competitors anticipate. The cost of developing the program has got to be paid for by hook or by crook. Sometimes this is by consultancy; other times it is via on-going support. However, it can and does disturb the market, as it makes it harder for less well-heeled competitors to charge the proper up-front price to recoup their costs.

Note Even the largest armies are unable to cope with sustained attacks on two fronts. So be wary of unwittingly getting into a situation where you are releasing two new products simultaneously. Concentrate your firm's attention. Stagger your releases. It extends the press coverage. Unless you receive an invitation you can't refuse, don't attempt to expand into two countries at the same time. Even the top names seldom have sufficient resources to do justice to two projects simultaneously. Consider every move you make to be a strategic one and think it through accordingly.

Competitions

Most competitions use some extraneous product or service as a sales catalyst. Prize offers are great where the product is fun, but they tend to supplant any serious product (people want the benefits of the prize more than they want the benefits of the product).

The best prizes are those that relate to the product, such as a free scanner with a new laptop, and they only work then if the lure is sufficiently tempting. The prize isn't necessarily something expensive. New technology is often appropriate for software. Digital cameras attracted a lot of recipients when used as prizes until the prices dropped.

Tip If you contact manufacturers directly, they will often give you products for competitions at reduced rates, as they appreciate the free publicity. They can also help you draft the key points to make and give you a few tips from their experience.

Some Final Tips

Timing is everything. When you are planning a launch, you need to have a plan B up your sleeve in case some unforeseen event occurs such as the Princess of Wales' untimely death. At the very least, you should establish a point of no return. If tragedy occurs up to point X, you abort. After point X, you carry on regardless.

Some events such as peak summer vacation time and a presidential election can be forecast. You will be wise to avoid periods when your target's primary attention is likely to be diverted by Thanksgiving or Christmas unless there is some peculiar spin-off (you write games software). Even events such as the Olympics, the soccer World Cup, or the Super Bowl and peak holiday periods may be better avoided.

Learning from Your Own Experience

The only other person who is ever watching you more closely than you do yourself is your competitor. So whichever way things turn out, it is important that you learn the most useful thing you can from every marketing experience. If you don't, you are simply dropping heavy hints to your competitors, giving them an idea (without cost or obligation) of what they should do. Philanthropy is supposed to begin at home.

A Word about the Bicycle

Products, like human beings, go through the same life cyle: conception, birth, infancy, growth, maturity, and ultimate decline.

✦ **Birth**—All products are at their most vulnerable during the first months after their launch. Those from unknown parents require announcements even more to spread the news. Court every bit of free publicity you can wangle. Spend time cultivating journalists. Brief them thoroughly to explain your program. You will also need selling power to get the goods off the nursery shelf.

✦ **Growth**—When sales increasingly amount to more than they cost, you are in the growth phase. Extra effort will hasten the rise and enable you to get a hold before competition takes up the slack. Products can usefully be diversified to exploit different sections of the market and bar them from competitors. The growth phase does not last forever. Sooner or later the market for your product reaches its maximum size.

✦ **Maturity**—As product sales peak, competition is usually at its greatest. Reinforcement advertising can be used to remind users of your product's existence and keep sales on a high plateau. New growth can only come from opening new sales territories. Most opportunities lie abroad. Product development still continues but you begin to run out of new features.

If you have not established value in the brand, you may be forced by distributors to drop the price.

✦ **Decline**—Sooner or later, the world moves on. For reasons no one could anticipate at the outset, every product becomes outdated, usually with newer products snapping at its heels. There's a great temptation to embark on promotions or reduce prices on the basis that what you lose in price is more than made up from sales from a much larger herd. It doesn't always turn out like that. Smart operators see natural decline years ahead so they build new products like a series of arches as they go. As one product goes down another comes up and the corporation floats forward from crest to crest.

Marketing Needn't Cost the Earth

Some of the most successful marketing campaigns ever have cost very little. What they all have in common is that someone will have attacked the problem creatively. Someone has used their brain rather than their wallet to solve a problem. This is the greatest marketing ally of any small firm.

There are exciting times ahead!

✦   ✦   ✦

CHAPTER 15

Going For Higher Volumes

If you have to sell in large numbers, you are going to have to get help with distribution. Distribution is the means of physically getting your product to the end user. Whether customers obtain your program via an Internet Web site or a local or chain dealer, distribution is the name and means of getting it from you to them. Distribution doesn't create sales. It just gives you the mechanism to deliver them.

The profit left after distribution depends on how you go about it. If you take one route, you may end up with less than 10 percent of the purchase price. If you take another, you may hold on to almost all of it. However, you may sell a million by the 10 percent route and only single figures by the 100 percent route. So it is essential that you consider the arithmetic of distribution with an open mind.

There's also another not uncommon situation. The obvious route may not alone tip you into profit. You may need a second avenue to strike home. The most advantageous answers sometime come from unexpected combinations. Frequently they start small and grow big. To arrive at the best combination, you need to weigh every option.

Now consider your avenue of choices. Distribution historically means packing the goods on a camel, trudging them across Asia, transferring the wares to a ship, sailing across an ocean, loading the goods onto a train, hoisting them onto a cart, and wheeling them across to some central wholesalers who then deliver the product to your friendly neighborhood dealer who sells them across the counter. Every time the product passes from one link in the chain to the next, there's a price hike.

Bulletin Boards for Selling

Ward Christensen began work on the first Computer Bulletin Board System (CBBS) during the Great Chicago Snowstorm in the winter of 1978 (January). They were predominantly used as an information resource for sharing text and files, much like the early FTP sites. They only began to be utilized for selling just as the Internet exploded onto the scene.

Ward also wrote MODEM.ASM, which became XMODEM, the first binary file transfer protocol, back in 1977.

Ever since software became available in the 1950s, high-value programs have usually been sold either directly from the manufacturer to the end user or via an intermediary, usually a consultancy or specialist reseller. However, the introduction of programs of near universal interest on the back of IBM's PC saw an awesome shortcut. Software began to be electronically coded, copied, licensed, shipped, and activated directly from the manufacturer to the end user via a phone line—an enormous advantage over traditional methods.

In the process, software houses adopted control techniques from many conventional markets, but in many cases it handled these transactions more efficiently than mail-order houses ever did in their heyday. For example, you can, at nominal cost, individualize software (like license plates on a car), allow people to sample it (like headphones in music stores), or allow a short period of use (like a library book).

Until the early 1990s, software distribution was still physical. Then people started using bulletin boards, FTP servers, and finally Web sites to deliver their wares electronically. Far from supplanting existing channels of distribution, electronic transfer introduced an additional one. By combining an ability to transfer software electronically with enormous rapidity with the control techniques already in place, it became possible to deliver software at the speed of sound (a technique so efficient it was adopted by Napster for the distribution of music tracks).

There are three basic routes for software distribution:

✦ Direct

✦ Web-based

✦ Traditional

Additionally, there are variants to explore. If you are to exercise an optimum choice, you need to exploit them all.

Meet the Players

Products don't appear through the door by magic, although when everything works smoothly it can appear that way. Here are the usual suspects that get the product to you from start to finish.

The Producer

The start of the chain is you, the creator, the entrepreneur, the manufacturer. Because volume of production is a pushbutton activity, software producers can handle all these roles.

Distributors

Every country seems to have at least one of these. These are wholesalers who sell exclusively to the trade (normally dealers), but never to end users, at least that's the theory. Large end users, corporations, and government departments frequently place significantly larger orders than many dealers, so distributors frequently suppress their ethical objections. The increase in electronic delivery and software activation makes this shortcut particularly tempting. Where distributors won't play ball, it is not unknown for large organizations to create trade fronts to enable them to purchase goods at trade discounts.

The main distributors may have literally thousands of dealers on their books, giving you an instant multiplier effect. Through their brochures, catalogs, and Web site, your product is available at a stroke to a vast array of potential purchasers. However, such opportunities come at a cost. Distributors will hardly ever take on a new product from an unknown source unless you can demonstrate the product and convince them of the need for it in advance. A common way of measuring this is for the distributor to demand that the manufacturer provide them with a sizeable initial order in advance to prime the pump.

Distributors do simplify things. You ship to a single address, submit one invoice, and deal with one set of procedures. They process the orders from all their dealers, collect the money, deliver the goods, handle the returns, and so on.

With software, distributors typically take around 60 percent of the end price to cover their own costs and reward their retailers. They run on surprisingly narrow net margins, often 4–10 percent. Such margins can only be viable where there is serious volume. They also have to insist that you simplify their lives by working to a strict set of procedures and remain responsible for quality and after-sales support. But they will pay you promptly as agreed.

Note Unless you are a big player, never even seek to change a major distributor's rules or ways of working. Apart from anything else, their systems are not equipped to cope with idiosyncratic variations.

Although large distributors have consolidated and grown larger since the late 1980s, some have recently introduced a hybrid service whereby they'll stock and distribute your products but not promote them. This limits their function to warehousing. In this case, they act as a shipping agent. The only tasks they perform are storage and delivery. Invoicing their dealers is normally left to you.

Once buyers know that a new product has been accepted for distribution by one of the big names, the credibility of a program is considerably enhanced. Apart from software that practically walks itself out of their door, distributors like products that continue to bring them money through periodic re-licensing for updates.

The trend is for domestic consumers to be provided with electronic editions of software. At present, distributors have to stock both. If and when electronic delivery spreads to the commercial sector, there appears to be little to stop software manufacturers from selling directly to the end user.

Pure distribution has always been available from small, specialized distributors who concentrate on niches such as leisure or graphic design. Distribution comes into its own with physical hardware and the software that is habitually sold with it.

Web-Based Distributors

Where software can be dispatched electronically, Internet-based distribution is an obvious solution. There are two types of distribution via the Web: traditional and facilitators.

Traditional distributors use their Web sites simply to sell products and take orders. The goods are stored, shipped, and invoiced manually. Shareware sites such as Tucows also list, review, and make software available for download and purchase (if found acceptable).

A newer phenomenon is that of facilitators. They sell the product. You ship directly to their customer. Invoicing, licensing, and cash collection may be handled by either party.

It is here that traditional retailing breaks down. Several Web-based distributors have taken to selling directly to the public at prices that are frighteningly close to wholesale. So the market and margins previously enjoyed by dealers are being eroded and they are casting around for other ways to make money. This may create an opening of one kind or another for you. With traditional distributors less keen to take on new companies and the ease of setting up your own Web site, there is nothing to stop you from becoming your own distributor. However, it might prove naïve to bypass the other avenues of distribution that could add more power to your elbow.

Dealers

Dealers are really local retailers, although they are often referred to as *Value Added Resellers (VARs)*. They typically sell everything from ink-jet cartridges to paper to fully installed networks. They may be called upon to supply any computer materials and equipment their customers demand.

Dealers are quite understandably (and rightly) customer led. Customers with the juiciest, most pressing orders call the shots. With so much software coming out each month, few dealers have the resources to assess the pros and cons of new offerings. They listen to what their customers tell them. Once they start getting requests and orders for your software, they'll be requesting prices and literature from their distributors faster than you can say "done."

As soon as they start to sell your software in any numbers, they will be interested to hear from you, meet your sales support representatives, and send one or two of their people to your training course.

End User

The end user is the client, the man, woman, or organization who actually buys your product to use. End users are the omega, the hero of every software entrepreneur's dream.

Tip

If you are writing specialized software, such as that used in financial centers, it makes sense to bypass distributors and deal directly with dealers in Frankfurt, Tokyo, London, New York, and so on.

Whether you are Bill Gates or Harold Doorknob, the first sale of your first product will almost certainly be a direct one between you and an end user. The user might be somebody who helped you develop the product or someone who found out about it and contacted you before any distribution was organized. Such contacts can provide an invaluable early warning system on what users are likely to think and the features that will finally convert them. They can show you how to sell your product before anyone else can.

Most ideas for software enhancements come from end users. Their suggestions are gold dust. While you will occasionally get a good idea from a dealer, it is almost unheard of from a distributor. So prize every direct sales contact.

International Distributors

If you want to centralize distribution into one county, you might set up a single point of distribution. This might be a separate branch of your own company or one of the main national distributors.

Large Retail Chains

Large retail chains work in a very similar manner to distributors. Typically, there is a single point of delivery and invoicing. Margins are high. What they lack in quality of clients they make up for in numbers. Chains are often reluctant to take on products that are not household names already or backed by substantial advertising. Quite understandably, they don't want to carry items that are not going to sell.

Regional Sales Offices

As previously explained, firms often set up a special division to act as their international distributor. This keeps the money within the firm, removes discord from rival distributors (they hate buying from each other), and allows them to fund local pre/post sales support, training, and hold directly onto the big buyers.

Direct Salespeople

You can employ salespeople yourself or hire them on a freelance basis. As a rule, freelancers will only sell yours or a limited number of non-competitive products. However, be warned: it's a rare salesperson who sells anything that cannot sell itself. They like the security of a successful company. If pressed about their lack of sales, they invariably plead a lack of advertising or a shortage of quality leads.

Be highly selective about who they approach. Salespeople are not missionaries. They are motivated by money. You are still responsible for training and backup.

Salespeople are usually remunerated on commission only or commission + basic salary. Given a choice, the better ones will go for commission only. They will only stay any length of time while the rewards stay interesting. The most effective salespeople often turn out to be the firm's principals.

Multi-Level Marketing

How do you sell a plastic bowl you couldn't give away into nine out of ten American homes? In 1951, Brownie Wise, an unmarried, single, working-class mother in Detroit thought she would have a go by holding a party to persuade her friends to buy enough to sell to other friends who in turn bought enough to sell to other friends. The Tupperware Party was born.

Gurus who investigated the phenomenon call the technique *multi-level marketing*, but this really is a dressed-up name for pyramid selling by a hierarchy of enclaves or a sequence of Internet chain letters. Success depends on nearly doubling sales at each rung.

The method goes in and out of vogue but often reappears when some eager beaver firm with a hot product and dreams of instant wealth reinvents it to kick-start sales. Multi-level marketing in theory can have an infinite number of layers. In practice, there is rarely enough money to spread further than four levels and barely enough customers to go beyond seven. Even then, success depends on recruiting strongly motivated people in the initial layers and falters the moment they appoint people less effective than themselves. The more levels there are, the more difficult it becomes to exercise control. To have a good spring and early summer with multi-level selling you need a peerless product, a thoroughly ethical approach, and a wall-of-death instinct to know when to stop.

Distribution Models

There are essentially five ladders of distribution. These are often called tiers. Just to confuse matters, the number of steps is one less than you'd expect. The manufacturer's ground floor doesn't count. Thus, a two-tier model goes PRODUCER ⇨ DEALER ⇨ END USER. Pre-sales and regional office staff and sales commissions paid internally are counted as part of the Producer's activity.

Table 15-1 shows the different distribution models.

Table 15-1 Distribution Models				
Direct	*Two-Tier*	*Three-Tier*	*International*	*Multi-Tier*
Producer	Producer	Producer	Producer	Producer
End User	Distributor or Dealers	Distributor	Importer	Level-1
	End User	Dealer	Distributor	Level-2
		End User	Dealer	Level-3
			End User	Level-4
				End User

Direct Sales

Most software manufacturers use this method to the extent that they can. It is the only method if you are writing a program to order. It is the favored method if your program commands a very high price among a very limited number of people. It is not a practical method if your recipe for success demands large numbers of sales at low unit prices. Where the break-even point comes depends on the creative investment, the program's intellectual complexity, the price it commands, and the feasibility of selling via the Web. The break-even point may also be affected by the capital available for promotion, the time it takes to engineer a sale and, in the case of repeat purchases, the cropping interval.

Some programs can only be sold by technicians to technicians.

Two-Tier Distribution

If the volume of sales your program can sustain is larger than you can cope with yourself yet falls short of universal, consider sub-contracting your sales. Appointing dealers gives many more prospects access to your program. There are more places where it can be seen and many more salespeople to help you, more than you will be able to afford yourself for a considerable time. With dealers, all the premises, organization, recruiting, and management are done for you. Web sites, such as online shareware vendors, bring instant outlets for low-cost programs and provide an excellent discovery point for reviewers.

As previously mentioned, specialized software is often better sold through dealers that specialize. These may be chosen for their location, customer profile, or technical expertise. Working upstream from similar or related software will usually guide you to them. While getting software accepted by a Web site is a relatively swift operation, finding, vetting, establishing, and supporting a network of dealers takes time.

Three-Tier Distribution

If your program is designed for a mass market and has to be presented in the traditional box, you need every stream of distribution. In next to no time you'll find you need a number of firms to handle the many thousands of dealers. Organizing the volumes of physical shipment is a major task in itself. Three-tier distribution gives you instant access to the distributors' dealer base that has been built up over a lifetime.

International Distribution

International distribution is another way of building up volume, but you need a secure and profitable home market first. It is, however, a strategy with few conspicuous successes. For one thing, international distribution requires a great stomach for travel. For another, it needs a deep pocket. Most people can tell you stories of overseas agents they appointed who did absolutely nothing.

There are two ways of handling distributors internationally: either ship to each distributor individually or have a single super-distributor handle their orders and liaise. This approach only has merit where the local distributor is also able to handle other trading issues. Ironically, when products become mass sellers internationally, the operation is usually taken in-house as a means of control.

Multi-Level Distribution

The main difference between pyramid selling and multi-level marketing (MLM) is that pyramid schemes make money from bringing more people into the scheme whereas MLM concentrates on selling product. This is only an option where your product has a universal, emotional, or sensual appeal.

It has to be universal for people who join halfway down the chain to sense that there are plenty more prospects to sell to. It has to have a wide sensual or emotional appeal because there are just not enough people with enough selling ability. Intellectual requirements have to be elementary, with little or nothing to learn, think out, or remember. If you have such a product and contemplate multi-level distribution, accept that at a very early stage you will lose control. There are just more sellers than you can vet.

One Success Story

So take a tip from Claude Ganz of Dymo. When he was very young, Claude bought a chunk of shares in a new company working out of a garage in Berkeley. They were distressing vinyl tape to form letters for signs. The other vice presidents didn't want anything to do with Claude, but he held a considerable chunk of the shares. One day when Claude asked yet again for a role, the others suggested he take over international sales. Claude, being adventurous, booked a world tour. Wherever he went, he demonstrated his plastic nameplate-making gun and appointed distributors.

Over a period of seven months he ran up a tab that frightened even him. When he finally got back to Berkeley and tentatively tapped on Dymo's garage door, he proffered his expense account in great trepidation. The vice presidents, much to his astonishment, welcomed him with open arms. Sales in two of the fifty countries he had visited had more than repaid his trip.

Armed with fresh confidence, Claude went back into the world, fired the non-performing agents, and (with more experience) appointed better ones. At the end of his second trip, seven countries were profitable. The rest is history. Claude eventually became president of Dymo worldwide.

The moral, however, is not just one of persistence. For every home country, there are over a hundred foreign ones, some with even larger populations. The odds are wonderful. So, while international corporations can't bank on success, there are always a few conspicuous successes. If you have one good home market of 100 million and only five out of a hundred small countries of 20 million come good, you have doubled your market.

Let's say each representative for your software has to bring five additional people on board each day. Allowing for such a modest conversation and no work on weekends, in less than four months every person on the planet would be signed up. Table 15-2 demonstrates this scale of recruiting.

The theoretical numbers generated by the techniques are enough to make a stoat gloat although the practice rarely delivers. If it did, we'd all be at it. However, as a one-off, one-step, limited time incentive, it can form the nucleus of a very effective sales promotion.

Table 15-2 Recruitment Demonstration for MLM		
Stages	*New Recruits*	*Total Recruits*
1	1	1
2	5	6
3	25	31
4	125	156
5	625	781
6	3,125	3,906
7	15,625	19,531
8	78,125	97,656
9	390,625	488,281
10	1,953,125	2,441,406
11	9,765,625	12,207,031
12	48,828,125	61,035,156
13	244,140,625	305,175,781
14	1,220,703,125	1,525,878,906
15	6,103,515,625	7,629,394,531
16	30,517,578,125	38,146,972,656

Third-Party Resellers

All good software has facilities for third parties to develop add-ons. This extends the functionality and expands the user base and the sales of your core product. Encouraging more people to be dependent on the product cements your future.

Consideration must be made to enable production, verification, authorization, certification, and distribution of these third-party resellers. If large distributors won't carry their versions, you can often sell them on their producer's behalf and pay them.

Selecting Distributors and Dealers

Many firms are so relieved to get a distributor, they pay scant attention to finding out what sort of job that distributor will do before they place their future in the distributor's hands. Then they wonder why little or nothing happens.

Don't just jump in because you must have distribution. Don't assume just because they have done a good job for X they will do a good job for you. You have to vet distributors and direct dealers as carefully and reflectively as you do when you are hiring staff. The process of courting dealers and distributors is theoretically very simple. The practice is long winded; so start as early as practicable.

Ask yourself what kind of distributor wants a product like yours? Looking at distribution lists for similar products can provide you with a short list. You then approach them to carry your product. Their receptionists will normally be able to give you the name and extension number of the person to whom you should speak. It's their job and they know one day it might be the next Microsoft/Oracle or Cisco calling. If this proves hard, ask friends or colleagues who deal with the firm for the best person to speak to. Once you've got the name the real fun starts. These people are terrifically busy, dealing with suppliers, handling hundreds and occasionally thousands of products, writing reports for their managers, analyzing sales figures and trends, and so on, and occasionally having time to vet new products. Getting on the ladder the first time is the hardest task. Contact each of them, find out their selection criteria, and what they pride themselves on. Ask also what they can do to promote your product. What is their success? What do they charge?

Once you're accepted updates are a formality and new products can be fast tracked as you've already passed a lot of their acceptance criteria, but first you have to gain their ear to be able to explain the product, its benefits, its market, well-known users, and sales projections. You need to be able to do this in less than two minutes. Unless you are an old hand at this, practice on your colleagues to fine-tune your delivery; then try your pitch on a relatively unimportant firm first. You don't want to blow your chances with an ace distributor because you are under rehearsed. It is one of the most important presentations you will ever make.

Distributors need to see the following:

- ✦ Sample of finished product and its packaging
- ✦ Sales literature (PDFs are now acceptable)
- ✦ Product presentations (PowerPoint)

✦ Business cards

✦ A well designed, informative Web site

✦ Clients lists and references

✦ Sample ads (if applicable)

They might also request to see the following:

✦ Your sales and marketing plan

✦ Sales projections

✦ Copies of the last audited accounts

If you choose a large distributor you will have no real control over their dealers, which is why it is better, if yours is a specialized product, to hand pick your dealers yourself. Whichever way you go about it, it is important to establish that there is no conflict of interest with any competitive products. At the end of the day, distributors and dealers will promote the products from which it is easiest to make the most.

Good relationships with distributors and dealers are worth working at, because they can be valuable in their own right. Software firms are not always purchased for their products. They are sometimes purchased for their access to distribution.

While it is hard work, it gives you the infrastructure for your current and future products. Your dilemma is simple. There are few key distributors in any country; you have to win the ones that are important to your business. People normally get distributors in place first. Dealers are thicker on the ground. If one isn't interested there are always 10 others you can approach. Ultimately, all they are interested in is making money. This must be the underlying thrust of your pitch. One way to resolve the distributor impasse is to start selling through dealers first. When you have established a credible sales record you can approach the distributors with more convincing sales and marketing figures. The dealers aren't likely to take offense provided you keep the communication channels in place that they have previously enjoyed. They will almost certainly purchase from these main distributors anyway, so all they are doing is switching suppliers.

Margins

With hardware margins (this discount you give) often falling back into single figures, distributors and dealers rely on software and services to make up the shortfall. As a result, you will be giving away more margin than you would have had to 20 years ago. Table 15-3 shows some typical margins:

Table 15-3 Typical Hardware Margins	
Selling to	**Discount off RRP**
International distributor	45–65%
Major chain	40–60%
Distributor	40–60%
Dealer	20–40%
End user (multiple sales)	0–25%
End user (single sales)	0%

In most manufacturers' eyes the real difference between a dealer and a distributor isn't their title but the volume of business they do. It is not uncommon for your largest dealer to outperform your smallest distributor.

To offer the greatest incentive, margins should be volume based. Even so, discounts should never overlap. Otherwise, promoting a massive dealer to a distributor offers no financial benefit.

Terms

These vary from country to country depending on legislation and accepted local practices. Thirty days credit from date of delivery is what most distributors boast. This is often interpreted as 30 days from the day on which they write once-a-month checks. In the worse case this means you are giving away 60 days credit if you deliver your goods on the following day.

Establish exactly how payment terms work so you can plan your deliveries and cash flows and not flag invoices as due before they really are. It is not uncommon for major distributors or chains to extend this credit to 90 days, especially when trade is slow.

With foreign distributors and dealers, ensure that the payment is made electronically for the exact amount in your local currency. This removes the uncertainty of the "check's in the mail" syndrome and ensures the right amount is paid into your account regardless of changes in exchange rates. For amounts less than $40/£25/€40, the cost of cashing a foreign check can be greater than the value of the check.

Who Does What?

The number of levels you add to your route to market will dictate responsibilities, as shown in Table 15-4.

Table 15-4
Roles in the Development Models

Area	Direct	Two-Tier	Three-Tier
Product Development	Producer	Producer	Producer
Export versions	Producer	Producer/distributor	Producer/distributor
National Marketing	Producer	Producer	Producer
Local promotions	Producer	Dealer	Distributor
Distributor Support			Producer
Dealer Support		Producer	Producer/distributor
End User Support	Producer	Dealer	Dealer
Manage Distributor			Producer
Manage Dealer		Producer	Distributor
Regional Sales Management	Producer	Producer	Distributor
Local Sales Management	Producer	Dealer	Dealer

Distribution Procedures

Distributors have strict guidelines that must be adhered to if you want to do business with them.

Delivery

Each distributor will provide you with strict guidelines as to delivery times, address, pallet sizes and weights, labelling, bar coding, and their own stock keeping unit (SKU) codes. Follow these instructions to the letter. Their staff are normally more than happy to help. With several hundred shipments each day, large distribution hubs cannot afford foul-ups, so it's in everyone's best interests to make sure everything works smoothly from the start.

Returns

Goods can be returned for any reason within a 30-day period. Thirty days is often a legal stipulation as well as the waiver period demanded by credit card companies.

The distributors/dealer may charge the customer a discretionary restocking fee on any goods returned. If they do, 15–20 percent is typical. You do not get any part of the restocking fee. Dealers have the right to refuse the return if the goods are incomplete (without a receipt) or not in a merchantable state (for example, they are scuffed/damaged).

Software can only be returned if it is unopened. Multiple software licenses can usually be returned provided the manufacturer has authorized it first. You should monitor returns to see if there is any pattern to them. Returns of less than 1 in 200 units are normally considered trivial.

Post-Sales Support

Most distributors will only sell your products if you provide support in the geographical area they cover. Some have small, dedicated teams to support their top-selling products.

OEM Arrangements

Here you brand your product with another company's name. Apart from setting aside your pride, original equipment manufacturer (OEM) deals are only done by established firms who have clients and distribution in place to take the product. Consequently, they will normally provide upfront costs to "brand" your product as well as some nominal fees in advance.

Apart from the welcome extra cash, they do produce a useful volume of extra throughput, which may enable you to improve your bulk purchasing arrangements and make more efficient use of your plant. It is also an ideal way to get sales into countries where you do not intend to set up an overseas office. Contracts need to include the following issues:

✦ Exclusivity (especially time and geographical limitations)

✦ Volume

✦ Price

✦ Call off times

✦ Termination

✦ Rights to client information

Updated Stock

You and your distributors need a clear understanding about whether unsold inventories shall be returned when your product is updated. Whatever you decide, keep dealer stocks low in the run up to any major upgrade; otherwise, you or your dealers will have significant amounts of outdated product to get rid of as best you can.

Local Duplication

How do you tackle key accounts such as large corporations and government departments who need the product at the drop of a hat and who, if they don't get what they want from you, can buy something comparable from another dealer or overseas source? You can authorize the corporations and government departments to issue software licenses for you. With Internet-based systems this can now be affected online so those problems of verification, auditing, illegal duplication, and misdirected sales are all taken care of.

Exports

There is more to readying software for a foreign market than translating the screen into another language. The product's position with respect to competition and marketing strategy needs reassessment. The name may need to be changed. Fresh trademarks and patents may need to be registered. Literature may even need resizing (the standard page size in the United States is Letter, in Europe it's A4).

 Note   A4 is 210x297mm and Letter is 215.9 x 279.4mm. It's interesting to note that although the pages are different sizes, the surface area for what you can put on the page is almost identical.

All the ancillaries have to be changed. Dialogues, help, manuals, sales literature, and training packs must not only be translated but checked by a highly literate speaker of that language. How often have you received documents from a foreign firm that have been translated into English with such imprecision that they get something wrong that robs the whole offering of credibility and authority? Having gone the final mile, go the final foot.

Press Copies

It makes good sense to give journalists copies of your software for evaluation/review purposes (try getting a review without offering this). Press software and boxes should be clearly marked "Not for Resale." Wherever possible, these copies best come directly from the manufacturer. This gives the journalist voice-to-voice (if not face-to-face) contact with the developers and ensures top-level support if they have any queries. The better their experience with your software, the better their review is likely to be.

Sales and Marketing

Many manufacturers find distributors excellent people to work with. Distributors know they stand or fall by their ability to market their client's products. A good distributor will produce regular sales catalogs, have extensive Web sites with special offers, arrange direct mail, and even work in conjunction with major manufacturers and dealers to produce jointly funded promotions. They do this so often they build up a massive working knowledge of what is and isn't successful in their territory. Naturally, they charge for all these facilities but the economies of scale that they command often make promotions cheaper than doing small runs yourself.

When dealers need training they'll ask for it. Often their request is not so much to find out how to use your product but how to sell it.

If your distributor has 50 dealers it could take you almost three months to visit them individually, so distributors often arrange product awareness sessions several times a year. These can provide excellent opportunities to bring dealers up to date and brief them on what's about to happen as well as to bring new dealers on board.

Managing Distribution

Setting up distribution is a task in its own right and involves the following:

- ✦ Monitoring, auditing sales
- ✦ Investing in the relationship
- ✦ Geographical restrictions, law
- ✦ Supporting the channel
- ✦ The reorder process
- ✦ Size of reseller base
- ✦ Not giving away more than you have to
- ✦ Quality control
- ✦ Sales

Recourse—Getting Legal

This is not an easy call to make. Let me take you through the two most common distribution disputes.

- ✦ You supply goods. They remain unpaid.
- ✦ Someone is copying your product.

These problems are even more complex when they happen overseas. Even in your own country it can take years to get justice. Litigation is also a major and demoralizing distraction. The only people who benefit are your competitors. The golden rule is that prevention is the best cure.

Write your contracts carefully. Deny transgressors any gray areas. Make sure the costs of putting things right fall on them. Have strict termination and punitive penalty clauses in place too.

Keep accurate, detailed records of accounts, phone calls, letters, and events. Watch delivery to payment intervals like a hawk. Keep the credit you allow low so if there is a problem you won't have to write off too much money.

Curtail the relationship with any distributor or dealer who defaults or colludes. If necessary, make your action public knowledge.

Outraged pride, no matter how justified, is never a good enough business reason to resort to law. Sometimes it is necessary just to warn people. Only take legal action when it is necessitated by survival policy and there is a clear, provable technical infringement. Behaving in a business-like manner reduces legal costs, but consider taking out legal insurance just in case. Build this investment into your manufacturing overhead.

Always have secondary distributors and dealers in the wings to replace your weakest dealers. These can then be brought in at short notice to replace any distributor or dealer who abrogates his contract.

Counterfeiting, Piracy, and Theft

In the United Kingdom, which is always regarded as being exceptionally law-abiding, the externally audited figures imply that one in four pieces of software in use are illegal. The internal audits by IT managers double that figure to one in two. The most common cause of this is people buying software once and copying it many times. In large firms uncontrolled software distribution can allow software to spread as fast as a brush fire. This is known in the trade as *under licensing*. It is likely to represent your biggest source of loss.

Pursuing individuals is as effective as trying to wipe out a colony of ants with the tip of a pool cue. Organized businesses are your real concern, such as a distributor who continues to sell your product long after your agreement has been terminated, or a large corporation who uses your software company-wide by copying an unlocked evaluation copy you gave them in good faith. However, the following also occurs:

+ **Counterfeiters**—Normally interested in branded products and even then they normally concentrate on their top-selling products.

+ **Software Incorporation**—One firm uses/embeds someone else's software into their product without paying for it. This is hard to spot but often a disgruntled employee will whistle blow or the software will exhibit some telltale sign that alerts you.

Whatever the offense and wherever the problem, you have to have a realistic strategy and a cool head. First, don't do what most people do: nothing. If you don't protect your intellectual property, your program, you can make it harder to protect your rights in the future. It is important to send out a clear signal that you are not to be messed with and you will protect your interests and recover monies whenever valid.

The trick is to know how to do this without taking up too much management time. You are meant to be running a software operation after all, not subsidizing the legal profession. This involves getting forceful rather than heavy and litigious at the outset.

Unless you are familiar with the procedures, your best bet is to contact your local software enforcement organization, such as SIIA in the United States or FAST for the rest of the world. They pursue thousands of such cases each year and they know the most effective way to deal with cheats. If you think you have a case you must gather as much evidence as possible to support your complaint. If nothing else, they will give you some practical advice. If they take the case, they will initially put the offending firm or individual on notice. If they persist from that point onwards, a judge would deem the defendant is contravening that organization.

Most firms settle at this point. In most countries the offenders and their board are criminally liable if found guilty. If they are selling the software illegally known customers can be served with similar notices.

If you don't get satisfaction, you will have to consider taking legal action. An official summons clears up many cases before they go to court. Although the police and Government Trading Standards departments are interested in these cases, they rarely have the resources to pursue them unless it is extremely high profile.

Are Dealers and Distributors Dead?

Someone asked this question the day the first piece of software was sold electronically. That was in the era of the bulletin board, long before the Internet reared its public head. I ran an extremely successful dealership for almost a decade. The most cynical thing that happened year in and year out was that hardware and software suppliers would come up and court you. Together, over a couple of years, you'd build up the sales, gradually growing some large and valuable accounts. Then suddenly, without notice, the manufacturer would switch to direct selling and keep all the money for himself.

The clients, irrespective of size, knew exactly what was going on and didn't trust the switch. They knew it would only last for a short period while times were rosy. Most manufacturers don't have the resources or staying power when times get hard. New products need explaining. End user problems pile up. The whole task becomes too expensive. Then they'd come back, hat in hand, and try and make up and then carry on as if nothing had happened.

As time has passed, hardware prices have come down dramatically so there is much less money than there was in distribution. Two-thirds of those who grew up on the back of the PC have shut down or become part of larger organizations. Those that remain, while by many measures larger, are naturally concerned about software manufacturers transferring completely to direct, Internet-based sales.

However, another type of distribution service has sprung up. It undertakes many of the tasks that manufacturers find irksome. These people sell consumables, mend equipment, and offer basic training. In a dynamic industry there are always opportunities for a smart new idea.

✦   ✦   ✦

Successful Selling

Forget about the genius who can sell a refrigerator to Eskimos. (It's quite easy actually. They use refrigerators to keep food warm.) Selling software isn't an act of mesmerism. It is the art of the possible. The only product your salesmen will sell is a product that can sell itself. Good salespeople simply accelerate the process.

At a throwaway price, a product has no option but to sell itself. At a steeper price, software needs a helping hand. Once software retails for more than the price of a laptop, you're in the business of wooing.

The Essence of Selling

The essence of selling is about putting yourself in your customer's shoes and explaining the product's advantages from their point of view. It's a knack. It's a habit. It's a way of thinking. It's being positive, and it is much, much more. Selling is about presenting advantages in the most acceptable way, and about giving others confidence to take a decision that is to their advantage in an area where they feel diffident about making a decision.

Selling isn't about taking advantage of buyers. That's not worthy of the salesperson or their company. Even when a hustler isn't caught out, people usually sense that something's fishy or doesn't add up. They distance themselves and don't come back for more. Real selling is white knight stuff. A salesperson is partly a master of ceremonies, partly a source of authoritative information, partly a diplomat, partly a pleasant companion. That's why selling and salesmen are so fascinating.

Fairly obviously, the amount of knowledge and skill required varies with the complexity and price of the product. Selling a $20 videogame may involve little more than putting the customer in a mood to enjoy himself and turning on a screen for a few moments. With a $200,000 program that may keep a chain of hospitals or supermarkets stocked, the sale may go through a number of stages that could last years. The salesperson needs a matching intellect and staying power for the decision level of the product. He or she also needs to be equable and well mannered so that his or her presence is not an intrusion. Salespeople also need to like people and be socially adroit to pick up signals from a situation, to not put their foot in it, to dispel tensions, and to engineer agreement.

This book is not about salesmanship. If you have never sold before, you would do well to visit your public library and pick out a couple of titles. Master salespeople have some wonderfully enlightening stories and what you will learn is going to be invaluable.

What a Sale Really Is

From a legal point of view, a sale is nothing more than an exchange of money for goods or services, but if you interpret it that starkly, you are endangering your own economy. An initial sale is the opportunity to start building a relationship. You don't just want to sell a customer your new products. You want to sell them the upgrades and major releases, add-ons, and new products that the company develops. You want them to be so pleased with their purchase they recommend it to their friends and colleagues. In a nutshell, you want them to help you sell your product. This can only happen if you look at the sale as a long-term relationship from the beginning.

The beauty of software production is that it normally gives a salesperson seven follow-up opportunities. On the back of the original program, these are:

- ✦ Upgrades
- ✦ Maintenance and support contracts
- ✦ Add-ons
- ✦ Lateral developments
- ✦ Custom-made developments
- ✦ Consultancy
- ✦ Bulk/OEM licensing deals

As you may appreciate, it takes time to build up the skills to orchestrate the spectrum. Even then, individual salespeople tend to have favorites.

Sales Costs

When they start a business, many people think sales cost nothing. Often they are right, technically. The CEO does the selling as part of his role, and usually very successfully. People love buying from a senior executive or founder. Who wouldn't like to buy their next Dell from Michael Dell? The other reason that top people are frequently such effective salespeople is they know their product inside out and give immediate, first-rate answers to every reservation. This gives doubters confidence and quickly wins them over.

The transition occurs when you start employing people just to sell. You then need to know exactly what they have to achieve to break even. You'd be amazed how many people don't know how many sales each one has to achieve per month before the company profits. However, the odds work just the same whether management knows them or not, and you are better off being aware of what they amount to. In the end you are the person who is going to have to find the money to pay for it all. There are essentially three figures to watch:

✦ The selling cycle

✦ The monthly cost of sales

✦ The profit

The selling cycle is usually considered a calendar month, which is why bills are normally invoiced and paid monthly all over the world. In retail outlets it can be much shorter, sometimes a day, though more usually a week. When selling in units of exceptional value (government contracts and so on) the cycle may be quarterly, bi-annually, or even a year.

One of the biggest factors that affect the length of the cycle is unit cost. Another is the time it takes to evaluate the product. A $25 utility program is likely to be bought on the spur of the moment, whereas a multicurrency, pan-organizational accounts suite is difficult to evaluate properly in less than a year. When you begin to develop your program, you can only guess what the selling cycle is likely to be. If in unknown territory, the best bet is to be guided by similar products.

Unfamiliar products and those introducing new thinking are particularly hard to predict. When Stac Software's Stacker disk compression software got going in 1993 (a point at which program sizes were growing faster than affordable disks to store them on), it took some time for even big names in the IT industry to latch on. The harder a product concept is to appreciate, the longer the sales cycle will inevitably be. Statistically, there is invariably some client who is an exception to any rule, a product evangelist who buys a new, unknown, and conceptual program quickly. Don't be misled by exceptions, however desirable. Sales cycles are averages, not *Guinness Book* records.

Knowing the true sales cycle, or rather the type of sales cycle your product is likely to achieve, is critical to the survival of your company. Most conservative guesses fall short of the mark. Companies can die, not because the product is flawed, but because the selling cycle is so long they go broke before customers sign the purchase order. If your products don't have any competitor against whom you can gauge your sales cycle, look for similar or cousinly products and find out theirs.

> **Note** With the Internet it's easy to establish your own sales cycle. It's the average time between downloading and purchasing.

The best selling cycle to adopt is the shortest meaningful interval across which you can effectively monitor progress. It's self-evident that the average interval between the first contact and handing over the money varies. Going into a newsagent to buy a magazine might take less than a minute; but a major airline might take years between evaluating the latest navigational system and placing an order, after which there's often several years before they take delivery.

Consider a three-man sales team that costs the firm $10,000 per month. Assume that the average monthly profit they bring is $20,000. Table 16-1 shows how the length of the selling cycle affects a firm's cash flow.

Table 16-1 **Impact of Selling Cycle on Cash Flow**						
Sales Cycle	*1 month*	*2 months*	*3 months*	*4 months*	*5 months*	*6 months*
Cost of sales operation	$60,000	$60,000	$60,000	$60,000	$60,000	$60,000
Sales profit	$100,000	$80,000	$60,000	$40,000	$20,000	0
Balance	$40,000	$20,000	$0	–$20,000	–$40,000	–$60,000

If the selling cycle is six months, you need $60,000 in cash to fund it before you start. It is a critical issue. Most software firms rely on regular sales for survival. If yours is one, you need to engineer as short a sales cycle as possible. The evaluation period provided will critically affect your sales cycle.

Individuals always make faster decisions than companies. The larger the company and the more decision makers it needs, the longer selling will take. Further confusing the issue, it is inevitable that sales cycles will alter between countries and market sectors.

When you are doing your sums remember expenses. Travel, recruitment, training, and expenses are all costs that have to be factored in. Probably the best way to stop expenses from going through the roof is to allot salespeople $X per month on expenses providing they make their basic sales target; anything left goes in their salary. You'd be amazed how expenses fall and pay packets increase.

How to Approach Selling

Marketing provides the road map. Advertising and PR, if you are fortunate enough to have them, set the vehicle in motion. With or without them, you have to start from where you are. Buyers aren't fools. Initially, they will be inclined to take you at your word, but they will feel let down if you deliver less than you promise. And they won't give you the benefit of the doubt a second time.

Sales managers have an old saying: "The more you tell, the more you sell." It is not quite true. It is the more you are *able to* tell that gives prospects the information they need to make an appropriate decision. So make sure your salespeople know everything about your product and can answer every likely question.

If they don't know the answer, the worst course is for them to make up an answer. The right thing for them to say is, "I don't know the answer to that one, but I will ask the person who does know and get right back to you."

When it comes to opening a sale, there are only three approaches: sell directly, indirectly, or both. Direct selling is where the producer's sales force makes direct contact with consumers so there is no middleman. Indirect selling is where the producer enlists an intermediate to sell to consumers and deploys a sales force to sell to distributors. This is best suited to products with which customers are already familiar and where success hinges on volume.

Which should you use? Indirect selling costs can be high. On the other hand, distributors have many more salespeople and contacts. Sales volumes need to be big for this approach to pay off. However, indirect salespeople have many more lines to handle, so there is less incentive to promote your program for more than a fraction of their week. In any case, how will they know how to sell your product if you haven't done so yourself?

When all is said and done, direct selling from a manufacturer is ideally suited for high value, custom-made products that require a high caliber salesperson to make personal contact with prospects. Where the economics are borderline, you may find yourself selling both directly and indirectly.

How Customers Think

Unless the purchase is very important, most corporate customers don't have the time to evaluate every alternative. They simply side for the market leader. They are also swayed by recommendations. The word of colleagues, friends, and trusted journalists carries a good deal of weight. Top-price products, however, carry much influence and little selling momentum. Price may make corporate decision-makers prick up their ears, but it rarely opens their wallets.

And it is easy to understand why. A top accountancy product may cost as much as $25,000 as opposed to the $250 that most firms spend. While the top end product may have 100 times more features, the popular ones almost certainly meet all the main requirements.

Salespeople who appreciate their buyer's situation are often deft at knocking their competitors' products. The best ones tend to speak with gentle authority. But all this is generalization. There is no such thing as a typical customer. The world is not made up of hoards of purchasing clones. So when you are picturing your customer, you are looking for character and purchasing types rather than a single exact fit.

The market research you do before you embark on the product reveals the types most likely to buy. Be prepared to fine-tune these if the product or market changes during development. When you are selling, it is a lot more realistic to have a flexible view of your customers than a single-minded one.

Unless you are a masochist, the best way to treat a customer is as you would like to be treated yourself: courteously, supportively, and fairly. Show them that you listen. Check back with them periodically to reiterate what you understand they've said. It doesn't matter if you don't agree with them. What matters is that they know you listen and acknowledge their reservations. Then when they stop, they feel they owe attention to you. What you have to contribute then falls on more receptive ears. Once it is apparent that you understand your customer's situation, they are much more likely to close the sale than postpone a decision until they can summon reinforcements. If you treat them fairly and they like your product, a few may even recommend you to friends.

One aphorism that should be crushed is "The customer is always right." It sounds good and it makes all purchasing mankind seem like demi-gods. Indeed the phrase has become so entrenched that anyone new to business begins by following this maxim to the letter. The truth is that customers are right a lot of the time, but they are pushing their luck when they try and return software that they have been patently still using, or pressure manufacturers to add a new feature, or demand major upgrades for free. They are just trying to extract a free lunch. The approach is disingenuous because they'll try it on a small developer but they'd never dream of asking big players such as Microsoft, Symantec, or Oracle for similar favors.

It is important that you treat customers well—this will pay dividends and build up customer loyalty—but question every request and if it's a ploy, politely, persuasively, and fairly explain the company policy. They may grumble initially but this technique has turned this situation around and won some of my companies their strongest product evangelists.

Why Customer Relationships Matter

When people asked Garfield Weston why, as the proprietor of a multinational food conglomerate, he still remained a baker, he used to tell them that there are few opportunities where a businessman can take a profit from a customer for the same product 365 times a year. The stark financial fact is that it often costs 10 times as much to make an initial sale as it does to engineer the follow up. Few businesses can survive on initial sales. Many go broke before this truth dawns on them. This is why the furniture business is so hard and why Terrance Conran, the main protagonist behind flat-pack furniture, was so successful when he concentrated on lower cost replacement items. Many startups fail despite having enough money to prime the sales pump. They just don't have enough to last until repeat orders come in.

The automotive business gauges this nicely. While Rolls Royce takes a lifelong profit at one swipe and their automobiles roll on forever, their rivals have another strategy. They ensure that their cars have a long enough life to offer unforgettable pleasure for the money, but not so long that their customers won't come back several times for a newer model.

The most vulnerable time in a fledgling firm isn't just before it first goes into profit. The most vulnerable time is just after the second release. If you haven't built up a good relationship with your customers by then, you have little chance of winning the more profitable second sales. An Eskimo who has to make a hole in the ice takes longer to get supper than the Eskimo who uses someone else's hole. It is the repeat sales that are the real lifeblood of any trading firm.

This process as a whole of being nice to customers is now known as *Customer Relationship Management (CRM)*. It isn't merely a pleasanter way to run a business. It is a smarter way.

Similarities of Scale

Your first big break may come from a large firm. Indeed they may have underwritten your project. However, if that's the case, it is an exception. Big firms generally prefer to buy from others like themselves. They can at least obtain compensation if all else fails. Confidence is the biggest factor. Big firms feel that others of a similar size are equally successful and will share similar views and values. This doesn't mean that big firms don't buy from smaller firms—they have to—but they typically buy smaller, fewer, and less significant products. So if you're a four-man band trying to sell a $50,000 accounting product to Mega Bucks, Inc., don't expect an undeserved break.

If you have a realistic proposition, targeting big firms makes sense in principle, but just because they turned over $1 billion last year doesn't mean they're going to give it all to you tomorrow. Be careful. Large firms are very good at wasting your time and dragging out the sales process or dangling tempting morsels for you on an endless basis.

Also remember that salespeople can be seduced by the rewards offered by big players. No salesperson would be accused of wasting time if he spent a year trying to sell to IBM. However, he would probably get fired if he squandered an entire month on a little known outfit.

Put yourself in the shoes of someone working for a large firm and look at it from his perspective. Every decision you make puts your job on the line, so understandably, you can't afford to stick your neck out. What you really want is a cast iron guarantee that the software will work satisfactorily, and make you look good.

So before you embark on the journey, think through the costs, extended sales cycles, and implications of selling to large firms initially.

About Viral Selling

A lot has been written about viral marketing and selling. This is where people, rather than paid time or space (advertisements), spread an infectious message. Prior to the Internet, this was done by word of mouth; now e-mail is used as well. Within our own time we all remember the avalanche of downloads Netscape received when it was first launched in 1995. Viral marketing suggests that by following a set of easy steps you can replicate these rare examples of feeding frenzy.

In the real world, Harry Potter–like conditions come together to hit a marketing sweet spot once in the proverbial blue moon. The launch of the IBM PC in 1981 and Stac Corporation's disk compression software just over a decade later were both runaway successes. Yet despite what many now assume, Microsoft Windows hammered away for eight years before it really took off.

Don't kid yourself or be kidded. Core elements of viral selling techniques make some sense for startup operations as they help spread the word and the cost is low, but don't think by following this path you will be deluged by wealth. Do build up mailing list databases. Do encourage customers to recommend the product to friends and colleagues. Do try and invent clever ways to spread the word (without resorting to Spam). Unfortunately, there is no magic lamp. Even so, there's a great deal most firms can do to polish up their act.

Extracting Blood from a Stone

If you are courting a major player and it's taking longer than you can afford for them to commit themselves, here are two ways of breaking the impasse. Offer for a modest yet useful fee to assess their situation professionally and write proposals. This breaks the ice. You are no longer a stranger. You are a supplier; not the most important one, yet still a supplier. Next you offer to prepare a consultancy document on the implications and implementation of your software (large firms commission consultancy documents all the time, so you are not asking for anything unreasonable).

These reports don't have to be long or expensive but at least they are paying for your expertise and time. Experience shows that the sooner you start working on a paid basis the sooner your software will be adopted. It's in their best interests that they start paying for something more tangible than a stack of paper.

Another approach is to buddy up with an original equipment manufacturer (OEM) or larger software/systems integrator firm who has a track record in this field. It pays to have one ready up your sleeve. This often gives larger firms the reassurance they crave. It makes particular sense to use this approach when the end product can be sold to several of the OEM's customers.

Managing Salespeople

Sales managers are often the best salespeople on the team. However, the *best* sales managers are simply the best at managing salespeople, and that is very much a matter of applying the experience of other sales companies in a systematic way. Like marshalling an army, the key to success lies in preparation.

Make sure your salespeople know everything about the product that any prospect might sensibly ask. Don't just tell them or show them. Make sure they can tell and show you. Training isn't like being at school. It is or ought to be much more fun. Give quizzes, and give little prizes for projects such as who has the best rundown on competition. Get the salespeople to teach each other. Build up team spirit by encouraging everyone to support each other and recognize each other's achievements. Something is always changing so training is a continuous process, and there are invariably points you will want to follow up on, such as after-sales service.

Most firms find it is enormously helpful to hold training meetings at a regular time each week. They don't have to be long; 30 minutes is enough in many cases. Monday morning is popular with management because people have a whole week to apply the knowledge they have acquired. Salespeople like meetings too. It helps to build a team spirit and whet their competitive edge.

There's no point in just announcing glorious targets. Targets, like carrots in front of donkeys, have to be individually positioned just far enough out of reach to encourage the salesperson to stretch, yet not so far away that the goal is unobtainable. You can only be sure that you have set an attainable target if you have sat down with each salesperson and explained exactly what is required in what time and have worked out together how the person can overcome any anticipated obstacles. Targets often work better where there is a mix of short and intermediate goals. This is partly because some salespeople are better at one than the other, but mainly because it gives a sales manger more scope to raise targets without raising hackles.

You can help salespeople by supplying leads, but they need to be doled out so that justice is seen to be done. It is also important to see that work is fairly shared among the team. There is no point in trying to present goodies behind anyone's back or unduly helping lame ducks. Everyone needs to know who is handling which lead to discourage poaching and squabbles over commission.

Hanging On to the Data

Unscrupulous salespeople occasionally have the idea that the client belongs to them and not the firm they work for. If you ever come across this attitude, remind the salespeople that if this were the case, they'd sign their own pay and commission checks. You should also be aware that it is a free world and legally, in most countries, there is nothing to stop salespeople from contacting past contacts. However, their contracts may be suitably worded to make it clear that they are not allowed to abuse their situation. You are paying them to work for you, not provide valuable information to your competitors.

The other half of the job is to monitor sales and not lose touch with your customer base. Customers are usually pleased to get a call from a senior person, especially when he or she is merely checking that everything is going right with their purchase. Client information is a great way to be alerted to effective ways of selling products and working out further opportunities. Clever sales engineers rarely jump in immediately when an opening shows. They note it and think their strategy through. Talking to customers can also give you a better idea of the way sales are going generally. Are salespeople pressing too hard or not hard enough? Is the market perception of what the company is doing in step with the company's intention?

Periodic contact at various levels not only nets valuable information, it also helps to extend your company's relationship with the customer.

Sales Analysis

Sales analysis isn't rocket science, although a supportive friendly attitude and a good help system are essential. The trickiest part of the analysis is getting accurate figures. If a customer's data is held on a CRM system, the orders are taken on a Web page (intranet or otherwise) and the accounts software produces the invoices automatically. How are you going to make sure the right salesperson is credited? When a customer returns an item, will your system recalculate? Integration of key data between different systems needs careful consideration from the outset—you'll need to be able to do this just to calculate sales commissions if nothing else.

Sales analysis may appear to be something of a dark art to newcomers. Reviewing individual performances is straightforward. Individual targets should always be graded against their experience, salary, and commissions levels. These should be adjusted to encourage them to achieve higher goals and reap bigger rewards. These should not be unrealistic or unachievable. Otherwise, failure is inevitable and all you are doing is reinforcing it.

Managers who expect continuous, exponential growth from their sales team are fantasists. Sales is like surfing. There are peaks and troughs. The management trick is to motivate through the troughs and keep the peaks profitable. What you are looking for are patterns in sales achievements; you need to be able to break down customers by market group, size, geographical location, and so on. This can provide you with insights into which market it is more profitable to concentrate on.

Here's a set of questions to ask potential customers, politely, if you can:

✦ Does the requirement actually exist?

✦ Who is responsible for this purchase?

✦ Has the budget for it been agreed on?

✦ Who signs off on it (rarely the same person)?

✦ What are the key expectations?

✦ Who are the real users?

✦ Are there any likely delays?

✦ What are the key motivations for this purchase?

✦ Have dates been set for delivery and payment?

Sales Teams

The cost, complexity, and degree of explanation and customization required to make a sale determines whether you need a sales team. Whether you run the team yourself or leverage the salespeople working for your distributors and dealers, the message is the same: sales require careful managing and monitoring.

As anyone who has run sales teams will tell you, sales teams are a mixed blessing. For sophisticated software they are often the sole mechanism by which to sell the product, but salespeople by their very nature are variable. Successful, long-established operations get around this by having evolved highly selective screening processes for salespeople and then training them in exceptional detail on how to sell a particular product. Startups that don't understand the process often chuck people in the deep end expecting them to be telepathic and inspired. Such people do actually exist, but not very often. Large sales teams, like large programming teams, don't deliver the obvious economies of scale. It's better to keep them small. Four to seven salespeople per sales leader is generally considered best.

How to Spot a Potentially Good Salesperson

Good salespeople generally exhibit many of the following characteristics:

✦ Good salespeople are good company. They are buoyant, thoughtful, and sociable.

✦ Good salespeople know when to hold their tongues. They listen almost as much as they talk. This way, the prospect does nearly half the work and, in many instances, talks himself into the sale.

✦ Good salespeople sell the product you have rather than the product they would like to have.

✦ Good salespeople have a good track record.

✦ Good salespeople are organized, self-disciplined, and methodical. They can recall names, times, and appointments at will. Average ones resort to CRM systems.

✦ Good salespeople create opportunities.

✦ They are believable. They don't need to exaggerate to make a point.

✦ Good salespeople are able to sell a variety of products. They are definitely not one-trick performers.

✦ Good salespeople know their time is money. They prioritize, re-schedule, and prune by value and speed of sale.

✦ They do not hang around in bad situations.

✦ Good salespeople know a sale is only a sale when the money is in their employer's bank.

One reason why it can be hard to distinguish between a good or bad salesperson is that bad salespeople are normally very talented at selling one thing—themselves. They normally go through jobs at an alarming rate so they hone this skill through practice. Look at their list of employers. Work out how long they stayed.

Indifferent salespeople believe they don't need to prepare, and they never do more than is asked. They are also prone to gossip. They disparage the customer in front of the company and vice versa, yet they never seem to analyze themselves. They sometimes mistake opening their mouths for closing a deal. They frequently demand what commission they have earned immediately.

Good salespeople are bright and sensible people. They are adept at putting themselves in their customer's shoes and working out what are the key issues for them. They are sensibly honest. They know how to make a fair case for your product and when to back off. Good salespeople build up a good name for themselves and for you. Customers quickly learn to respect this, and fundamentally, people buy more readily from people that they like. Bear these points in mind when interviewing and add your own.

Rewards and Cautionary Tales

Creating a suitable selling environment is sometimes compared to pushing water uphill. For a sales team to work it has to be hungry, greedy, and managed. Members must be aware of the result if they achieve nothing, must salivate for the riches that come from success, and realize that the best way to achieve this is through a controlled reward structure.

Good salespeople are extraordinarily smart and learn at a phenomenal rate. Carrots come no bigger than a vested self-interest, so it is hardly surprising that salesmanship attracts powerful personalities. What they are especially adept at is articulating their own remuneration, often with an eloquence you will hear from no other segment of your organization. For everybody's sake, it is vital that you avoid this cuckoo feeding frenzy. Your firm can afford to pay its salespeople what it can afford. If that is insufficient, you just have to get the business off the ground by some other means.

If you can afford salespeople, it is essential to devise a fair incentive system that rewards the successful. Average salespeople on a fair base salary do little to justify their overhead. A good salesman will want a low basic and negotiate as high a commission rate as he can wrangle because he knows his capability. Unsuccessful salespeople live from mouth to hand. They often demand their commissions on the nail. Whereas they are very prepared to take the money, you'd have though that Krakatoa was about to erupt when you mention subtracting commission when a customer cancels his order.

A sale is not a sale in law until the money changes hands for the goods. Where commissions are paid against orders, it is not unknown for friends to invent orders so that the salesperson can collect the commission and disappear shortly afterwards. The only fair arrangement to both parties is for commissions to be paid only after the customer has paid for the goods. This encourages the salesperson to keep the sale sold. However, keep in mind that sales staff, just before they plan to leave, can get very concerned that they won't be paid for orders that are fulfilled after they depart. Their best indication is how their predecessors were treated.

When commissions are astronomic or times are hard, it's not surprising that people start squabbling over money. Anything from answering a phone call from the customer and passing it on can be grounds for claiming a cut. As previously mentioned, unscrupulous salespeople start behaving as if the customer belongs to them. Such people don't usually last long, though they often try to exploit potential customers they have met through the company at their next job. To avoid such issues taking up company time and sapping morale, it is essential to draw up and enforce rules that each salesperson must agree to with management in advance.

There are three useful ways of discouraging client piracy:

✦ Nip it in the bud. If a salesperson interviewee offers you a competitor's list as an incentive, tell him to leave then and there. If they are that unscrupulous to their current employer, how do you expect them to treat you?

✦ Make it clear and write it into their contracts of employment that sales and client information is the sole property of the company employing them and it is a criminal offense to steal it.

✦ Finally, make it very hard to download sales contact lists in any loot-worthy volume. This is perhaps the best argument for having your own sales lead researcher, preferably someone out of house who is paid by a combination of numbers and quality.

Caution   Sexism costs. It's a long-held belief that most salespeople are men. Statistically-speaking, this is correct. However, in IT, there is nothing to stop women from being equally successful. In fact, the most successful salesperson I know is a woman. She has worked at the highest level of European sales for a succession of blue chip organizations. She would typically hit her annual targets, which were not insubstantial (7 digits +), in under her first month at the job.

Training

When Tony Pontin took over as CEO of the Dymo Corporation for the United Kingdom, they had 18 salesmen and were in danger of folding. These young men (average age 22) were tasked to sell plastic alphabet guns to stationers. These guns distorted adhesive vinyl tape so they produced sticky labels. It was a great idea. Unfortunately, few people in the United Kingdom at the time were using labels. These salesmen typically gave notice at the end of three weeks.

Thanks to Tony Pontin's successor, Reg Melluish, who had been the fantastically charismatic sales manager of Remington Typewriters, Dymo was able to replace these salesmen with other youngsters of incredible quality. Tony Pontin introduced a number of changes that extended the life cycle of the sales force to nine weeks.

After 18 months of a still fraught existence, Tony Pontin took a brave step. He hired a 37-year-old (who wasn't a particularly good salesman) to train his youngsters. Initially this was on a catch-as-catch-can basis. Everyone thought Tony was mad, but learning quickly by experience, they soon developed a training system whereby every new salesman got a week's full training before he hit the road. He then had three days working in tandem with a more experienced man and three further days by himself. He then came back for three days' further training and then went out for two weeks and had a day's training refresher.

These trained salesmen soon began to make headway and being successful, they stayed. Within two years they were selling more Dymo tools and tape in the United Kingdom than the entire American sales force were in North America. Tony was promoted to senior vice president of Dymo Europe. Within 15 months Dymo Europe was accounting for more sales than the rest of the world combined.

While I could cite numerous examples of similar successes, sales training is not as widely used by software houses as it deserves to be. So plan a training course for your salespeople while the program is being developed. It is one of the few areas where resource and method can replace the need for money. Sales training takes the knowledge already within a company to create a multiplier effect. Selling techniques are long established, so you can read how other companies have turned sales around by every technique from teleselling to personal, face-to-face visits.

There are two ways to overcome initial resistance: by pulling or pushing. Push sales kick in when advertising and other marketing devices are employed to drive customers into phoning or e-mailing you, possibly by filling in a coupon expressing an interest or by circling a box in a magazine for further details or calling the phone number given in the ad. Pull selling is when you approach potential customers cold. Once a product becomes established, sales teams inevitably end up using both. Either way, you must know the following:

✦ Who the customers are likely to be

✦ The main things they will want to know

✦ The strengths and weaknesses of competition

✦ How to open a sale

✦ Typical hurdles that have to be surmounted

✦ Financing options

✦ How to close a sale

✦ What the fallback position is if the customer says "No"

Cold Calling

Universally understood products *can* be sold by cold telephone calls, but getting hold of customers is hard. Typically two in five will be busy, in meetings, anything other than able to take your call. Once you have the person on the line, providing you come across as smart, useful, and seem genuinely concerned about finding out about their business so that you can offer them something of genuine usefulness, they are often prepared to listen. Surprisingly, big-ticket items can be sold this way.

Good telephone mannerisms often come down to nothing more than treating others on the phone the way you'd like to be treated yourself: polite, informative, and not wasting other people's time. Introduce yourself quickly and cleanly and try to throw in a point of contact even at the start. "Good morning, I'm Harold Doorknob, vice president of sales at XYZ. I was speaking to your CEO last week and he suggested I have a word with you. Can you talk now?"

Put this way, your respondent will often say, "Now is as good a time as any."

If you have something interesting to say people will listen. So start off with an intriguing statement that prompts further discussion, such as "We've developed a new piece of software that may save you at least an hour a week. Knowing your workload, Charlie Topdog was wondering if you'd like to evaluate it for the company."

Don't sound too urgent. If you are really confident about the benefits, you are the one who is doing the customer a favor. The main benefit of course is the one for which your product has been specifically developed to deliver, the one succinctly described in your development plan.

It's useful at this point to have a list in front of you of the key product points so you can introduce them as the conversation develops. Different points will carry more weight with different customers so use it flexibly.

When you have achieved your target, which isn't always a one-call sale (it may be the transmission of a trial copy or an appointment to discuss the possibilities), wind the call down politely. Remember to leave a tag in the adieus so you have a valid reason for calling back. For example, you might say, "That's great. I'll make sure your software is dispatched this afternoon and I'll give you a call in about a week to make sure its working well."

If you don't overstay your time, the recipient will be more prepared to speak again. However, unless your product is a simple one, don't expect people to buy it sight unseen on the strength of a single, unsolicited phone call.

Note   It is counter-productive to call business people at home unless specifically invited. In the United States, households are beginning to employ firms to screen out unwanted calls, and the federal and some state governments are instituting no-call lists.

Software Can Do a Lot of the Donkey Work

If you are a one-person band and must be for sometime to come, you can manage your leads on spreadsheets. Otherwise, ask everyone you can what is the best CRM software out there. The trick is to know the features that will be most helpful and find the best match. A lot of CRM packages may appear overtly complex, which is odd because the task they try to perform is actually very straightforward. Once you have installed your chosen CRM package, make sure it is always used unfailingly.

Site Visits

The financial and cultural switch from using salespeople to sell via a telephone to selling in person is massive. The time, support costs, and payback escalate and can only be justified on top ticket items (> $5,000) or high-volume sales (100 x $50 upwards). These figures are highly subjective as it depends on the sales cycle of your product and the average number of visits required to convert a customer. Table 16-2 shows an example of a firm selling a $5,000 product. Look what happens to the bottom line as selling costs vary.

Table 16-2 **Bottom Line Sales**	
Aspect of Sales Cycle	*Cost*
RRP of product	$5,000
Average sales cycle of product	3 months
Average number of visits	3 (1 a month)
Cost of each visit (travel expenses, time, and so on)	$500
Cost of sale	$1,500
Salesperson's commission (30% of RRP)	$1,500
Gross profit	$2,000

So on a $5,000 sale your real profit (after production, marketing, and sales costs) may only be $2,000 (see Table 16-3). However, when you start to factor in the success rate (the number of clients you must visit to affect each successful sale) watch how evenly this profit can slide into a loss.

Table 16-3 **Profit versus Loss**				
Success Rate	*1 in 1*	*2 in 3*	*1 in 2*	*1 in 3*
Cost of product sold	$5,000	$10,000	$5,000	$5,000
Cost of visits	$1,500	$4,500	$3,000	$4,500
Salesperson's commissions	$1,500	$3,000	$1,500	$1,500
Sales profit	$2,000	$2,500	$500	–$1,000
Average profit per sale	$2,000	$833	$250	–$333

The figures obviously vary with product and company, but when you bear in mind that a good salesperson will win about half their leads and on average about one in three or four, you may appreciate how closely you have to watch results.

For low-value sales, the figures hardly add up. It's only when you make inroads into large companies and get a taste of pulling off volume deals that salespeople stand a chance of being viable, as illustrated in Table 16-4.

Table 16-4 **The Large Deal**	
Figure Work Behind Large Deal	*Cost*
Value of sale	$250,000
Average sales cycle of product	6 months
Average number of visits	12 (2 a month)
Cost of each visit (travel expenses and so on)	$500
Cost of sale	$6,000
Salesperson's commission (30% of RRP)	$60,000
Gross profit	$184,000

With large sales, a salesman may need to succeed only once in 31 times to net you a profit.

There is no rule of thumb. You have to use what facts you can establish and work out the odds for yourself. (This was discussed in Chapter 13 on pricing.)

Presentations

Contrary to what most people expect, software presentations that work best barely show the product or demonstrate it. They concentrate on dramatizing the benefits, often just including the odd establishing shot towards the end partly for the following reasons.

+ All software discs look so similar.
+ They want to show that the product exists.
+ Software houses think they are selling their product.

Customers know they are buying a solution. A good presentation is a compilation of many people's selling experiences.

Keep presentations short. Five to six minutes is ideal. Twenty minutes is absolute tops.

To Buy or Grow Your Own Contacts

Even in the good old days, when the world was stable and hardly anyone had a car or went abroad on vacation, one contact in six vanished every two years. They moved, died, emigrated, got hospitalized, or whatever. Most of the lists were sold by mail order houses on the principle of used cars: while they were still capable of some mileage.

Things haven't gotten better. Cheap lists have a significant proportion of out-dated companies, contacts, and phone numbers. In addition, their poor unsuspecting listees will have been punished by many other uninvited mail order firms.

Lists that claim to be carefully screened come at a premium, sometimes costing 10 or 20 times more than cheaper counterparts. In a good list, almost all the contacts will exist (sellers will normally give you a guarantee as to the efficacy of the list). Furthermore, all the people on the lists will have been contacted, typically within the last three months.

The most reliable lists are those you build up in-house from the following excellent sources:

✦ Previous customers

✦ Respondents to ads

✦ Competition entrants

✦ Tradeshow visitors

✦ Logged telephone inquirers

✦ E-mail newsletters subscribers

However, the combined numbers from all such sources are rarely sufficient.

Sometimes salespeople are good at building up their own additions. More frequently, this is a task for someone else who is particularly good on the phone, but they have to have terrier-like tenacity. Building up a list requires intelligence and patience, takes time, and costs money. Most people find it tiring. Because of the high run-off of energy, some can only cope with it in 30-minute stretches.

Telephoning is a great way to let respondents know that your program exists, particularly if you use the opportunity to simply whet their appetite and refrain from any attempt at selling.

Customers Who Give Themselves Up

When people up and ask (or almost ask) for the product, your firm's principal need isn't for a salesperson; it's for an order taker. Sales departments often exert pressure on management to route all such orders through them. There is only one reason for this—money. Once they touch the client they have a genuine claim to a commission from any resulting sale.

Ironically, customers that contact you directly have been 100 percent sold on your product. Once such imminent sales are re-directed, conversions drop noticeably. Salespeople don't handle such inquiries that fall into their laps as positively as those they have generated themselves. Customers sense this and hesitate. The best thing you can do with an unsolicited order is to accept the order gracefully and process it immediately. Gather additional details casually if you can. Three or four weeks after they have received the goods, pass the details to the most suitable member of the sales team who can find out how they are getting on and begin building a regular relationship.

Big Leads

When leads from big companies fall out of the sky, you need to know which ones are dead ducks and which ones are gold. Discerning is not always easy.

Leads from large corporations sound impressive but are they expressing a genuine interest in your product? Or are they checking the value you offer against an existing supplier? Or is some minion in a big firm simply filling time?

When big numbers are intimated, even the best salespeople can find it difficult to draw basic information out of the buyer's man who is suddenly curiously shy. Trying to combine selling and fact finding in a single call is rarely productive if the prospect is being coy. The best solution is to split the process and find out everything you can about the lead before you arrange a time to open the sale. Small companies are usually more frank about what they are doing, but your ability to win additional or repeat orders is low.

With any lead, large or small, you need to get a feeling of the situation. Establish the following:

+ Level of person you are dealing with
+ What they are ideally looking for
+ When they expect delivery (this can be telling)
+ Who makes the purchasing decision
+ Delivery and contact addresses
+ The value of their order and their payment policy (some expect four to six months' credit)

Be guarded. Don't give large firms anything you wouldn't give a small one. They are quite capable of wearing you down.

Monitoring Sales

Just as market research helps you focus the product during development you must continue this process after launch. Ask yourself the following questions:

✦ What are people buying (if you have a range of products) and why?

✦ Which features persuaded them to buy?

✦ How critical was the price?

✦ What other products did they consider?

✦ How did they find out about yours?

✦ Very importantly, how long was it between the time they started looking and the time they signed the check?

Prioritizing Prospects

Prioritizing prospects is second nature to good salespeople. They do it without thinking, but you are going to need the same self-discipline from everybody. There have to be some company measuring sticks. The potential volume of business is an obvious criterion. However, you may have a cash flow crisis looming and need to convert the easy orders as soon as possible. At the other extreme, a new product release might be on the horizon. The priority then is to build up leads before the launch and not to press for immediate sales. Controlling prospects can be done with the same finesse that you apply to the accelerator pedal in an automobile.

To ensure your team prioritizes leads in the way the company needs, it's best for the person in charge of sales to spell out the company policy and go through leads with each salesperson individually, either at the weekly sales meeting or privately. It's a hard decision, whatever the size of the firm, to decide between chasing a $250,000 lead from a government department that might take six months to get through the door or another 20 to sign off against a $10,000 lead for a two-week delivery from a small firm that is unlikely to provide any repeat order for years. In practice, you try to pursue both, but the prioritizing will determine in which one you invest the bulk of your time. Sometimes cash flow will dictate the option you have to choose.

Having taken the right steps, you at least have the comfort of knowing that you have tried to make optimum use of everyone's time.

Selling through Other People's Teams

Firms with vestigial or non-existent sales teams often delegate selling to their dealers and distributors' salespeople. While this appears to sidestep the immediate problem, it comes at a cost. The most obvious is lack of overall control. Outside sales forces have their own profile of contacts, which may or may not dovetail with yours. They also take time to influence, encourage, and assess.

For an outside team to be able to extend your operation, your communication strategy has to be thought through systemically so as much as possible is made easy. Remember, there are dozens of other manufacturers who are also vying for their time and attention. Never expect that because a dealer agrees to get his salespeople to sell your product, they will devote 100 percent of their time to this task.

You will need to furnish an outside sales force with the following:

- ✦ Sample products
- ✦ A demonstration
- ✦ Documents explaining the product and its features
- ✦ A rundown on competitive products
- ✦ A sample selling letter
- ✦ A sample telephone spiel
- ✦ Product literature
- ✦ Reprints of product reviews

But how do you train the dealers? One popular way is to hold an open day. Another is to visit individual salespeople. Unless you are the market leader, the chances of a dealer sending his staff to you for a day is low. A better bet is to run a seminar at the major distributor's product showcases. Most hold these two to four times a year.

Visiting the dealers individually is a strong way of winning their commitment. It enables you to see for yourself that your software is correctly installed, and to take their sales teams through a typical demonstration and answer all their questions. You can discuss their prospective leads and explain which features might be of most interest to different types of contacts.

In practice, a salesman would be fortunate to visit more than three dealers a day in an urban area or two adjacent counties. For this reason alone, you may still be better off working indirectly than employing any salespeople. Dealers have swathes of customers that they have worked with for years. They know instinctively which products are appropriate.

To start things rolling, some software houses fund a bulk mailing to their most promising customers. If you take this approach you must stay in regular communication with the dealer to monitor your progress and help them with their problems. Dealers have short attention spans. Nothing holds their attention longer than success. If they spend time periodically to sell your product and nothing happens, they will soon give up and find more profitable lines to promote. Conversely, there is nothing like quick early sales to encourage them.

The Customer Relationships

The moment a prospect signs the sales order that makes him a customer, a bad sales-person will scamper faster than a rat down an aqueduct. Good salespeople hang around. Why? Politeness, certainly, but a good salesperson is also making sure the customer stays and won't suddenly come to his senses and cancel the order. A good salesperson makes sure the customer feels good about his buying decision. A good salesperson will want his customer to continue to feel good, so he will want to repeat the process.

As the post-sales conversation goes to and fro, a good salesperson begins to form an opinion about whether his customer would benefit from training, support, or a little consultancy. What the salesperson is doing is building trust. This alone will make it easier for him to sell the next product and for his customer to buy it.

With low-cost products, this dialogue goes via e-mails, newsletters, and news of forth-coming special offers. With high-ticket items it takes the form of visits, lunches, and invitations to prominent sporting events. All of these techniques are keeping the prospect warm and keeping your company and your product constantly in mind.

Building the Customer Dynamic

Just because a customer has given you an order doesn't automatically mean they become your best buddy. Some people you naturally warm to more readily than others, but most people soften when someone sympathetic offers help. It just takes some customers longer.

Once the initial sale has broken the ice, begin to develop the relationship. A frater-nal approach often works best, concerned but not invasive. Check that they're get-ting along okay—has the software installed easily, are they up and running, has customer support been helpful? Stay in contact and be approachable at all times. Let them know they always have a receptive ear to contact.

As your customers get to know your product, you need to get to know them. The more you know about them the easier it is to see where other opportunities lie. Being able to converse with customers, almost as if you were a member of their staff, makes their making the right decision much easier for them. Your range of products won't suit everyone, so don't try and sell it where it is bound to fall short. Salespeople who withdraw their product because it isn't suitable have an enormous amount going for them when they come back with a product that does fit.

In IT you'll often find the customer base is valued in takeover situations more than the products your company delivers.

Web-Based Selling

Your Web site is the common font of selling information that all software companies use. It is the fastest, most secure monetarily, and cheapest way to sell. Succeed here and you succeed. Fail and you fail. Period.

This section isn't about how to design or structure your site; only you know your business. What it offers is a master checklist to ensure that prospects have a better chance of reaching it.

This is such an important issue that I separate it from other modes of selling. I have gathered together the essential checklist of Web site content and Search Engine optimization to ensure your site is comprehensive, legal, and highly findable.

You can't make a sale if no one knows your product. The first step to getting a sale is to spread the word. How are you going to make this happen? Inanimate products such as washing powders use staggering amounts of advertising expenditure to push the customer towards the sale. How are you with a comparatively negligible budget going to be making the world aware that you are there? The obvious answer is to utilize a Web site on the Internet. Unfortunately, there are millions and millions of Web sites. How will you ever get noticed? The first step is to find out what everyone else is doing. Make a list of your favorite Web sites. Chances are, they all have one thing in common—they allow you to find what you want easily (it's a good idea to add such sites to a favorites list for future reference). Nothing is worse than for willing customers to visit your site to purchase and be unable to do so, or than when a search engine says some information is on your site when it patently isn't.

Now Find Out What You Need to Say

Irrespective of the goods you are describing and online methods of selling them, your site should contain the following information and navigation:

- ✦ Home button
- ✦ Copyright statement
- ✦ Full contact details
- ✦ Legal statement
- ✦ Privacy statements

The following are also useful depending on the complexity of your site:

- ✦ Terms of use
- ✦ Search facility

Home Button

Web sites take on a life of their own. What starts off as five or six pages ends up in no time being 50 or 60. It makes it so much easier for a user to navigate around the site if there is a simple Home button on every page that will transport them back to page one.

Contact Details

There seems to be a growing tendency for large Web sites to omit contact details or to make them hard to find. Full contact information is essential for some customers. A large, international charity, for instance, might wish to place an order with you but can only do so with a written purchase order. With no contact details and being unable to use credit cards, what do they do? They go elsewhere.

You should always include the following contact details:

✦ Company name, full address, and postal/zip code

✦ E-mail address (possibly a special one for your Web site so you know the inquiry origin)

✦ Phone and fax numbers (if available)

✦ Some sites include company banking details—account number and name, bank, location, and sort code to help people wiring money through

What does need consideration is whether you release telephone numbers if you don't have the staff to deal with calls. Large organizations list various contacts so that callers can work out for themselves the best person to contact.

Copyright and Legal Statements

Theoretically, anything you originate is your copyright as a right. In practice, if you forget to put the copyright symbol on your Web site, anyone can pilfer your contents with impunity. To protect the site, it is important not only to display the copyright on all pages, but also to do so correctly.

The correct format is: © Edward.S.Hasted 2002-2005.

List the copyright symbol, company/person, and years in which it was first applied. The copyright symbol can be hard to enter in some processors (try using Alt-0169). If that fails, you can use the long form with brackets: (c) Copyright E.S.Hasted 2002-5.

The easiest way of making sure the copyright statement appears on all pages is to include it as part of the common index/header or footer of the page.

Legal Statement

If you do not complete your Web site's legal page you leave yourself wide open to being sued for software being unfit, products being copied, and so on. The legal page protects you, so state the following on your Web site:

✦ **Terms and conditions**—The terms and conditions under which you make the information on your site available.

✦ **Copyright**—Restate the copyright notice.

✦ **Trademarks**—List all your registered and common law trademarks. Remember to include any third-party trademarks, if relevant.

✦ **Use of software**—Stipulate the terms and conditions attached to software and documentation that can be downloaded from the site.

✦ **Use of information on the site**—Again, spell out the agreement under which information from the site can be used, copied, and disseminated.

✦ **Warranties and disclaimers, limitations of liabilities**—Restate these as for the software.

✦ **Product and service availability**—Unless you are providing worldwide roll out, make it clear that just because something is announced on the site doesn't necessarily mean that it is available in every country.

✦ **Submissions**—Explain how you store credit card information securely, the implications of sending unsolicited ideas, and that you won't knowingly tolerate libelous, obscene, or pornographic transmissions.

✦ **Linking to your Web site**—Spell out your procedure and terms for people to link to your Web site.

✦ **Governing law and jurisdiction state**—The laws and jurisdiction under which cases shall be processed should also be asserted, as appropriate (for example, the United States District Court of North America or the English Courts).

You may need to include export control laws if any of your products fall into that category and any government/citizen's rights that need to be stated for your particular jurisdiction.

If you've never done this before it will seem like a mouthful. Luckily, you only have to do it once. My advice is look at the content of similar companies that operate in your state/country and check the points they cover. Build up your own master list of what you feel is relevant. Then pass your compilation to the company lawyer, or a friend with legal training, to make sure it's all present and correct.

Cross-Reference   For more information about this, refer back to Chapter 10.

Privacy Statements

These are becoming increasingly common. What they state is what information you store about people who use your site, what information you might store in cookies on their PCs, and what you do with such information. Issues to cover include the following:

✦ Statement of intent—Information you gather and track

✦ Information on visitors and how you use that information

✦ Who you share it with

✦ Customers options/opt outs

✦ Security of information

✦ Cookies—What they are, and how to find and control your cookies with your browser

✦ Web site traffic

✦ Links to partner sites

✦ Other privacy considerations

✦ Policy changes

✦ Access to your private information

✦ Contact information regarding privacy issues

Again, I recommend taking a similar approach to the Legal page. It only has to be written once. Look at other relevant sites and get a consensus of the points they address. Then add additional issues for your products and company. It makes sense for whoever is reviewing the legal content of this page to go through it at the same time they review the Legal page, as between them they need to cover all eventualities.

Terms of Use

This one is a hard call. Some sites have a separate section for this. Others call their Legal section "Terms of Use" to sound less litigious. The important thing is to make sure that terms of use are clearly spelled out wherever you place them.

Search Facilities

Search facilities are not essential. However, if your site is going to contain information about masses of products or certain third-party products that run in conjunction with your product are sited elsewhere, a search facility is essential if customers are to find and use the most suitable product.

Note   If your site is simple enough to be able to hand index, it almost certainly doesn't need indexing in the first place.

Secure Transactions

Whenever you are requesting confidential information from customers, such as credit card details, your Web pages must be secure. Many customers, very sensibly, won't provide such information unless they see their browser display the lock/key icons at the bottom of the screen to reassure them that they are on a secure page.

A security key may be already embedded in your Web site or it may have to be purchased separately. If you are using a third party to process your credit card transactions, liaise with them and ensure your transactions are secure.

This procedure may seem a little torturous the first time. It's often advisable to get a friend to help you who knows the ropes.

A secure Web page encrypts the data to and from the page to a secure server. This means the transmitted information can't be intercepted and decoded. Secure Web pages start with HTTPS:// where the S stands for Secure. Secure Web pages should be stored in a separate folder within your Web site (such as https://mydoamin.com/secure/orderfrom.html). Note that the www prefix has been dropped.

Search Engines

This is the big catch-22. If no one knows your site exists, how will they find it? There are billions of Web pages on the Web. How do people locate the page they want? They use a search engine. These are IT's computerized equivalent of the Yellow Pages. Eighty-five percent of all users who discover new sites do so by using search engines—they are that important.

A search engine is made up of three parts:

+ The first automatically spiders or crawls along the Web looking for new or updated pages. It then reads each page and analyzes its content and ranks it. If there are any links on that page, it will follow them.

+ An indexer keeps a copy of each new or modified page the spider accepts.

+ The actual search engine software is what users use on the Web to enter and download their searches. As you may imagine, search engines are among the largest databases on the planet, as they are keeping a copy of the Web.

Just to keep you on your toes, every search engine works in a fractionally different way. Fundamentally there are two types: Search Engines and Search Directories. Engines such as Lycos do the indexing automatically with material supplied by the spiders. Directories such as Yahoo! have a team of human beings who vet the information prior to inclusion.

Processing Electronic Orders

The process of handling orders that come via the Web is the same, regardless of the quantity. The cost of processing Web-based orders is small.

To prove the theory can work in practice, take a look at RS Components. Started in 1937 selling radio spares (hence the name), they now carry an inventory of over 300,000 products that businesses need—literally anything from a switch to a safety shoe. What is more, they process over 35,000 orders worldwide taken by telephone, fax, over the counter, and on the Web every day. Each order has on average over four different items. They ship these to customers in 160 countries from 24 strategically located distribution centers around the planet. Virtually 100 percent of orders received by 8pm are shipped the same day, and a staggering 99 percent of products are held in stock at any one time. Their returns rates are close to zero because their distribution system is almost failsafe and the product quality is high, so the chance of defective goods is low. They calculate that a return takes three to four times as much to process as the original order. Several well-known online retailers have run at significantly higher rates.

To have people come back again and again for items purchased on the Web, you must set exemplary standards of efficiency. For example, up to 5 p.m., all orders should be dispatched the same day. All sales queries should be acknowledged and, if possible, replied to within 60 minutes by e-mail, telephone, or fax.

Make particularly sure you do the following:

+ Have taken down the order correctly and that you have complete dispatch and billing addresses
+ Dispatch the right goods promptly
+ Deliver prompt and pleasurable service to the client

If you do these three things well, you have opened the way for future communications and sales. When you send the goods, there is an opportunity to include information and other offers that may be useful to your customers.

As soon as you receive an order you should acknowledge it with a confirmation by e-mail (immediately preferably). The acknowledgment should include the following:

+ Confirmation of the goods ordered
+ An optional dispatch note
+ Invoice
+ Newsletter
+ Promotional offers

The only difference between ordinary orders and those from the Web is that in the latter case all the goods and confirmations are electronic and dispatched by e-mail.

Dealing with Delays and Returns

You can't always ship an order the same day. The accounts system might be down, or you might need to wait for the customer's check to clear or a newer version to be released. Whatever the reason, e-mail the customer to let them know and specify when they will receive it. If you don't know, tell them so. If you can, tell them why, and tell them that you will contact them the moment you have more information.

Outstanding orders should be monitored particularly carefully; otherwise, they can be forgotten. Remember only to deduct the cost from the customers' credit card on the day of dispatch.

The returns policy that will win you the most respect is to have what appears to be a "no questions asked" policy. To the customer, you come across as a more than reasonable (and confident) firm. In practice, you scrutinize every return transaction.

If the customer pays by credit card, they are legally allowed to return the goods within 30 days. Unlike with physical goods, what is to stop the customer from opening the software pack, installing the goods, copying them, and then returning them so they end up getting the product for free? As a result, software is rarely sanctioned for return if the package has been opened. Wherever possible, embed records that log the date and time whenever a copy is made.

A reasonable return policy might be as follows:

✦ Goods may be returned on a bona fide basis within 30 days.

✦ The packaging, literature, and so on must be in good condition.

✦ The purchaser must be able to prove that the goods have not been opened or installed.

✦ If incorrect goods have inadvertently been sent, your firm will refund the return postage.

✦   ✦   ✦

How to Keep Customers

A program without support is like a table top without legs. Responsibility for your program doesn't end when the customer buys it. The way you support your program is the only means by which customers can measure your commitment after they have handed over their money.

Apart from helping those who have put their trust in you, support is a fantastic way of building goodwill, finding out how clients are using your program, getting suggestions for improvements, and helping you make up your mind about priorities.

Well-handled support leaves clients with a strong, positive view of the program and its company. Support really does matter.

What Support Can Do for You

You should ensure that the support you offer is set up to accomplish the following:

- ✦ Help new customers install your product and get it working
- ✦ Help customers to make the best use of the program
- ✦ Tell you what customers want future releases to do
- ✦ Give you information you might not otherwise get
- ✦ Create an opportunity for you to make further sales

The Price of Perfection

No one ever says anything openly, but we've all seen managers wince when the subject of support costs come up. They equate the size of this budget with their programmers' failure. Yet the truth is, as any of the companies producing familiar brands (such as Procter & Gamble and the cola companies) will confirm, there is no such thing as a perfect product (each will readily cite their competitors as proof). And some of them have been producing the same product for over a century.

Trying to fine-tune your program until it is perfect, the costs will become infinite and you'll miss the market. In reality, products are ready for market when the benefits outweigh their cost, and support is a benefit every buyer expects of every product. It is a measure of achievement, not failure. Support is your means to the end.

How Customers Think

Contrary to popular belief among embattled support men, people do not call the support line because they are lonely or have nothing better to do. Most of your clients are people not unlike you. They will try everything they can, within reason, to get their program working. They see this as a challenge. They want to get on with their work as quickly as possible. They will normally only contact a support team as a last resort.

So when you start to plan the kind of support that you will offer, think how you would like to be treated yourself. Think what your colleagues and friends like and dislike about the support services they have to use. Consider the following questions:

- ✦ Do you have an aversion to automated voices?
- ✦ Do you dislike having to choose from multiple options by pressing the corresponding number on your phone?
- ✦ Do you dislike having to hold on for more than five minutes?
- ✦ Is the music playing while you wait inappropriate?
- ✦ When you eventually get through to the right specialist, is the advisor only semi trained?

Don't think what you can or can't afford. Write down a full wish list to start with. Then consider the practical options.

Your Options

Your support service may range from doing nothing to personal on-site visits. Ultimately, you have to select the modes that best serve your aims.

Inevitably the answer will be a compromise between what you can afford to give and what you have to gain. If your operation is like most software houses, your support service will cluster along the scale in Figure 17-1.

None	Help	E-Mail	Newsgroup	Web	Phone	On-Site

Figure 17-1: Support service scale.

The subsections that follow further explain each option on the scale.

None

Even a child knows how to use a can opener. It is simple and has a single purpose. It doesn't need 24-hour support. Even the most basic computer program by contrast is far more complex.

Take a tip from the software equivalent of the can opener, PKZip (the universally used file compression/decompression software). Even they supply the program with comprehensive help both built-in and online.

None is a theoretical option but not a practical choice.

Help

The first place any customer looks for guidance is in the program's own built-in Help section, or failing that, the manual or other documentation that came with the program. Not only are these the fastest and most convenient means of solving your customer's problems, but they are also the fastest and cheapest means for you. Every problem solved this way is a phone call or e-mail that you don't have to answer.

As mentioned in Chapter 10, you need to plan the Help section as thoroughly as you plan the rest of the project. To work, it needs to cover everything. It needs to be keyed to search words that customers use habitually in their trade or calling, not words the programmer suspects might be appropriate. A good Help system describes how the program tackles tasks and provides a separate guide of function.

Printed documentation is particularly useful where explanations are inescapably complex and where purchasers may experience problems getting the program started the first time.

E-mail

All professional software firms have a dedicated and obvious e-mail address for support along the lines of *support@yourdomainname.com*. This is essential for people who need to contact you during or after business hours. In theory, this electronic address has a resident who has to examine his post at reasonably regular intervals. In practice, many otherwise successful software firms set up an e-mail address and then promptly never check it.

Note   The one pitfall to having an e-mail address is that it opens you to bombardment from cranks. It doesn't happen very often, but you should think carefully about how and to whom you will give your e-mail address.

The main problem with e-mail is that each query needs an individual response. If you happen to be dealing with sensitive personal issues such as finances or health, e-mails are ideal, even essential. However, if most of the problems raised are generic, e-mail is usually inefficient, although you can cut and paste prepared replies if you get repeat questions.

If you install an e-mail channel, make sure your support replies really do give support. They need to be clear, comprehensive, and polite. The aim is to deal with each question completely in one reply, not incite a correspondence.

Newsgroups

By far the most efficient, cost-effective, and least onerous vehicle for supporting most software is via newsgroups.

Newsgroups are public discussion areas on the Internet, dedicated to a specific subject, in your case, your program. Access is now universal via the Web, e-mail, or dedicated programs. Subscribers post messages there and every other subscriber can see them. Your support team reads the messages and injects replies as necessary.

Newsgroups are ideally suited to supporting technical products that have mechanical problems that can be answered tangibly (for example, *Which update must I be on for this program to work?*). They are less suitable for answering subjective questions, such as which shade of gray is the most suitable background for cloud shots. This is because, in practice, clients will answer other clients' questions, as well. With open-ended questions, every subscriber will have his own opinion. However, with specific questions, end users really can help each other. You end up with a support team far more numerous than the one you employ. For example, Internet software that I developed in the 1990s had a formal support team of five, but we ended up with several thousand helpers. This slashed the response time dramatically and meant that very few questions were unanswered at the end of a day. The support team double-checked all answers and clarified points if required.

Newsgrouping doesn't mean the support staff does less. It simply enables them to achieve more, including giving more time to the trickier questions. Newsgroups also have an advantage in being self-logging.

Newsgroups remain a surprisingly underused Internet gem, so be prepared to educate your customers on how to use your newsgroup if you set one up.

Web Sites

Web sites are currently the first port of call for anyone looking for help. The golden rule is to make sure you have a help icon displayed prominently on the home page. Break support down into products and categories, questions and answers as much as you can. Finally, list the other forms of support you offer, how to reach them, and state the hours of operation. Clients will try to make the most sensible use of this. The more effort you put into the Web site, the fewer calls you will get.

Telephone and Video Telephone

Support is particularly useful to users who have no real knowledge of computing and need to speak to someone who can explain how to escape their predicament in plain language.

Tip

It is common to record telephone support (they always say for "training purposes"), but if you do, remember that in some countries it is legally necessary to make customers aware that you are doing so.

In time, it is likely that video will enter the help equation, allowing support staff to see what is on the customer's screen and prompt them through corrective steps. Until then, the needs for a good telephone help line are the same as for other help media.

✦ Widely publicize your Help hours.

✦ Don't keep the customer waiting longer than three minutes.

✦ Have the answer (or find out and phone them back).

✦ Be polite regardless of the provocation.

✦ Have good search systems on your side.

Site Visits

When everything else fails, a site visit is the ultimate course of action before going back to the drawing board. As a rule, site visits are only viable when the clients are relatively close. A two-hour call to a customer's premises 80 miles away will effectively take the better part of a day. If you do go, make sure you take with you everything you will possibly need.

Whether or not you visit clients regularly, it is a good idea to keep a complete duplicate software/help kit in your car. It saves last-minute fussing looking for that vital missing manual or screwdriver.

Clients really appreciate their supplier going the extra mile, providing of course you sort out the issue. Visits are also first-class opportunities to find out first hand what customers like and dislike about your program and what they'd like to see in a future version. They can also provide a natural opportunity to lay the groundwork for further sales.

Scheduling Support

Whether you are a one-man band or a million-dollar monolith, the key to acceptable support is regularity. Clients are happier when they know when they can reach you.

Organizing support effectively leaves you free to proceed with other tasks with minimum disruption. Make it very clear in manuals, packaging, and on the Web site when and how support is given. If you don't do this, interruptions will continually cut into your work time.

Note   When providing support nationally or internationally, remember to state your time zone.

Costs

Even though keeping your customers happy is vital, it comes at a cost, as Table 17-1 shows, where 0 = Nothing, $ = Low, $$ = Medium, $$$ = High.

Table 17-1 Support Cost Comparison						
Item	**None**	**E-mail**	**Newsgroup**	**Web**	**Phone**	**On-Site**
Cost	0	$	$	$	$$	$$$
Personnel	0	$	$	$	$$$	$$$

Realistically, the most effective combination of support for most software programs includes the following:

✦ A comprehensive built-in Help program

✦ A scheduled e-mail and newsgroup

✦ A Web site constantly updated with development issues

✦ Telephone support where appropriate

✦ Site visits reserved for fact-finding or sensitive or valuable installations

Support Staff

The following subsections explore the many factors you must consider when building your actual support team.

When Should You Switch On Support?

Once you have planned your menu of support, don't wait until you launch the product before you shop for your support team. Bring support to life when you start beta testing. This way, you can train your personnel and fine-tune the operation and have all the procedures and frequently asked questions (FAQs) smoothly in place when the product goes live.

What to Look for When Choosing Support Personnel

Good support staff come in all ages, genders, and sizes. Yet they have certain qualities in common. They are good listeners. They know their product inside and out. They are sensitive to the caller's situations. They can pick problems apart and communicate solutions in several different ways (customers are not all homogeneous). They respect the caller. Good support staff don't kick callers off the line the second they are finished but ask if there is anything else the caller wants to go over.

Good support requires a rare breed of personnel. They are much like every student's ideal teacher, people who are interested in other people's problems and can talk them through their issues, and people who derive satisfaction from helping others. These people don't necessarily cost big bucks but they must be properly trained and motivated.

When to Buy in Your Support Service

There is an accelerating trend for software houses to purchase support services from third-party providers. The success of these third-party operations is presently mixed. For programs that generate a limited number of simple problems, using outside support can work. However, remember these organizations are in business to make money by keeping their own costs low. You will never get more than you pay for.

If your product is sophisticated and the pleas for help are varied, you're better off keeping support in-house for the time being.

Training Support Staff

Support staff who can't help your customers can't help you. They cost money. They take up valuable square footage. They annoy customers with limp or plainly wrong answers. At the same time, you can't expect these people to know every detail of something you've been keeping secret. You have to find a routine way of training them.

I was called in to run the operations side of a Web hosting firm a few years back. The powers that be wouldn't let me train their support staff. The guys came in at nine, picked up the phone, drank coffee and ate lunch at their desks, and left when it was time to go home. They did their best by the seat of their pants, but calls took distinctly longer than they should and turnover among the support team was high.

With a new product, you have to find the best way by trial and error. By the time your product is established, you should have an embryonic training course in place. The training syllabus should include the following:

+ An understanding of how and why customers will use the program.

+ Some software houses have all applicants sit in on the support room assimilating what is going on so they get an idea of the issues that concern customers before they join the company.

+ A thorough acquaintance with the program.

+ Be familiar with the FAQs, answers, and reasons. If you sit beside a programmer answering users' questions in an alpha test, you will soon realize that the bulk of user questions boil down to a limited set of answers. It's the old 80/20 rule. Keep a record of these. Work your way towards the clearest most satisfying answer for each. Rank questions in order of frequency.

+ Be able to explain other forms of support to customers and teach them how to use those alternatives. Make sure that classic answers to FAQs are repeated in the program manual, in the Help program, and on the Web site so users can help themselves.

+ New staff members should take dummy runs with other staff members before they are let loose on customers.

+ Administer an examination of their knowledge and skills before they take the help seat.

One technique used to shorten the learning process for support staff is to recruit respondents who shine in their newsgroup replies. Give priority to those who clearly know the product well, live locally, and want a job.

How to Deal with Mr. and Mrs. Angry

Every so often you will come across a client from hell who will decide to pick on you. No matter how Teflon coated your product is, they will accuse you of all the failings of other programs, of wasting their time, and unless you sort it out in two shakes of a gnat's whisker they will telephone the boss personally and get you fired then and there.

You will know from the tone of the voice when you have this kind of person on the other end of the line. It's their frustration they are giving vent to, not yours. Do what you would do with any customer. Introduce yourself, and be polite and reasonable. Get them to explain the problem from the start. This will take them time, exhaust them a little, and give you a chance to gather as many facts as you can. Make it clear that you want to get their problem solved. Get it right and these customers will become your staunchest ally. People like this don't just pick on you; they pick on everyone. So if they go around saying that yours is the only software manufacturer with decent support, others will listen.

Unacceptable Language or Behavior

If a customer is rude to you or your staff consider the following approach:

1. Don't take it personally.

2. Ask the customer to stop.

3. If they persist, explain that you are going to cut the support call off and ask them to call back in 30 minutes when they've had time to calm down.

4. If you think the nature and severity of the outburst warrants another voice at your end, ask them to call your supervisor.

5. Log what has happened. Inform your supervisor.

6. Take a short break. Such incidents can be emotionally draining.

7. Get back to work.

Similarly, if an abusive message appears on your newsgroup, withdraw it immediately. Most times, users will flame it down. However, it is your newsgroup; you are the moderator. You must take decisive action. Unmoderated newsgroups are potential anarchy.

Escalating Problems

Some problems can't be resolved by support staff immediately. The problem may be a new one. The staff may not know the answer. If you find yourself in this situation, take the following action:

1. Go over the problem with the caller to make sure you have grasped it correctly.

2. If you can't solve their problem, be honest and tell them.

3. Explain that you know the person who can and you will go and see them and call them back.

4. If you can, give your caller some idea of how long this might take.

5. Make sure you have the customer's name, work designation, and contact details.

Never invent an answer in this situation. If you think you are correct, you may say, "I think I know what the answer is, but I am going to make sure for you." Go and discuss the problem with your colleagues. One of them may have already been through the same hoop. At all stages be clear, coherent, and honest. Go back to the customer on or before the agreed time, even if you haven't got the answer.

Keep Your Programmers in the Loop

You can't, and indeed you don't want to, isolate your programmers from the real world. On the other hand, if you want your software developed on schedule, you don't want them to be constantly interrupted. Yet it is important they see for themselves the sort of problems that are coming in. It is the only way they may realize there are problems they haven't anticipated. The realization alone can alert them to working on it from a different angle and enable them to revise their coding so the problem doesn't occur.

There are times when the support team can only resolve their customer's problem by talking it through with the programmers. The best way to balance all these requirements is to agree on discussion times in advance. When programmers and support staff do get together, support personnel should have the call information on hand.

In my experience, programmers are not only willing and concerned to see problems that are brought to their attention, but are invariably already aware of the problem's existence and wrestling with the cure.

Measuring Support

Unless you measure the support you provide, you will have no idea of how effective it is. The barometer equivalent for software support is usually as follows:

+ Number of calls

+ Maximum wait time

+ Average length of call

+ Type of call (categorized as you need)

✦ Success rate on first call

✦ Percentage of subsequent calls

✦ Support staff per customer/user/new user

Unless the only support you offer is via a newsgroup, the only way you will be able to measure the efficiency of your support is by logging all calls so that issues emerging can be taken up by other departments. Logs are also necessary where support staff work in shifts or stand in for each other over holidays and illness. Drawing attention to the need for logging is not an invitation to insatiable bureaucracy. Don't implement anything more complex than strictly functional requirements dictate.

Categorize the calls you receive; you will have to make your own rules. The suggestions in Table 17-2 are offered as a guide.

Table 17-2	
Call Categorization	
Level of Importance	*Description*
Trivial	Existing FAQ, misunderstanding, or handholding
Medium	Technical issue that takes time to resolve
Serious	Bug, omission, or inaccuracy in help or documentation

It is often an eye opener to demonstrate the support load by plotting the numbers of support calls against time for any given product graphically.

Charging for Support

It is ironic that the cheaper the product, the harder it is to charge for support, yet customers take it as law that they will pay thousands of dollars for a maintenance program on a million-dollar software suite. If you are going to employ staff to support your program, the cost of their support either has to be built into the software or charged separately.

Consider carefully how you will charge your customers. If customers don't get the program installed they will return the program, bad-mouth the product, and shovel shame on the company. It's a lose-lose situation. If software support is required before the program is working properly, provide it for free. If customers ask for the company's expertise to provide additional benefits after the program is working, the company is in a position to charge.

Take Note

In the 1980s PCs were new and technical; support was vital for questions that are now grist for *The Weakest Link*. Without the manufacturer's support, every dealer had a lot of disgruntled customers on the telephone.

When the support became farcical, sales dropped, dealers complained, and emergency action was taken to beef up the support department. Two years later they had a large team of first-rate people. Support calls were answered almost immediately. The quality of effective responses was over 90 percent. However, this was achieved at a price. Costs by this time were stratospheric. In marched the bean counters and took a scythe to the bulk of the operation. Much of the support staff either wound up in some other part of the firm or were let go (often straight into the hands of competitors). The remainder were overworked (and often followed their former coworkers to competitors). Then sales fell. Dealers complained. Support oscillated between brilliant and rubbish.

Support wasn't managed consistently. In more than one case, what could have been a brilliant international corporation became an abandoned brand. Hardly anyone remembers Apricot today.

There are only a certain number of ways you can levy a charge.

+ You can build support into the software price.
+ You can offer free support for the first so many days after registration.
+ You can offer help on a premium rate telephone number.
+ You can make a flat charge per issue.
+ You can offer an annual maintenance contract.

Ultimately, the tariff or tariffs you choose may be dictated by what perceived competitors charge. You may of course turn this to your advantage by providing something better. It's your call.

If you or your staff have to make a site visit, it is not unreasonable to charge for travel expenses and time. Agree with the client on a rate in advance and get confirmation in writing (fax is fine) in case they query it afterwards.

Making the Customer Feel Good

Support isn't just about fixing the problem. It's about making the customer feel warm towards the product and its developer. If at the end of a support call all your staff has communicated is a technical solution, you have missed an opportunity.

However, keep in mind that no matter how strong the support you provide for your product, its quality and competitiveness is critical. Before 1990, everyone using a word processor was familiar with WordPerfect, which was synonymous with DOS word processing. WordPerfect held 56 percent of the entire world market. Apart from a very comprehensive product, WordPerfect support was legendary with its toll-free numbers and really helpful staff. WordPerfect had a large team of knowledge-able and enlightened people who could talk you through any issue you couldn't iron out yourself. When Microsoft introduced Word for Windows in 1991, WordPerfect thought their phenomenal support record would carry them over until their Windows version came on line (16 months later). It certainly delayed the decline, but the reality was that a weaker product was released too late and by then the market had swung over. The moral is: Consider your support as part and parcel of your overall strategy.

Using Feedback

The positive side of a complaint is that you can learn from it, and if you don't, your competitor will. Support is the most reliable yet most under-used area of user research. Every time someone phones and reports a problem, note what the problem is. Note what you did to help the client and what you did to make sure you don't get any future calls of this nature. Note anything else of any significance.

Each week the support manager should collate the call sheets and summon the team. The entire team should discuss the issues and produce a feedback report that compares the following with the prior week:

- ✦ The total number of calls
- ✦ The principal bugs by number
- ✦ Issues that need to be addressed urgently
- ✦ The updated wish list

The support manager should also keep a record of generic problems so that when you deal with the next generation of products you don't repeat the same mistakes. This provides a ready-made feature list for your next release. It also provides a record against the corporate memory loss that often accompanies departing personnel.

The product development manager should give the support manager an indication of when these problems will be addressed (if 80 percent of the calls concern a new bug, the priority is to fix it immediately) and report on progress with previous issues.

Always keep your support team in the loop. When they are cut off from the main-stream development, they will feel they are only being used to keep customers quiet. If the result isn't a riot, it's demotivation, and neither of those options is appealing.

Take a Tip from Sage

With more than 3 million users and a turnover in excess of $800 million, Sage is a familiar name to everyone who handles payrolls and accounts in the United Kingdom. In addition, Sage has recently acquired a number of U.S. accountancy software firms. So how over the space of 20 years did four men sitting in a Newcastle pub build a business that now employs over 5,500 people worldwide? Ian Wright, who is the General Manager of Sage's Customer Division (with over 300 support people), says quite simply, "Sage offered first-rate support from the start."

The founders knew that the bulk of their customers would be accountants, and once they bought the program, support would be the only recourse back to the firm. So there was never any possibility of building a business by being anything less than professional.

Sage provides support free for the first 90 days so purchasers and their staff can learn to use the program in every circumstance that occurs in an entire trading quarter. Afterwards, when they need support, they already know that prompt effective help is available.

Sage levies only modest charges for subsequent help. Because of this Sage can't afford to take on support gurus who are fully qualified accountants. They have to be able to train ordinary people. The secret is a long thought out, unhurried induction. Initial interviews, though relaxed, are probing to assess the general competence of candidates and see how they handle others under pressure. Over the years Ian Wright's staff have built up personality profiles that match successful supporters. Selected candidates spend their first week learning about customers and business so they can appreciate the problems of financial accounting and be sympathetic to those who turn to them for help. Only when candidates have a sound understanding of Sage's customers do they learn about Sage's products. When these newcomers are ready, typically after a month, they are gradually eased into Sage's support team. Initially they just sit and listen to how veterans deal with things.

When they are sufficiently knowledgeable and at ease, they are paired up with an experienced buddy to answer customers' calls on a closely supervised basis. The one-to-one buddying trials last at least a month. Then the new employees are moved into a working trio, where one experienced member buddies two new ones. After six months under close supervision, each team member is evaluated to make sure that both the firm and the team are satisfied with his or her progress.

Sage views support as their best medium for market research. With 300 staff taking 20,000 calls per day, they literally have the ear of their market. As Ian said, "There is no point in listening to your customers if you don't take any notice."

In addition, always let your testers know that you are aware of their problems and are working on a solution, and never set a date for release until a satisfactory number of issues have been resolved, tested, and found to work robustly.

✦   ✦   ✦

Plugging the Hole in the Boat

Fortunately, most companies prosper. Sadly, most of those who fail don't need to. This chapter, accordingly, isn't about some miracle cure that magics money from nowhere but how to manage what you have wisely. A shortage of money brings with it other problems. When money is tight, more management time is spent looking after it. Other issues, such as deadlines, tend to get pushed to the back burner.

The Other Golden Rule

While everyone knows that "cash is king," the other golden rule you also need to understand is that corporate liability will protect you personally only if you remain within the law. So when times get hard, stay honest.

What the law, quite rightly, does not allow you to do is abuse it and conduct business when you don't have the money to meet your creditors—this is called trading insolvently. It's also fraudulent to use money you don't have. Directors of firms have the responsibility of knowing the trading position of their firm at all times. Having said this, most firms will, at some stage, trade while they are technically insolvent. There are three types of breach. It is important that you can recognize with which one you are dealing.

✦ **The stretch (a trivial violation)**—A client is late with a check, sales this month are low, but the forward order book is strong. The firm doesn't have the funds to cover its overheads; technically it's insolvent. Provided the situation is transitory and you lend the firm the money or your bank manager gives you a temporary overdraft facility, you should be alright. Even so, discuss the situation and agree on a course of action with your other directors. Providing the loan is repaid, preferably with interest, it's irrelevant.

✦ **The tight rope (worrying)**—The situation here is less clear-cut. The firm is running short of money. Although the future is rosy, you have no idea how long it will take for the balance to right itself. Again, discuss the situation with your fellow directors and agree on a course of action; then inform your accountant and confirm it in writing. Get his view of the seriousness of the situation.

✦ **The void (whoops!)**—If you are already overstretched, the future looks dim, and there are no easy marketing fixes, call a crisis meeting. Arrange an immediate discussion with the company accountant and your directors. Consider very seriously pulling up stakes while the firm is still technically solvent. It's cheaper to call the administrators in and close it down.

Money is every software firm's Achilles heel. Money gives you altitude. As you lose height nothing adverse seems to happen. For a deceptively long time you still feel free to do anything. Then suddenly the ground is coming at you at an alarming rate. If can't pull out of the situation very, very fast, wham! You're dead. While we have all used money from the day we bought our first package of candy, managing corporate money is an altogether different business. As an individual if you fall on hard times, the state will come to your assistance to some degree. If this happens to a business, it is terminated. There are no safety nets or second chances.

Financial shortages have been known to affect even the most outwardly healthy and well-known firms. If you miss a deadline, a major client pulls out of that mega-deal, or you stop managing your creditors, but you still have money in the bank, you're safe. If you don't, you're history.

The accrual, spending, and overall management of money, therefore, require special consideration; so let's start at the beginning. There are a couple of words used a lot in this chapter that you probably know, but their meaning runs counter to our instinctive expectations:

✦ **A debtor**—Someone to whom you owe money

✦ **A creditor**—Someone who owes money to you

Bank Accounts

It's good practice to keep private and company money separate. If you don't, you won't know what is whose. The easiest way to do this is open a new bank account for your business. This also enables you to have a clear record of the money you have transferred to fund the firm. If you've incorporated your firm, you'll be able to use its business name. Your bank will ask to see a copy of the document of incorporation. This is a straightforward task.

The big difference between running a business account and a private account is cost. Whereas banks rarely charge for personal checks, they do for company checks, and for money you pay in, statements, quarterly management accounts, and so on. It's not heinous but it certainly adds up.

If you are just dipping your toe in the water it often makes sense to set up a new private account to keep costs down. Nowadays you might prefer to use a low-cost, online bank. That allows you to pay suppliers electronically.

If you want to have a corporate account, make a point of meeting your bank manager. Pass your project by him and gauge his reaction. Bank managers look after hundreds of businesses and they have a canny knack of knowing what will and won't work. It will cost you nothing and you could come out of it with some excellent, free advice. Other important areas in which bank managers are invaluable include the following:

✦ Providing emergency overdrafts (temporary)

✦ Loans (longer, fixed term)

✦ Expediting setting you up with your own credit card handling facilities (discussed later in this chapter)

If these are necessary, it is prudent to set up overdraft facilities at the outset, as they take time. In an emergency you might need the facility immediately.

At your meeting with your bank manager, get a rundown of all the costs associated with the account. Keep a record of these so you can incorporate them into your financial cashflow. When the bank manager has told you what they're getting out of the relationship, get him to explain everything that they can do for you.

 Note   Another ally is of course your accountant, which was discussed in Chapter 12.

Accounting Systems

Unless you are selling some very highly priced custom-made software and just sending out the odd invoice each month, you really need accounting software. It more than pays for itself by speeding up the computation of wages and invoice dispatch and shortening the time it takes to produce statutory tax returns such as VAT/TVA in Europe and state tax in the United States.

A good accounting package will allow you to customize invoices to your requirements and deal with any issues specific to your organization. It often speeds things up to no end if you use the same accounts software as your accountants. Then data can be transmitted in real time. I strongly recommend that you get your accounts software up and running long before your software hits the streets. This will give you time to get to know it and record all the money you have spent before then.

One of the things a good accounting system will also tell you is whether you are funding your customers. If they aren't paying you on time, you certainly are. Most firms, especially the smaller ones, have no idea, but your accounts software should be able to print this out in an instant. Presuming you are working on 30 days' credit, it will list money outstanding by time: 3 months plus, 3 months, 1 month, and outstanding but not yet overdue. It is good practice to examine the debtor list each week and decide what action should be taken.

Credit Cards

Are you likely to get more orders if you accept credit cards? In the trade, if you have this facility, you are called a *merchant* by the credit card companies, who are called *merchant service providers*. However, becoming a merchant is not as easy as the abundance of outlets that take plastic would lead you to believe. Since the arrival of the Internet they have tightened up their criteria for acceptance, either wanting to see a couple of years' audited accounts or be provided with a refundable deposit. If you're a startup venture you won't have audited accounts for at least 12 months. Furthermore, merchant service providers have been known to ask for deposits up to $50,000 to cover them against abuse (with electronic payments machines you can generate refunds as well as take money), depending on the perceived risk of your business.

Every major country has several merchant service providers, so it makes sense to shop around for the best rates. There are also different types, notably Visa, American Express, Diners Club, and MasterCard. They are not interchangeable, so if you have a Visa arrangement you still need to approach American Express to take money with their cards. Pay careful attention to their validation and anti-fraud procedures. It is important they spell out the correct procedures for when cards bounce and how you can best protect yourself. Contrary to what they will tell you at the outset, if you are doing a serious level of business the rates are negotiable.

Having credit card facilities in-house has the following advantages:

- ✦ More orders
- ✦ Lower costs
- ✦ Professionalism—it's your name that appears on the transaction
- ✦ Promptness—you get paid immediately (often the next working day)

The disadvantages are that you need to administer the process yourself. To manually process a credit card order and generate an invoice takes up to 5 minutes, irrespective of the order being for 100 items or one.

Ideally you want to integrate and automate the online payment procedure. When the order is placed it is verified, the payment authorized, the request to the dispatch department made, and your accounts system updated simultaneously.

Remember to route all online transaction Web pages through to a secure server. With credit cards, money should only be taken from clients when the goods are ready for dispatch.

Credit Card Fraud

Credit card fraud comes with the territory. As the merchant you are the piggy in the middle. Consumers like credit cards for ease of use and if there is any dispute (goods don't turn up, not as advertised, whatever) they can cancel the order. In the United States customers' liability is set to the first $50 by federal law; in the United Kingdom it's zero. However, if you take an order, the card number is correct and all other verification is followed, and the customers default for whatever reason, you pay. If you are selling hardware where you might be running at a 10 percent margin, you'll need to make 10 new transactions to make good that loss. Luckily for software producers, the margins are higher so you only need to cover your internal costs, but that's not the point.

Use Third-Party Online Facilities

An alternative that grew up to service the Internet boom was third-party merchant service providers. WorldPay is the best known of these. For a startup and transaction fee they take the monies on your behalf. The customers pay the money to them and they, in turn, pay you. This facility can be set up overnight. Some include single or multi-currency options and fraud screening as part of the service. The downsides are the costs and the time you have to wait before you get paid.

Invoicing and Credit

You must take invoicing very seriously. A lot of firms don't and go out of business unnecessarily. They actually forget to send out the invoices they could. (Do they expect their customers to remind them?) The inevitable happens—financial strangulation.

Most successful, cash-rich businesses operate on a policy called *negative working capital*. This means they sell the goods and get paid for them before they have to pay their suppliers. If this sounds too good to be true then read on. McDonalds had a negative working capital of $698.5 million between 1999 and 2000. Amazon.com estimates they turn over their inventory 20 times faster than superstores and 50 times faster than small specialty bookstores. Dell is another proponent of this technique. If nothing else, it makes it unnecessary to require overdraft facilities or waste time dealing with cashflow crises.

As a software developer, you are the product manufacturer as well, but you might still have to buy in manuals, CDs, packaging, and so on. Treat it as a game and see if you can sell each month's production before you have to pay for it. Realistically what you are aiming for is prompt payment. The advantages are obvious:

+ Solvent (money in the bank)
+ Failsafe (no chance of items going out uninvoiced)
+ No bad debts (per se)
+ Less administration

If you don't take the negative working capital approach the opposite happens. Staff will be tied up pursuing bad debts, and you'll end up funding overdrafts to cover times when debtors are in arrears. It's a no-win situation. Don't even get into it. For small, one-off orders my advice is clear: cash with order. How customers do this is their choice (credit card, check, money order, or cash). Once they pay, it's your call, however, with checks only release the goods after the checks have cleared (typically allow 2–5 days).

Over the last decade, a noticeable change has taken place in the way that large companies buy small products. Ten years ago they'd generate a purchase order, you would then send the goods and an invoice, and sometime down the line a check would turn up. Today they invariably pay on the spot with a credit card. If they still work the old way, blue chip companies are normally a safe bet; although if this is the first time they've dealt with you, there may be some delay while they enter your company details into their accounting system (so you can be paid). So if you get a purchase order, it's often best to phone and check the company's payment procedure. Nowadays, most members of staff have corporate credit cards, which allow them to make small purchases on the spot.

When smaller companies approach you and you have grounds to be wary, ask them to ship a check with their order. While this might appear draconian, it will pay for itself immediately with less administration, higher bank balances, and reduced hassle.

If you have to give credit, you may choose the terms. Although 30 days is the norm, think seriously of the advantages of settling it at 7 or 14 days to bring the money in faster. Protect yourself further by stipulating an interest rate for overdue accounts (typically 4 percent over the bank base rate) on an annual basis. If you don't do this, you can't claim it.

Tip One tip from a senior bank manager about opening accounts for new customers is to ask for three times the amount of credit clearance they say they will actually need. If there are any impending problems, the exaggeration is likely to reveal it.

If you are worried about people's preparedness to pay up front, don't. Dell turned over $31.1 billion in 2002 and almost all their transactions were done on a credit card/cash-with-order basis.

Credit Control

The beauty of running a credit card/cash-with-order operation is that you don't have to waste time on credit control, although statistically you are bound to get a rogue credit card transaction at some point. In the real world government departments, large corporations, schools, and so on will use purchase orders. If you want their business you'll have to make an exception to your rule—even Dell offers credit when pushed.

Downtimes Are the Norm

A recession is defined as a contraction in the economic cycle and is measured from the peak to the trough when it stops. The picture is made worse when you add in all the major stock market falls that don't have the decency to coincide with the start of or impact on recessions. Recessions are a lot more common than you might think. There were over 20 in the United States during the last century, as illustrated in Table 18-1. And bad debts soar when the economic climate clouds over. No firm is immune, so you must know how to plan for them.

Table 18-1 U.S. Recessions			
Recession	**Started**	**Ended**	**Length[1]**
1	September 1902	August 1904	23 months
2	May 1907	June 1908	13 months
3	January 1910	January 1912	24 months
4	January 1913	December 1914	23 months
5	August 1918	March 1919	7 months
6	January 1920	July 1921	18 months
7	May 1923	July 1924	14 months
8	October 1926	November 1927	13 months
9	August 1929	March 1933	43 months
10	May 1937	June 1938	13 months
11	February 1945	October 1945	8 months
12	November 1948	October 1949	11 months

Continued

Table 18-1 *(continued)*			
Recession	**Started**	**Ended**	**Length**[1]
13	July 1953	May 1954	10 months
14	August 1957	April 1958	8 months
15	April 1960	February 1961	10 months
16	December 1969	November 1970	11 months
17	November 1973	March 1975	16 months
18	January 1980	July 1980	6 months
19	July 1981	November 1982	16 months
20	July 1990	March 1991	8 months
21	March 2001	November 2001	8 months

1 Measured from Peak to Trough

Source: National Bureau of Economic Research

Spotting the Early Warnings

Half the time it's boom; half the time it's bust. No business that cannot survive tough times will keep its shingle up for long. The sooner you recognize the symptoms of a general economic downturn, the more likely you are to weather the worst of the storm. Your business sector may be hit earlier or later than the rest of information technology. And IT itself may be among the first or last to be pinched depending on whether it is considered cause or effect of the latest economic fluctuation.

You can't rely on the press or TV to give you an advanced warning that heavy weather is coming your way, so always keep you eye out for the following:

- ✦ Sales slowing
- ✦ Customers extending payment cycles
- ✦ Production costs creeping up
- ✦ Major contract approvals are delayed
- ✦ Large orders get cancelled
- ✦ Promotional efforts bring disappointing returns
- ✦ Cash reserves begin to dwindle
- ✦ Staff turnover declines

First you have to ask yourself the fundamental question: Is this recession likely to be a short or a long one? The average length of the recessions shown in Table 18-1 is 16 months, but this is only the bottom of the down cycle. Trading conditions that affect a business adversely may be twice that long.

In a recession men and women have the same intelligence, skills, and abilities as they do in a boom. So the only thing that can reverse the spiral is what the bankers and politicians do. Until they take effective corrective action to restore people's confidence in themselves, nothing beneficial can happen.

Companies That Take Early Action Are the Ones That Survive

Your best bet is always to invoice as early as you can and never let up. If someone has ordered your software, received it, and reneged on their agreement to pay, don't waste time philosophizing. The sooner you accept the situation, the more options you have and the more likely you are to be able to sort the situation out. Never dither; if in doubt, do the following:

1. Call the accounts team together. Using the latest aged debtor list, attack the largest overdue amounts first—typically 10 percent of invoices account for 90 percent of outstanding payments (these are the most useful bills to be paid).

2. Get your accounts department to telephone them and ask for immediate payment. Failing that, ask when the amount will be paid. Depending on your business the phone calls should bring in between 40 and 60 percent of outstanding monies in around seven working days (much of the time, people just need a reminder). The threat of debt collection should collect a further 20 percent.

3. You will now have to confront problem payers. If the time is too long or you don't trust their answer, pass the debt over to a debt collection agency. Do this with all non-strategic debts.

4. If your accounts department is ineffective, find someone who can bring the money in or give the job to a proven collection agency. The money is more important to the firm's survival than individual niceties.

5. Senior management should go through the outstanding debtors list once a week, and the senior financial officer has a duty to blow the whistle on any client of whom they are suspicious. The best day for this is Monday. You can then pursue them right through Friday.

6. Once you start chasing, never let up. Be firm. Be unflinching. Be polite. Remember, it isn't for nothing that professional debt collectors behave like barely restrained terriers trying to savage rabbits through barbed wire. The person who gets paid first isn't always the person who deserves the money most. People at the other end will often pay "Mr. Nasty" ahead of others just to stop the phone calls.

Forecasting

The best computer model to create for your business is the cash flow forecast. In its simplest form, it is the sum of all your normal incomings and outgoings, totalled on a month-by-month basis and extrapolated into the future. This sounds easy, but where do you start? A cash flow, as you would guess, is best calculated on a spreadsheet program, as it takes care of all the adding, subtracting, and carry forwards that are straightforward to do but devilishly easy to make a mistake on.

The next thing to know is that there is an unwritten format and conventions for the way cash flow is laid out and calculated. So don't just rush and start slapping figures anywhere. Accountants and other friends with financial training can help here.

In Figure 18-1 I've assembled a condensed cash flow forecast sample. You can add entries that occur to you that are relevant and particular to your business. To condense the layout I've placed several entries on the same line. The standard convention is to list them individually, line-by-line. By convention, money in is always listed before money out. Whether you include employment tax in the salary or as a separate item is up to you, as long as you don't forget it.

Theoretically, you can run a cash flow forecast forward several years, but the further ahead you extrapolate, the less accurate it will be. Six months ahead is generally considered as far ahead as is realistic. Cash flow forecasts also provide an excellent model for you to see what might happen if you double your staff or move to larger premises (the "what if" scenarios).

If your forecast is going to be close to accurate, it's essential that you allow realistic delays between sales and purchases and the money being received and dispatched. Remember, your staff needs to be paid on the button at the end of each month. Most of your suppliers will give you 30 days' credit.

In a startup situation there are two break-even dates that especially interest investors:

+ In which month is the firm notionally able to take more money in than it spends?
+ When will the operation pay its debts and become profitable?

These critical dates are typically referred to by numbers of months. Being able to say, "We first go into profit in month 11 and the operation becomes cash flow positive in month 18" tells investors how long they have to wait before the firm is self-supporting.

	Month 1	Month 2
Cash Inflow		
External Funding		
Sales		
Product Sales (New/Upgrades/Maint)		
Maintenance, Consultancy, Bespoking		
Other Revenue		
TOTAL INFLOWS		
Cash Outflow		
Salaries		
Management, Development, Sales, Admin		
Product Manufacturing Costs		
Media, Packaging, Distribution		
Marketing Costs		
Origination, Production, Media, Exhibs		
Development Costs		
Hardware, Software		
Premises		
Rent, Rates, Insurance		
Heating, Electricity, Security		
Cleaning/Maintenance		
Professional Fees		
Audits, Legal (setup/contracts)		
Insurance (Business/Empl/Prof Indemn)		
Administration Costs		
Stationery (Corporate/Office)		
Postage/Telephone/Fax/Mobiles		
Training/Recruitment		
Leases/Entertainment/Travel/PC		
Other Costs		
Bad Debts, Bank, Interest Charges		
TOTAL OUTFLOWS		
Net Cashflow		
Cumulative Cashflow		

Figure 18-1: Sample cash flow forecast worksheet.

You'll have appreciated by now that cash flow forecasts combine both fact and fiction. While the past is known, the future has to be estimated. While outgoings are quantifiable, sales and other forms of income are initially wishful thinking. As such, the cash flow is one of the most useful yet potentially misleading business aids you have.

As your business gets started, or your product is launched, you will be able to supplant fictions increasingly with facts. Update your future forecasts using the current week's figures. In time you'll learn the seasonal trends associated with your product—typically people buy less during vacation months, and sales trail off before an upgrade and temporarily mushroom when it comes out. If you are unfamiliar with these just ask a friend about other software operations. Again, build these fluctuations into the spreadsheet, and remember to include future payments or known contracts that should come in.

Tip   When the future is uncertain, it may pay you to have two forecasts, a best case and a worst case.

When you start to introduce variables, your forecast becomes a model. As such, it can be an incredibly valuable and valid tool. Apart from an up-to-date cash flow forecast, you will need a financial model so you can play with impacts of overruns and various levels of sales and know which elements really make the biggest difference. Information on recent sales is the best indication you can get of how future buyers will behave; whether there is likely to be sizeable repeat business; the probable value of updates; and what you can expect to earn from maintenance contracts. You can also analyze niche user profiles.

Caution   Cash flows are private documents. The information is sensitive. Never make copies. Never show them to anyone who does not need to know. When they must be presented, they should be presented well. Lay yours out so it is easy for any bank manager to understand.

Paying Suppliers

It is better to have a limited number of suppliers that you know well and manage them. A model company treats everyone equally. Make sure that your suppliers get paid with the same promptness that you would want to be paid yourself. This practice ensures a good working relationship but also has hidden benefits. You might need to call in a favor at short notice (Can you double the CD run for next Friday?). With a good payment record they have every incentive to say, "Yes."

If you are going to be uncharacteristically late with a payment, the best policy is to let the supplier know. There isn't much they can do about it at this stage. Explain the cause so they can appreciate the problem and let them know when they will receive payment. Add on a couple of days' contingency; it's always best to be cautious with timescales. They'll appreciate the call and you won't be pestered by their accounts department.

Creditors typically get paid in the following order:

1. Secured creditors (for example, the tax man, bank loans)

2. Staff

3. Suppliers (on a strict first-in, first-out basis)

4. Directors

In most jurisdictions it is illegal for a director to receive payment if the firm has more debts than money.

How to Spend Money

Money is both a luxury and a scarce resource. Mismanagement is another reason why a proportion of firms hit trouble. New cars for the sales team, prime time television commercials, or another administrative assistant; all of these might do wonders for someone's ego, but they can melt the corporate cash reserves faster than the Sahara sun melts butter. And when it's gone, it's gone.

In the 1980s I ran a PC dealership; it's still open today and operated by my co-founder. A lot of people think he's tight with money. In fact, he's prudent. In good years he squirrels money away, in bad ones, he disgorges to keep staff on when competitors are laying them off. This provides him with a continuity of corporate knowledge and skills, which other firms can't afford. When it comes to spending money you should always ask, "Is it really necessary?" and "How is it going to benefit the firm?" If you husband the firm's resources consistently, your firm will be sound.

Note   Just remember that when you eventually taste success, it's no time to take your eye off the ball. People who have experienced success previously know that rewards are fine, but this new and far more pleasant situation brings its own challenges.

✦   ✦   ✦

Handling Growth

"If you want to be a big company tomorrow, you have to start acting like one today."

—Thomas Watson, founder of IBM

Striving for success is exhausting. Achieving it is intoxicating. Growth does not follow a big win automatically.

It has to be planned for long in advance and nurtured.

Success, of course, brings money, kudos, and relief. You know that sales will be well above the waterline; that bills can be met; and that staff can be rewarded for all their hard work. It also creates the opportunity to choose what to do next:

- ✦ Grow personally
- ✦ Select your next goal
- ✦ Learn from your success
- ✦ Advance management skills
- ✦ Get into the next phase of marketing
- ✦ Move to better premises
- ✦ Organize the finance for it all
- ✦ Possibly to venture abroad

Success Sifts the Comets from the Stars

This is a period where, provided the money is rolling in, you can afford a limited number of mistakes. However, this window of deceptive immortality is brief: six months, a year, 18 months at the outside. During this time, you either learn to expand or success gradually falls in on itself.

If you are wise, you won't expect to get rich during this period. This time isn't about Rolls Royces and nights on the town. It is about using the opportunity you've earned to grow bigger. It's about finding out what you never knew you could do. Companies that grow through this period successfully make big mistakes, but never mortal ones.

The best time to plan for such success isn't when it arrives. You need to start dreaming sensibly long before that.

Selecting Your Next Goal

Some are astounded by their program's success. Some set off an avalanche of ideas and they don't know which one to tackle first. Most are not quite sure what the next right move is.

Not knowing where you want to go is like thumbing a lift without having any destination. Opportunists invariably end up in Las Vegas. Luck, however, isn't a reliable mechanism on which to build any ongoing security for your colleagues, to say nothing of yourself.

In your chosen field there's no shortage of brilliant ideas. Software is a mine of opportunities, and the people who work in information technology have some of the best minds in the world. If you are uncertain about your ideas, someone else is very likely to implant their objectives. Initially, attractive as they may appear, they may not take you exactly where you wish to be.

To avoid confusion, it is important for you to quietly reflect on your next strategic aim *before* the business takes off. Practically as soon as they were able to move out of their parents' garage, the teenagers who started Microsoft knew that if they could control the market for a computer's operating system, they could afford to produce all the other programs on which they had set their hearts.

Intel knew that by making their processor the de facto choice for the IBM PC (and therefore its clones), they would be able to capture a slice of the market that would enable them to out research all competition.

Cisco knew that by introducing new routers faster than anyone else's they would remain the market leader.

Once you have a clear picture in your mind of what the firm needs to be and do to succeed at the next stage, the decisions that further your aims virtually identify themselves. You may have many objectives in mind, including the following:

+ Develop your program
+ Write something new

✦ Raise sales higher still

✦ Concentrate on a particular niche

✦ Win a particular client

✦ Reorganize

✦ Find a bigger space

✦ Smarten up your image

These are all good objectives and everybody has them. Yet they all miss the point. You don't want to pick from the menu while there is a chance of buying the entire restaurant. The real question is which of these objectives is the magic word to invoke the others? Sometimes the answer is already on your list. Other times you can only put your finger on it if you start to think tangentially.

Once you have a definite strategic vision, sound it out among close colleagues until it's honed. Then, when success arrives, share the next salutation with your team. It's their lives you are dreaming for, too. Once they believe that you can see over the next hill and know how to get there, any blaséness and arrogance that creeps in with success is supplanted by fresh motivation as feet touch the ground again and the firm's morale rises.

As soon as you have the cardinal concept in place, most of the subsidiary choices make their own priorities. Everyone around you will be dying to help. Good ideas should always be encouraged and valued. You just have to ask each volunteer, "Does your idea fit in with company strategy? Can you demonstrate that it is practicable?" If their idea passes these two tests, analyze its business worth with the same severity that you used to pick your original winner.

Learning from Your Own Success

This isn't as easy as it sounds. During the late 1980s Apple realized that their Mac was selling well into the creative, graphics studios. So they forged strong links with the first graphics program developers and established a stranglehold on that market that persists to this day. What they didn't do was analyze the steps by which they achieved their preeminence. Indeed, considerable time passed before they realized that graphic programs demand much more powerful processors. Even when they had built them into the Mac, they didn't appreciate that graphics capabilities are necessarily of a higher order than those required for word processing and number crunching.

With judicious exploitation of their strength, they might have been where Microsoft is today or larger. As things turned out, Apple lost their window of opportunity, maybe literally.

My advice? Listen carefully to what dealers, users, and journalists say. Be wary of flattery. Though you may laughingly dismiss it, it has a way of sneaking in.

Some deserve success. Some have success thrust upon them. However, success that is based on luck isn't repeatable. If you just happen to be lucky, don't put yourself down. You are among the many not the few. Be smart. Appreciate your luck. Work out why you were lucky. Take steps to repeat it. If your program is selling like hot cakes or you've pulled off a couple of mammoth sales or presold your software to a major player, you are clearly doing something right.

When Bird's Eye, a very sophisticated marketing company, analyzed the frozen food lines they launched during the 1970s (there were over a hundred), it turned out that the products that failed were the ones that required more cooking knowledge than most homemakers had at the time. By contrast, the lines that succeeded were mainly "just pop it in the oven" jobs.

Most of the good answers are simple ones. The key to any firm's success is usually very straightforward and may even sound mundane. Don't underestimate a business principle because it sounds humble. "Stack 'em high, sell 'em cheap," said Wal-Mart.

What counts is what it's worth at the bank. A definitive answer to the question "Why is my program successful?" is vital.

The Real Driver behind Growth Is People

If you want to expand a programming capacity, seven is generally regarded as an optimum team. If you are embarking on a new project you'll need additional programmers and another manager. At this stage, there is no need to increase the size of the sales, support, and administrative teams.

Rather than take on one person at a time, you might feel tempted to take on half a dozen. And when the sales operation doubles, you will need an additional team leader and to appoint one of them as sales manager.

When the firm reaches a certain size (around 32) you may find you need a human resources manager. Perhaps one of your administrators has a natural touch with people and knows the legalities to handle this?

From the outside, a firm that is rocketing upwards looks as though it's going from seamless strength to strength. From the inside, it feels more like a series of lurches from imbalance to imbalance. Only as you begin to get used to the bumping do things start to settle, as the effect of newcomers is dampened by sheer numbers. People who have survived growth often have a feeling that certain firm sizes work better than others. Fours and fives, 12s, 20s, and 32s tend to work more harmoniously than any numbers in between. Such are the building blocks of teams and the administration to manage and sell them.

With a modicum of luck, it is only a question of months before you will have staff working for staff. Then you will realize, if you haven't before, that while it is people that will help attain your goals, it is their team leaders who augment and implement the policy that make success happen. If you are going to move ahead, you are going to need rowers, the strongest, most dexterous, and most supportive you can find.

When you are starting from a pinhead, it is more practical to begin by bringing in new staff one angel at a time so new faces aren't too disruptive. A little later, it may be more convenient to hire in twos and threes. When you plot your recruitment schedule, take this into account. However, take care that you don't inadvertently engineer your own decline. While taking on more staff to ensure the business multiplies, remember that this also multiplies your wage bill, running costs, and gear.

Alas, past success is no guarantee of future solvency. Should, owing to circumstances beyond your control, the firm's revenues decline, you may be left with a mountain of bills. Studies at Harvard Business School and INSEAD (see note that follows) invariably demonstrate that the manager who plays things conservatively risks less and learns most, and although he starts like a tortoise, he ends like a hare.

Note Is INSEAD an acronym? What does it mean? Forty years ago, when the school was first started, it was common to refer to the school as the European Institute for Business Administration. However, over the years, the school has extended its European roots to Asia, and has become increasingly known as INSEAD (pronounced IN-SEE-ADD). It is no longer known as European Institute for Business Administration, nor is that name used. Like Harvard is Harvard and Wharton is Wharton, INSEAD is INSEAD.

Top Management

It is almost impossible to manage a static company for any length of time because there is no room to maneuver. To manage successfully, you have to be able to steer, at least a little. And you can't steer effectively unless you are making some headway and there is room to grow. Growth is as essential as oxygen.

The more brilliant you are, the quicker your company will grow to a size where even you can't do everything. It is therefore essential to get the right team together. Some of the rowers may be with you already. One or two others you may have to find as soon as you prudently can.

While the bloom of endless future possibilities is still on a company, it's relatively easy to attract outstanding employees. This bloom, however, doesn't stay upon on a budding company forever—seven years at most. After that, most of the great team players will have already gravitated to the larger corporations. Small firms are left with the mavericks who can be brilliant and adroit. Their companies can be extremely profitable. However, such prosperity comes at a price. They are far harder to manage.

While every member of the team matters, it is the handful at the top that steer the destiny of any firm. Getting the right people at the top is essential. Often it can take as little as one person to affect an entire company's mood. A new senior man can as easily break as make a firm. It is in everyone's interest that you be circumspect. Take your time selecting and screening the candidates. Have as many meetings as you need to explain the business and get to know each other. Make sure that the chosen candidate is sympathetic to your aims and has an instinctive feel for the business. The crucial thing is what the candidate can do for your company. People who make the difference often know the answer before they ever join. Do not accept put offs along the lines of "I can't tell until I actually start working." Find out how the candidate plans to get you from where you are to where you want to be before he is appointed. Calculate the cost the operation and its options between you. This way, you should be able to gauge whether he or she is likely to deliver.

Before drafting any letter of appointment, ensure, by e-mail or exchange of letters, that the situation, goals, and resources are clearly understood and agreed to. There is no point in fudging. We have all seen or heard stories of high caliber people brought into IT firms to effect some decisive change with ample resources, only to be told on their first morning that the cupboard is bare. That's an exit strategy from the start. All that will happen is that your would-be savior will do his ostensible best while making other arrangements. Someone else will soon snap him up.

It is not what people say that matters; it's what they actually do. The irony of Watson telling everyone, "If you want to be a big company tomorrow, you have to start acting like one today" is that from the day he started buying up punch card operations, he knew that a machine would one day manage data more cheaply and more efficiently than his Hollerith machines. In the interim, he trained his staff and built his great corporation. Successful sales managers were continuously trained and promoted. IBM staff were the elite.

Fifty years later, the product that IBM was built for began to appear. Instead of behaving like a big company president, Watson dithered, fretting that his now withering punch-card business would be taken away. Indeed, he would have blown it had not the U.S. Department of Justice brought a suit against IBM for monopolizing the punch-card business. Watson was scared. Fifty years earlier, he had been sentenced to prison for an antitrust violation brought against National Cash Registers (NCR). Only a presidential pardon (thanks to the firm's election predictions) saved him. In the maelstrom, his sons forced him to stand down. They then put together a top-notch management team and within three years IBM emerged as the undisputed leader in data processing. To the outside world nothing had happened. IBM had simply taken its rightful place in the information technology world order of that time.

Watson was afraid to let go of his early, enormously successful idea. In the IT industry, it usually happens the other way around. The founder has too active a mind to fit into any conventional business. Management then becomes a relay race with the business as the baton. If you discover that you are a born pioneer rather than a settler, revel in your gifts and find another frontier. Pass day-to-day management to a capable person in whom you can trust and keep control of your firm. This way your business acquires twin towers of strength, each doing what he or she does best.

Relocation without Dislocation

Moving offices is not only a signal to distributors and customers that you are moving up, it is also an opportunity for you to remind them how efficient your firm is. The implication is that the major transformations you can reap for yourself, you can reap for them as well.

However well you plan a move, it is by nature disruptive. The best tactic is to set up a small working party to shepherd everything along, usually with a jolly sergeant major as the moving marshal, and a practical, do-it-yourself programmer to take care of the mechanical contingencies. The prime objective is to interrupt normal business as little as possible. Inevitably you will incur a double set of costs during the changeover for items such as office rents, utilities, insurance, and telephone lines, not to mention business fees to the government.

Part of the trick is obviously to switch premises in as short a time as possible. Be sure to schedule the move for the absolute end of your rent cycle. Your best bet may be to move over a Saturday or over a long weekend. The office can then close down fairly normally on Friday, with as much as possible boxed beforehand. By the time your staff hit their new offices at the start of the week, their equipment is set up in its prearranged space and already working.

The devil is in the preparation. Get the boxes from your movers in advance so that you can pack up in an orderly and non-time-consuming manner. Work need not get behind if things are gradually packed into boxes in order of priority. Then if there is a panic late on Friday, everyone knows where to unearth that crucial item.

It also helps if you can take groups of staff over to the new place before you move in. They can then figure out how they will travel to work and decide how they want to arrange their office space, producing a small sketch outlining where everything is to go for your movers. This isn't, you will no doubt point out, an invitation for everyone to become an interior designer or Feng Shui consultant. It is an exercise in making the new place functional.

Be warned that telephone providers rarely work over weekends or holidays so it is important that switching the old numbers to the new ones is booked and confirmed in good time. Make sure, also, that the Internet connection is live before you move in. This gives you a means of communication should the telephone system not be connected as promised. If you are hosting servers in your offices and the IP numbers change, propagate the change with sufficient time. Check, to the best of your ability, that as many of the internal systems are working as possible before people arrive to work.

Last but not least, advise clients and suppliers of when and where you are moving. Back up change of address cards with "Hi, I'm here," phone calls. People are usually sympathetic. Everyone moves from time to time.

The ideal is that people come to the new offices as if they had been working there for years. In practice people like to sniff out their new environment, work out where everything is and who is where and generally exercise their nesting and maze-learning instincts. To avoid losing focus completely, provide for an exploration period but don't let it drag on. Make sure everyone arrives on time (or half an hour early and you supply breakfast). Set aside a specific period so everyone can explore the new offices. If you've employed a designer to lay out the new office, get him or her to give everyone a short, practical explanation of how things are laid out. Formally show everyone where restrooms, kitchen facilities, fire exits, and so on are located. At the end of 30 minutes, ring a bell and everyone can get back to work as normal.

Your moving checklist should include the following:

✦ Change of address cards printed and dispatched (alternatively, use e-mail)

✦ Stationery reprinted with new address, phone/fax numbers

✦ Answering machine or voicemail messages updated with new numbers

✦ Fax machine reprogrammed with new fax number

✦ Telephone directories given new details

✦ Mail forwarding order for sufficient period

✦ Tax, post office, and any other authorities notified of your change of address

✦ New office signage ordered

✦ Internet connection working (for Web, e-mail, and so on)

✦ IP numbers propagated (if necessary—remember HTPPS)

Turning on the Sales Tap

Although it is amazing how much can be achieved with modest marketing budgets, you're going to have to use marketing differently as your program and markets mature. The examples and explanations of launch marketing described in Chapter 14 are designed to give your baby the best chance of a successful birth. However, below-the-line campaigns can never build national recognition. You are going to need to soften up much larger numbers of prospects by laying the foundation of a desirable brand image. This does not mean opening the financial floodgates but beginning to put your toe in the public arena. Seek some professional marketing help perhaps to develop your Web site, to make the best use of a notable space at a major trade exhibition, or to create a little cinema advertising. Or devise some clever teaser posters. You may want to alert your public to new releases or to synchronize a competitive launch with your own special offer. The important point is to make the move to being professional.

Expansion Abroad

Offices abroad bring glamour and international travel to an industry that could otherwise do it all from a desk. The only acceptable reason for opening another office in another country is to develop overseas markets for profit. No corporation is rich enough to support overseas operations on an altruistic basis. The sharp business reasons for setting up abroad can be many. Trade is already growing at such a fantastic rate you need to organize it properly. You have been offered a whale of a contract provided that you have a locally based operation. Or there may be some other major fiscal advantage.

Because trading conditions vary, there is no hard and fast rule to guide you through setting up overseas territories. Nevertheless, here are some thoughts to consider:

✦ **Have you done your homework?** Do you know before you make a move exactly what you are getting into? Have you studied the country closely? How many fact-finding trips have you made?

✦ **Is X the best country to start with?** Do surrounding countries speak the same language or follow its lead (USA and Canada)? Is it part of a block (Denmark, Sweden, and Norway)? Is it a good springboard for neighboring countries (Switzerland)? Is it a center of technical excellence (Silicon Valley, Cambridge, or Sophia Antinopolis)?

✦ **Can you possibly make better use of your national distributor?** Might he be able to let you have a little spare space? It is an excellent place to set up camp while you gauge the local market and work out where you'd really like your offices.

✦ **Have you found a local manager?** Having a foreign national on your side can smooth out a host of bureaucratic problems as well as being a source of sound on-the-spot advice.

✦ **Will supervision strain the home staff?** Someone is going to have to commute regularly. Will your ambassador be split between the company headquarters and the new operation? Can he or she do both jobs well? Are the travelling costs supportable?

✦ **Recognize the language barrier.** Do they speak English there? Can English remain the company language? If not, do you have a senior headquarters person who's fluent in the appropriate language? Is the language of the country one that might be useful elsewhere (such as Spanish)? What provision have you made for language training?

✦ **Do you appreciate the outlay?** Setting up overseas offices always costs more than many expect. Get quotes for all aspects of the exercise including setting up the firm, renting premises, paying staff, and transferring key staff from the head office. Just in case, take into account your wrap-up costs, as well. In some countries laying staff off is prohibitive and office rents have to be paid in full to expiry.

✦ **Is it easy to repatriate the profits?** Is the government stable? Is the country tolerant? Are you likely to be affected by changes in international currency rates?

Financing

Even when you are successful, you can never be successful enough. Very few firms generate the excess cash to grow without seeking some outside investment. Although Cisco was turning over $250,000 a month in their early years, they had to resort to venture capital to kick-start their business.

Now, armed with an excellent track record, you are in a strong position to approach potential investors. Your sales achievement diminishes the early doubts, and you yourself are more assured. Doors may open at speeds you would never have believed previously, but don't fall in too quickly. There is probably no need to take out a second mortgage on your home to underpin your overdraft. Your bank manager will be more than happy to extend your credit. Additionally, you may now have the option of a stock market flotation. Your have the following main options:

✦ Bank loans

✦ Venture capital

✦ Flotation (or selling part of the shareholding)

When approaching venture capitalists or banks you will still need a business plan. You will probably find it a lot easier to write now on a foundation of facts, leaving less for aspiring conjecture. It may not need to be as detailed as before. Proposals should always include copies of your latest audited accounts.

In Conclusion

Growth without bona fide goals is a delusion. In the same way you engineered your original product launch you have to keep working and planning a long way ahead. Growth does not automatically follow success. It has to be planned; and the planning never stops, but it's worth it and great fun. I wish you success.

✦   ✦   ✦

Preparing for Further Success

If you continue to be successful, sooner or later your business will hit its natural ceiling. It will have reached as far as it can without radically extending its objectives, taking on considerably more staff, and becoming another animal. This invariably means raising a great deal more cash.

Whether you elect to do this by becoming a quoted corporation or striking some private deal, restructuring inevitably means exchanging a large part of what you have now for a lesser share of what you have next. The expectation, of course, is that the value of this lesser holding will become infinitely more valuable.

If you are in a position to take the public company route, you will be offered all the advice you may need from the merchant bank you retain to handle your flotation. Unfortunately, software houses are 100 times more likely to receive a takeover offer out of the blue. If, like the majority, you come to some private arrangement, you may or may not gain what you expect; especially if the buyer has, unbeknownst to you, been stalking you with an eye to taking you over.

Consider a Cautionary Tale

An Internet development firm with an outstanding reputation is sold to an offshoot of a major U.S. corporation with one of Silicon Valley's real legends on the Board. The corporation gets the firm. The proprietor goes for an exceedingly valuable bundle of shares about to be floated on the U.S. Stock Exchange. The purchaser takes over the premises, staff, equipment, checkbooks, records, Intellectual Property Rights (IPR), and so on—and then doesn't float.

In that position, what can you do? Sue them? You have no money as the transactions are entirely in the form of shares, which still have a two-year Securities and Exchange Commission embargo on them.

The next day they call you and trump up some charge that you are in breach of contract. When countercharged, they offer to give you back your firm and return the transaction. That might have been interesting a few months ago but you had mentally been psyching yourself up for a new venture and working out on which Caribbean island you were going to build your dream villa. In the meantime, they subleased your premises, fired most of your staff, transferred the best contacts to the parent organization, and sold every asset they could. Someone tips you off that the purchaser desperately needed extra credibility in an attempt to get itself publicly listed. A few months later the corporation sells what's left and shortly goes into liquidation.

This story, though far from typical, is far from unknown in one form or other. Success is not a full stop. When you reach your first objective, you have to decide what should come next. Unless you are planning to sell, this means beginning all over again, albeit in a better situation.

You have been through it once. You know where you are strong. You have a certain amount of money, and premises presumably, as well as people and contacts. You may have a very definite idea or possibly too many. The big question is to what extent are you truly suited to what you are going to decide?

Running a large outfit doesn't appeal to everyone, and it is not automatically more profitable despite what friends and family may think. If you find a larger operation daunting, and most people do at some point, the most mature thing you can do is to set your pride aside and broker the business while you are holding the aces. You don't have to sell it all; you can retain that slice of the action where you truly excel. You will do much better for yourself in the long run being best at what you *can* do than scraping by at what you can't.

Whatever you decide, it is an important decision. My advice is take a vacation. Recharge your batteries. Listen to those you hold most dear. Consult your inner voice. Take your time; but not too much time. Competitors are bound to have noted your success. They will be looking for your program's limitations. They may underestimate the difficulties of improving it and overestimate the money to be made. So one of your prime objectives will probably be to tighten up your program. The better your program, the more people will like it and the costlier it will be for any competitor to steal a slice of the action.

Competition can come from three sources:

✦ Small outfits who don't know their limitations

✦ Bigger outfits who are angry that you developed an area they were always about to move into

✦ Really large firms who are determined to have the lion's share of your cake

You are going to have to watch all three. The small outfit may just be very smart indeed. The bigger outfits will probably invest much more money than you did and come out with an unremarkable product with one significant plus. A really big firm may well wait years; then just as you are about to make the big time, they will put in an offer. If you don't sell to them, they may well develop a competitive product and swamp you. By the time they get in touch, they may have executives and technicians who have been watching you for several years and know almost as much about your business as you do.

That's the way business is. Some people thrive on it. Others don't. You just have to be true to yourself. If you are sensible, and you would hardly have read this far if you weren't, you will probably come out well in the end. In the interim, you inevitably will have to make some important decisions. The most crucial one is likely to concern staff. Those who have helped you deserve appropriate rewards. In some instances this may take the form of a raise or a title. However, it could easily take one or more of the following forms:

✦ Recognition

✦ Share options

✦ A company car

✦ Other perks and prizes

✦ Further training or some assistance with their personal development

Doling out the goodies is an act of acknowledgment not propitiation. So there's no point in making things hard for yourself. Ask yourself whether the people who have helped you so far are the people you need for the next leg of the struggle. To decide this objectively, you are going to need a fresh staffing plan. Inevitably, some people will fit and others won't. It may be possible to move some of the square pegs into slots better suited to their capabilities, but if you haven't got room for them, you haven't. Bear in mind that holding on to them may prevent them discovering their real areas of excellence. When you sever the cord, remember that no one who chooses staff is ever infallible; be humble, even apologetic, but firm.

The next thing you have to consider is what changes you need to make to working conditions and rewards to keep the people you do want. Motivation isn't necessarily about more money or options or cream in their coffee; it can be spending more time listening to them so they feel they have more of an input. It can be sending them on courses that increase their expertise and enable them to grow. The most successful leaders are those who build those underneath them.

As you may have gathered, there are a lot more adventures in store once you achieve your first major success. One of the most practical things you can do to get up to the next level is to go back to the beginning of this book and go through the process of creating software successfully again.

Is It Too Good to Be True?

A takeover is probably the last thing you were anticipating when you first considered writing a program. Yet any successful software house is several times more likely to receive a takeover offer out of the blue than it is to float its parent on the stock exchange. If you ever get an offer be courteous and business-like but be very, very guarded.

The offer may come in an unexpected telephone call, be dropped in the course of a social drink or business lunch, or be made by a stranger turning up unannounced at your office. Stand by to repel flattery. Your reactions may give away more than you mean to. Your body or voice may signal that you are desperate to sell at any price. Your proposer, no matter how disinterested he strives to appear, will be watching closely for unconscious signals that will tell him how to act next. It's often prudent to make some excuse to withdraw as soon as you can, if only to collect your thoughts. As soon as you are alone congratulate yourself. Give yourself a well-deserved pat on the back. Then wipe the gloat off your face and recognize the offer for what it is: acknowledgment in someone else's eyes that you have succeeded.

Are you going to tell them to get lost (rarely wise), play them along (potentially dangerous), or are you going to display some mild interest? When you've decided, go back in and pick up the conversation. You have a much better chance of displaying the required come-on coldness if you know in advance that takeovers, like dating, have their own rituals. First there's the initial pass. Then there is a line to see if you are likely to be receptive. Then both sides go for a clinch to see if there is any basis for a deal. Next both sides check out the merchandise to ensure that they are really going to get what they want. Finally, there's a short ceremony at which titles and presents are irrevocably exchanged.

The only thing you can be sure of at the start of any negotiation is that your reactions will be reported in every detail to the prospective buyer. The right or wrong conclusions he comes to will frame all his next moves.

Don't pass up the opportunity to open up communications at the highest level with another company. It is the perfect opportunity to make a dummy run. You never know what the future will bring. Do the hi-tech equivalent of putting on a clean shirt. Take pains to make a good impression.

Have They Sent the Right Person?

Unless the offer is made in person by the head of a company or via someone you know well, ask the intermediary the following:

✦ What his/her title and authority is

✦ Whether this is part of his/her everyday role

✦ Whether he/she is on some special assignment

✦ Whether he/she is part of some brokers

✦ Who he/she is reporting to

✦ Who is paying him/her

You could ask whether the possible purchase is being made on behalf of a company or a parent or associate, but at this stage you are unlikely to be told or even recognize the truth. Get rid of the intermediary a soon as you can and check his credentials.

It often happens that you know the person or his company already. Perhaps you play golf with them or have already done business. Even so, still treat him in the same detached, inquiring, and highly professional manner. Remember that this isn't a round of golf. It's the endgame of all endgames. And you are playing for everything you have worked so hard to build up.

If you know anyone who works for the company you may be able to get some background about the tentative purchaser. Another good source of information is the trade press. If you are not satisfied, trust your instincts and have nothing more to do with a deal. However, if it all seems straightforward, write directly to the CEO and ask for written confirmation that they are seriously considering an acquisition and that the person to whom you have spoken has been entrusted with negotiations. If you consider that their representative is insufficiently senior or that the chemistry is wrong, write back explaining that you are only going to feel comfortable exploring possibilities with a more appropriate person. It is in both sides' interest to make sure that you are dealing with a person as high up in the hierarchy as possible bearing in mind the scale of the takeover. If you deal with too low a person, he won't have any real influence. Negotiations will hiccup along as the intermediary takes time to get a yes or a no.

Note   Don't be afraid of upsetting the other company's head man. Any CEO worth his salt will not be put off by a tough nut. Tough nuts are a challenge. What a good CEO fears is a fool. Nobody can make money with fools.

Do They Have an Adequate Reason for Buying?

Historically, this is one of hardest and most important questions to answer, because in many instances the purchaser doesn't know himself. Nevertheless, the answer is most important because it determines what the buyer may be prepared to pay. If you follow the financial papers, you will know that in many cases, the purchaser discards or dismantles the company he bought with great pomp. Perhaps the symbiosis isn't as promising as the purchaser thought. Perhaps the purchaser gets caught up or caught out by something grander. You, on the other hand, may be in a better position to be objective. If a sale doesn't make functional or emotional sense to you, beware. Often in these situations it may make more sense to you than it seems to for him. You have an extra trump card in your hand; but you will make the decision on whether you should use it.

How to Spot a Trojan Horse

How do you know the person courting you isn't a spy, that he isn't simply trying to find out facts to which he has no legal right? When a company needs to get inside information on a competitor quickly it often takes a disgruntled ex-employee to lunch. If that fails they may try questioning a salesman in a demonstration. If that fails they may try the bogus takeover. There are two principal give-aways to this ploy:

- ✦ Their pleasantries are unnecessary or seem insincere.
- ✦ The purported negotiator begins to probe deeply at too early a stage. "When are you planning to bring out the next version?"

The spy's main aim is to extract the information and run before he gets unmasked.

Other earmarks of a hoax are that it is unprofessional, talks are peremptorily called off, and no future date is set. Another clue is that the CEO is never available. CEOs will hide facts or create a false impression, but they usually draw the line at flat lies.

Of course, I am talking about amateur inquirers. If you are ever done over by professionals, you may never feel the anesthetic. However, take comfort. Whether or not they ever come to anything, most takeover approaches are genuine.

When You Make the First Approach

The perceived wisdom is the only reason one firm puts its hands up to another is that it is on the verge of trouble; not a very promising way to begin. This isn't to say that you may not have good reasons for casting your net around. Perhaps you are seriously ill or due to retire, want to emigrate, need to fund development or extend your distribution, or the other firm holds the nut while you hold the bolt. Not all of these warrant yielding control.

The most common way to approach a potential buyer is to drop hints to a well-placed, common acquaintance. With luck, he will sow the idea in his boss's mind so the other fellow thinks he is approaching you. Astutely done, this keeps all your cards in your hand. However, being devious doesn't mean being unscrupulous. It is unfair and dishonest to ask your contact to do anything that is not in his best interest. Incidentally, if any member of the other side questions you about your relationship you must be frank even though you play it down.

If they ask you why you want to give up, you must be direct. Draft your case in writing even if you are going to give an answer verbally. It is essential that your response makes business sense. If you have to take the initiative with their CEO (deal only at the highest level), don't talk about a takeover. Talk "mutual business." Sound intellectually exploratory.

A more interesting angle is to make your approach to more than one firm. Then you are not selling, you are exploring all possibilities. You can say, "My board has always had a great respect for yours. I was wondering whether we should meet to discuss a more constructive proposition."

How Do You Run Your Business *and* Sell It?

The idea of being paid handsomely for all the work you have done for so long, for so little, is intoxicating—so intoxicating that a surprising number of firms actually go under during takeover negotiations because they fail to keep their business going. The solution is to use a business broker. These organizations typically work on a percentage or charge a modest fee. As they sell any number of businesses a year, they are very experienced at negotiating. Additionally, they have a vested interest in selling your business at the best possible price. They don't get paid otherwise. In the process, they isolate you from all the emotional toing and froing.

Note This is not the main reason they are so widely employed. The main reason they are used is that they are able to conduct negotiations without the seller's staff being alerted.

Heads of Agreement

As soon as both sides are sure they want to look further into the matter you should get together with your counterpart and draw up a *heads of agreement*. This is an informal, non-binding agenda in which both parties set out the negotiating criteria:

✦ The intent of both parties

✦ The issues and concerns that need to be addressed

✦ An outline of how the takeover will work

✦ The status and implications for your company, products, rights, and employees

✦ The timescale envisaged

Good heads of agreement are clear and straightforward. They do not overstate or over promise. While they commit neither party legally, they may form a useful lever for negotiating if there is any serious departure. For example, if you want to bind the purchaser to pay for any update of your current financial situation, you should put this in a separate short-form interim agreement, probably by an exchange of letters.

Hassle

Takeovers often involve endless meetings, conference calls, video links, interruptions, correspondence, visits, and trips abroad. This is partly because there is so much to discuss, but it is also because everybody's nervous. CEOs of even major multinationals don't buy other companies every day. There's a great deal at stake. So don't immediately assume that the other fellow is being tricky. The best policy is to be endlessly patient, open, and honest. If and when you disagree, say so. Your view will be respected. After all, if he was in your shoes (and very shortly he will be) wouldn't he be raising the same point?

Be Prepared

Sooner or later the buyer is going to want to go through everything with a fine-tooth comb. So get your paperwork in order well in advance. The biggest obstacle is likely to be your lease. No purchaser wants to be saddled with an unbridled upward rent revision, susceptibility to flooding, and so on. (If you haven't already discussed any such problem with the potential buyer before he asks, he is likely to assume you are desperate to sell.)

Buyers are similarly loath to take over firms in the middle of any potentially serious legal dispute. Sellers frequently find it wiser to set aside their legal rights and settle, thus losing something small to gain something big. Such a sacrifice may go against the grain, but you should always defer to your own greater interests.

Having everything in impeccable order demonstrates that yours is a well-run organization and thus worth serious money. Here's a list of paperwork any potential buyer is bound to check:

✦ Rights to ownership of the company, its premises, leases, and intellectual property

✦ Annual account of past years' trading including the very latest year. Larger firms should be audited. Smaller firms may get by with a financial synopsis.

✦ Securities and Exchange Commission requirements

✦ Changes in registered address, directors, and corporate administrator

✦ Filing information relating to shareholding structure

✦ Up-to-date tax returns

✦ Company minutes and register

✦ Register of share certificates and dividends issued

✦ Litigation; any ongoing legal disputes

✦ List of disputed invoices and credit notes

✦ Complete register of assets, all hardware items, date of purchase, serial numbers, location, original costs

✦ Software licenses

✦ Leases and titles to all the company's real estate (probably held by your attorney)

✦ Names, addresses, and full contact numbers (including e-mail IDs) for all the company's advisors, including bankers, attorneys, patent officers, accountants, and so on

✦ Other statutory obligations such as employer's liability insurance, data protection legislation paperwork, health and safety legislation, log books, and so on

Don't be put off by the length of this list. There's nothing here you shouldn't have already as the head of a well-managed firm.

Due Diligence

This is lawyer speak for a detailed check on the facts. The buyer needs to inspect the books, make sure your records and contracts are up to date, and that your products actually do what you say. Typically, due diligence is conducted by the buyer's lawyers, accountants, Human Resources, and technology specialists. They may be part of the firm or hired from outside.

When you get the request of due diligence to be conducted, agree to the following:

✦ Dates and places

✦ Names and positions of those they wish to send

✦ What they need to see

This enables you to get everything ready and protects you against unacceptable requests. For example, you might be working on classified military contracts. In this case, make it clear what they cannot see and explain your commitment to client confidentiality.

If the inspectors are doing their job correctly, they will be adequately briefed, polite, professional, but probing. It is their job to find issues. If they don't like what they find, you may take it that the deal is off. It is very important, therefore, to have staff and advisors present to assist the buyer's representatives. The people you select should have a helpful attitude and be able to answer all questions competently and promptly. If there is dithering, stand by to see the valuation plummet.

If the prospective buyer does not ask for due diligence, ask why. It could lead to later allegations of inadequate disclosure. If you ever find yourself in such a position, make sure that you have it in writing that the buyer was offered every opportunity for due diligence but turned it down.

Can You Use Due Diligence in Reverse?

If someone is promising you the earth, you want to be certain that they can deliver more than compost. You owe it to yourself to understand the credentials and financial worthiness of the firm taking you over. If the prospective buyer is publicly quoted on the stock exchange there will be a good deal of information already in the public domain. Otherwise, set your experts digging. I suggest you do the following:

1. Examine their audited accounts. They should supply these willingly. Otherwise, get the latest details for a modest fee from your state's business governing body. Ask your accountant to decipher them.

2. Speak to people who have recently been taken over by the buyer or who know and trade with it. Listen carefully to what they say. Investigate anything you don't like.

3. If money is involved, ask the potential buyer's bankers for a statement that there is sufficient money to close the deal. If the reply is "No," abort the deal.

Tip

Unless your attorney and accountant have practical experience with takeover legalities, you would be well advised to retain specialists to consolidate and present your case. Make sure they aren't going on vacation and won't otherwise be tied up at the crucial time.

Valuing the Firm

Certain factors help to establish a ballpark price, such as what similar firms in your sector have fetched, and how extrapolations of their profitability, overheads, and debt compare. Your accountant will say it is arithmetic and there are formulas. Your lawyers will say it is the law and there are precedents. You and your buyer will know that the endgame is nothing short of poker, unless, of course, you are a publicly quoted company who can put a market value on your ever-fluctuating worth.

Always remember your strengths are also your weaknesses. If yours is a startup operation whose products are just about hitting the market, you have no track record. If yours is a mature operation, clearly things are getting long in the tooth and you need serious reinvestment. Don't be surprised either if in the closing stages the buyers suddenly turn their logic upside down and the value of your business with it. They are just sparring and will try to convince you that only their newly produced method of valuation is kosher. If the numbers are large they may argue with considerable forensic conviction because if they win, they'll save their client a small fortune and justify their existence.

At the end of the day it will all come down to what you and the buyer agree to. Before you even discuss the figure with anyone else, you must have worked out the bottom line figure for yourself. Consider what you have invested in money and time, and what profits you can expect shortly. Add your assets, both material and human, and your developments in progress. Try your valuation on your accountant. In negotiations never say "I guess my company must be worth X." Say "It *is* worth X for the following very good reasons." Don't be afraid to ask for a price down to the cent.

How Do You Maximize Value?

If all your paperwork is in order and there are no outstanding legal issues, you have done yourself a major favor. It is very hard for a would-be purchaser to cite irregularities later as an excuse for beating you down. The best and only proven way to maximize the sale price is to introduce another serious buyer. At one fell stroke you transform an argument into an auction. Blood pressure rises and what people are prepared to pay suddenly goes through the roof. If you fear it may come crashing back to earth, insist on sealed bids.

The Contract

The usual arrangement is that both sides pay their own legal costs; but if the deal goes through, the buyer inherits your bill. In practice, this results in the buyer drafting the contract and paying for the bulk of the legal work even if the deal falls through. Nevertheless, the seller has the right to stipulate what the contract must include. When you get the initial draft, go through it phrase by phrase with your lawyer. Sometimes these contracts are surprisingly short and well written. Other times, they are a cobbled together assemblage of templates. Your attorney will explain the tricks and traps and advise you what changes you should insist upon.

The games, posturing, and scams that can be paraded as you come up to the finish line are a legion. Keep a cool head, concentrate on your final objective, and be professional and in control at all times. Do not be surprised if they decline, accept, back off, halve the offer, or double it all in a single telephone call. Anything and everything can happen. If you behave dispassionately you won't get exhausted. The result of patient courtship is usually that you end up with a contract that is more than they want to pay and less than you would like. All that's needed now is the signing.

The Deal

Unless you have second thoughts, the deal should be sealed as soon as possible. Otherwise, the buyer's share price may drop, you may lose a crucial order, or some other external factor beyond your control may intervene and botch the deal. You must agree who should be present at the signing, where and when it shall take place, and what documents you need. Prepare pre-drafted company minutes with all the relevant directorship papers, resignation papers, affidavits, and new share certificates as agreed. Again, have your attorney present to oversee the process.

Caution   It is not uncommon for people to try to change the goalposts even now. If they try this on you, look them in the eye and ask them to stop wasting your time. Give them five minutes to come to their senses or the deal is off.

If money is being exchanged it must be in the form of a banknote. A company check is worthless, as it can be cancelled any time prior to payment. If money is promised at some future date it must be backed up by watertight personal guarantees from the most creditworthy member of the buyer's board. If you are getting shares in lieu of cash, the certificates must be vetted in advance.

It is legal fiction that the signing, exchange, and transfer of all documents take place simultaneously. What you actually do is sign all the company minutes, finalize the share certificates, and so on, and carefully and slowly pass them to your attorney. Then both parties sign the contract making sure it is correctly dated and witnessed. Some directors like to initial each page. When this is clearly completed, the attorneys exchange the paperwork, directorial forms, share certificates, banknotes, and so on. Your attorney then passes the boodle to you. You all shake hands.

That's it.

The deal is well and truly done.

✦   ✦   ✦

Search Engine Optimization (or Winner Takes All)

This appendix explains how to optimize your Web site ratings in seven steps:

1. Decide what you want your Web site to achieve.
2. Familiarize yourself with HTML.
3. Select your search engines.
4. Make your site search engine friendly.
5. Compile your key words.
6. Index your Web site for maximum exposure.
7. Submit your site and monitor progress.

Your Web site is likely to be the most powerful selling tool your software program will ever have. There's no point in creating a fascinating site to promote your much-wanted program if no one else can find it.

There are only three ways searchers will find your site:

1. **They already know (or guess) its name.** However, it has to be well known, or be so outrageous that no one ever forgets it. If searchers are not to go astray, the name had better be short, unambiguous, and hard to misspell.
2. **Chance.** A friend or magazine article mentions it, or they run across a link in another Web site.
3. **The searcher uses some kind of search engine.** This is by far the most common way to find a Web site, and the one addressed in this appendix.

In the beginning (which was only as few years ago), anyone who created a Web site was like the first astronaut on the moon. Teenagers fell off skateboards and curious computer people checked in from miles around just to look. Now everyone from the president of the United States to lifers in jail have Web sites. If you search for the word "software" on one of the major search engines, you could get over 590,000,000 hits.

Today, the task of finding any one site is daunting. When you have created a Web site, the work of getting it seen has only just begun.

As the creators of search engines soon realized, helping people to find needles in haystacks is not a new problem. Cartographers, genealogists, linguists, and librarians have been grappling with it (pretty successfully) for centuries. However, to get your site indexed with the search engines, you have to follow the rules.

The secret is twofold: Include the mechanisms the search engines are looking for, and construct your site in a way that search engines can index it.

Not only must your Web site be found, but for users to be bothered to follow the results, you should also appear on the first page of results and as close to the top as you can. Any site can be found. What you are aiming for is *high rankings*. The steps outlined here will help you get just that.

Step 1: Know Your Audience

State your objectives with as much care as you gave to creating the program itself. Answer the following questions:

- ✦ What is your target audience?
- ✦ What information do they need?
- ✦ What is the effect you want to achieve?

Then explore the Web. See what others are doing on Web sites for similar products. Note any trends. Take a leaf from other people's notebooks if their ideas are good.

Then rewrite your objectives as specifications, in order of importance. Keep them realistic. The purpose of Web pages isn't always to sell a product or service on the spot. It is often to offer information and support or encourage would-be buyers to take a closer look. Then list what callers will need to know about your software and think about how you want to present that information. Make the points simple and avoid anything too intricate.

Step 2: Familiarize Yourself with HTML

Fortunately there is only one universal language of the Web, irrespective of the search facility, hardware, or operating system anyone uses: Hyper Text Mark-up Language (HTML).

Note HTML was created by Sir Tim Berners Lee and his colleagues at CERN, Geneva, Switzerland in 1989.

To create a Web site and appreciate its scope and limitations, you must understand the vocabulary (HTML syntax). (It's not difficult.)

HTML is essentially a set of simple instructions that sit among the text and images that you wish to create. You can see the HTML by viewing the source in your browser (select View ➪ Source in Internet Explorer or Views ➪ Source Code in Netscape and Firefox). Scanning the code will give you a pretty good idea of what they do as well as what is and isn't possible.

Designing a Web site is a naturally self-contained project. If no one on your team has the time or aptitude, and you have resources or friends schooled in the task, it makes sense to parcel this out. To speed the process, take a tip from most professional site designers and use a Web generator such as Dreamweaver or FrontPage.

Step 3: Select Your Search Engines

Despite the hundreds of search engines and tens of thousands of specialized directories on the Internet, there are only a handful that matter to most users. These 20 or so control the bulk of the world's Internet search traffic, and most of these are powered from the four core search engines.

The search tools comprise two species: *directories*, such as the Yellow Pages, which simply list sites, and *search engines*, which crawl around the Internet trying to find what the users say they want. The directory variety uses human editors to analyze and describe what each Web site is about. The true search engines crawl around the Internet tasting the contents. These crawlers visit Web sites on a regular basis. The more popular you are or the more often you change contents, the more often they will visit your site and update your contents.

As this book goes to press, a single directory, Yahoo!, still accounts for half of all referral traffic, with Google (a crawler) and Inktomi (another directory) in the number 2 and 3 positions. (Inktomi, incidentally, provides the technology that drives both types of engine it powers, such as both MSN and AOL Search.)

Commercial gateways such as altavista, Excite, and Lycos pull users into all the sites that match the specified keywords until the enquirer declares a direct hit.

The four main search databases are Google, Yahoo, MSN, and Ask Jeeves. Their databases feed all the key search systems. Following is a more complete list of the major search engines (entries are listed in alphabetical order):

- ✦ Alltheweb
- ✦ altavista
- ✦ AOL
- ✦ Google
- ✦ HotBot
- ✦ Lycos

A list of the most popular search directories (in alphabetical order) follows:

- ✦ AllTheWeb
- ✦ Ask Jeeves
- ✦ Complete Planet
- ✦ Excite
- ✦ Google
- ✦ Hotbot
- ✦ inktomi
- ✦ iWon
- ✦ LookSmart
- ✦ MSN Search
- ✦ Northern Light
- ✦ Open Directory Project
- ✦ Yahoo! About

The situation is continually changing. Check the current search engine ranking yourself. Sites such as http://searchenginewatch.com cover recent developments.

The one thing all these engines have in common is that each search tool has developed its own algorithms for ranking who should appear and in what order in response to a search. Unless your site appears on the first page of a search reply, your chances of being checked out are close to zero, which is why I say, "Winners take all." Major corporations recognize this and employ full-time site search engineers to make sure their listings stay on top.

Step 4: Make Your Site Search Engine-Friendly

There are two design options you particularly need to consider before constructing your Web site: *framed* versus *unframed pages* and *static* or *dynamic pages*. You decision will affect how easily search engines read and index your site.

Figures A-1 and A-2 provide a simple illustration of the difference between a page that is framed and one that is unframed.

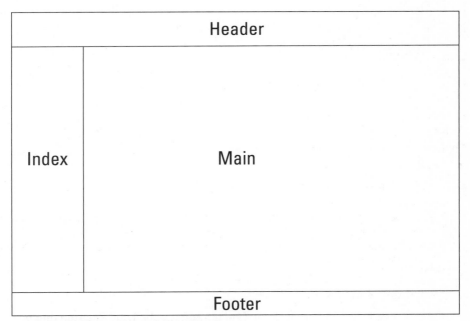

Figure A-1: Illustration of a framed page.

To Frame or Not to Frame?

Frames are display boxes within a page. Their big advantage is that you can change one box at a time instead of the whole page. So, for example, if you are offering people monthly gardening advice that talks about what's currently right for planting, you only have to change a single frame. Frames have clear benefits. And frames make it easier for laymen to construct well-organized Web pages.

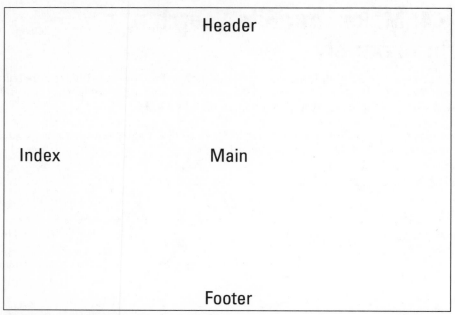

Figure A-2: Illustration of an unframed page.

However, there are two drawbacks to using frames:

✦ A frame-based site usually has a master page that issues the instructions that call up the frames on all the other pages. This is called a *frameset*. After the initial frame page is presented, subpages only get generated when the reader requests them.

Search engines, unfortunately, don't push menu buttons. They can't index what they can't see.

✦ The other problem is that if you find a framed page with a search engine, it will only see the selected frame. This will look out of place without the other frames around it.

These limitations are easily overcome, but they do have to be incorporated from the start.

If you use frames, add code to test whether they have been loaded within the frameset. If not, add some code that checks for this condition and loads the page in its correct frameset.

Note Creating frames and writing code for its proper placement is really a job for a professional Web designer. Keep that in mind when the time comes to create a site for your product.

Static or Dynamic Pages?

Another option is to use pages that only exist when they are summoned. You've probably used dynamic pages without knowing it every time you've purchased something online. Almost every shopping site from Amazon upwards uses a mixture of HTML, programming, and databases to maintain its Web site. Instead of trying to create a new static page every time an item is added or deleted from their list, it is much more practical to use a display from a database that holds details and images that can be continuously updated. So the page you are viewing is created dynamically, on the fly.

The problem, of course, is how to persuade a search engine to index these ephemeral pages. The solution is to produce a permanent master page with all details and links relevant to the page when generated. Thus, when search engine spiders visit these, they will pursue each link in turn and index the details.

Step 5: Compile Your Key Words

When people search the Web, they enter keywords.

So if you were looking for someone to update your Web site, you wouldn't type into the search engine anything like, "I am based in the Bay Area of San Francisco and need a local firm to update my Web site." You'd simply pick out the key words *Web design firm, San Francisco,* and *Bay Area.*

If you really want to get your site onto the crucial first page of search results in your category, you are going to have to display the fistful of trump words and phrases that carry the most clout. In advertising, these might be *new, amazing, free.* On a golf site, the top keywords might be *Tiger Woods* or *U.S. Open.*

A smart use of keywords ensures high search engine ranking. To help you find them, there are specialty Web sites that list the most popular words for particular industries and products. The keywords are what people actually search for. For the search engines to select your Web pages, the keywords must be embedded on each page of your Web site.

For example, if you opt for *marketing,* you may find, in descending order, the key names and phrases listed in Table A-1.

Table A-1
Key Names/Phrases

Ranking	Keywords	Hits
1	Marketing	6166
2	Internet Marketing	2788
3	Online Marketing	1705
4	Search Engine Marketing	1298
5	Network Marketing	1176
6	Web Marketing	895
7	Marketing Plan	889
8	Search Engine Marketing Firm	845
9	Email Marketing	825
10	Strategic Internet Marketing	735
11	Search Engine Marketing Company	722
12	Direct Marketing	635
13	On-line Marketing	628
14	Website marketing	508
15	Salon Marketing	487

Source: www.wordtracker.com, February 9, 2005

Such sites not only prioritize the keywords according to how often they have been requested recently from search engines, but they also show how many times they have been requested (Hits Column). Use these as a prompt and pick those most appropriate for your site.

Program writers sometimes try to beef up attention, rather like journalists, by incorporating words that have a high buzz value: sex, money, danger, sensation, health scare, arrest, and so on. This may attract attention to your site, but not necessarily from the searcher you want to go there. What you want is not just attention, but attention that leads to a hit.

If the keywords you choose are too common, your site won't end up on the first page of a search. If too obscure, they'll never be requested. It's your decision to get the balance right.

As search engines get more sophisticated, the way they grade Web sites changes. To counteract the scams and tricks that used to mislead searchers in the past, they now count increasingly on descriptions in the body of the copy.

While search engines still don't understand linguistics, they do respond to statistics as they hoover up your site and submit it to their indexing engines. Hitting the sweet spots of the search engines is the trick. So you need to infuse your copy with the trade terms, phrases, and intelligent guesses that searchers might use. Consult your thesaurus and ask customers.

Modern search engines are getting very smart at discounting hype and marking Web pages down. So an important rule of assembly is to concentrate on keywords that are relevant to your product or service. Also, if you have something tasty to offer, make sure your audience can see it.

Keywords will color the structure, headlines, navigation titles and tags you use throughout your Web site. Good ones won't guarantee you a place on that critical first page, but they will immeasurably improve your chances of appearing.

To broaden the appeal of your site, the keywords should be distinct for each page. The current wisdom is that two or three keywords per page is about right. The best place to put them is at the top.

Repeating top keywords on each page may seem like a good idea. It certainly hooks the eye. However, done heavy handedly, this is called *spamdexing*. The moment the search engines realize you are besieging them, their automatic reaction is to demote or remove such pages or sites.

Tip   To avoid rewriting, select your keywords before you write the copy.

Some Keyword Dos and Don'ts

Following is list of things to keep in mind when settling on your keywords:

- ✦ Use lowercase throughout.
- ✦ Don't be too ambitious.
- ✦ Make sure every page is different.
- ✦ Use the find words that customers use.
- ✦ Plant keywords in every title, header, subhead, frame, tag, text, and picture caption.
- ✦ Use 3 to 4 keywords per page, 20 per site.
- ✦ Make sure the keywords are relevant; tailor them to the context.
- ✦ Eschew hype. No advertising or slogans.
- ✦ Keep common misspellings and variants in mind.
- ✦ Limit titles to 20 meta words.

+ Delete spaces around commas.

+ Limit text to 300 words a page (1,024 characters max).

+ Give every frame a page title.

+ Program each page so it can be summoned from any of its frames.

+ Add dynamic data to a standing template with all indexable data.

+ With animation, caption every clip.

+ Link widely and wisely flit from one address to another.

+ Include a thumbnail map.

+ See that titles and contents correspond.

+ Test the lot before you finalize.

Step 6: Index Your Web Site

As search engines get ever more sophisticated, they use more complex strategies to index and rank your Web site. There are several components you need to insert, not just in the copy on the page, but also in special indexing instructions written into the HTML. The instructions that follow should be applied to every Web page on your site that you want to be found.

If you look at the text of any Web page, the topmost HTML will have a header line (between the <head> and </head> tags) that looks something like this:

```
<html>
<head>
<meta http-equiv="Content-Language" content="en-gb">
<meta http-equiv="Content-Type" content="text/html;
charset=windows-1252">
<meta name="GENERATOR" content="Microsoft FrontPage 4.0">
<meta name="ProgId" content="FrontPage.Editor.Document">
<title>Index</title>
<style type="text/css">
</style>
<link href="../css/hasted.css" rel="stylesheet"
type="text/css">
</head>
```

Meta Name (Keywords)

Meta name keywords reside in the HTML header. Look for a line like the following:

```
<meta name "keywords" content ="" ..."/>
```

Replace the ellipsis (. . .) with the keywords for the site or page. If you are using words that are frequently misspelled or spelled variously, include both versions, as in color/colour or theater/theatre. Also cover singular and plural variants where relevant. Keywords are separated by commas, as in the following example:

```
<meta name "keywords" content ="wheel,round,tire,tyre
cycle,transport,automobile,car,caravan,aircraft,
automobiles,cars,motorbike,plane"/>
```

Try to limit your keywords to 20. Note too that lists longer than 1024 characters are usually ignored.

Don't repeat words more than three times and never together. While some search engines will up your ranking, most don't.

Ironically, most search engines turn the commas between keywords into spaces, but strings of keywords are much easier to read with the commas left in.

If you are using framed pages, put the keywords in the frameset *and* within each frame.

Titles

The *page title* is the wording displayed at the top left-hand corner of your browser. Search engines give high priority to the titles on each page because they are easy to locate. The title on your home page is the most important one, so make sure yours tells visitors who you are and what you offer. Try to express this in less than 40 characters and spaces. There are no marks for perfect English. Say what you want in short pithy phrases.

Remember, too, that good slogans make bad titles. Searchers aren't looking for advertisements. They are looking for nuts-and-bolts help. It is a critical distinction. So where an advertising tag line for a program that helps people with their tax returns might boast the headline "The greatest tax software in the country," a title version that simply offers to tell an inquirer "How to reduce your tax liability" actually includes more words that searchers are likely to type in to find it.

Every Web page has a title space at its top left-hand corner. In HTML-speak the instruction sits between the <head> and the </head> and is enclosed in the line that begins <title>.

The trick is to make each title different, yet relevant to its page, and thereby add to your Web site's appeal. Put yourself in your visitors' shoes. Ask yourself what you would want to know.

If by any chance there is no title on a page, it is not uncommon for search engines to display, by default, the first couple of sentences they come across.

Crawler Pages

Some search engines, notably *Yahoo!* and *altavista,* only allow you to submit one Web page for rating. They then examine that page and index the keywords in it before following up the Web links it mentions. Ideally, this *crawler page* contains links to all the key pages on the site that you wish to be indexed. This should be done without any text. It only exists to help the search engines, so it doesn't have to be viewable. To prevent the crawler page from appearing in the search engine results, put a redirect on it so the searcher is passed straight to your home page.

If your site is extensive, link the master crawler page to sub-crawler pages, which list other working pages.

The maximum indexable content per page is limited to 100K. Any excess cannot be indexed.

If you are using framed pages, make sure they don't exceed the limit by getting your crawlers to test the links between the `<noframes>` and `</noframes>` sections in the master page that generates framed pages.

The More Links the Merrier

A link is a pointer to another page or Web site. All the major search engines add cumulative weightings when they find links to your site. So to increase your ratings, the theory is just add links.

First, consider other Web sites to which you want to link. Are they home pages or sub-pages? A sub-page won't boost your ranking because the search engine won't credit it to you even though you originate it. You need to develop a strategy to get your site usefully linked.

I advise you to set up quality, long-term links with Web sites where there is a genuine reason for cooperation (for example, another site owned by your company, a site selling your product, or perhaps a magazine review).

Sometimes such links are reciprocated; at other times, not. It is always possible that the linkee may adopt your software. Either way, it can do you no harm to include keyword phrases in your description, such as the following:

```
<a href=http://www.yourwebsite.com> Description with
Keywords </a>
```

Work methodically to cultivate links that add value. They will pay dividends in the long run, but be aware of the sub-industry that has built up around contrived mechanisms for increasing search engine rankings. While conjuring tricks such as these appear to work, they are fairly obvious. Furthermore, search engine operators resent attempts to hoodwink them and are constantly devising ways to torpedo such ploys.

My advice is don't waste your time trying to get attention from people who have no natural interest in buying your service or product. What you want is genuine data that will attract the maximum number of genuine prospects.

Simplify Your Web Address

A Web address is usually referred to as a *URL*, or *Universal Resource Locator*.

It will come as no surprise that search engines like URLs that are clean and easy to decode. In other words, URLs that contain the address and nothing but the address, which in turn means that simple addresses are more crawlable and therefore more likely to be found.

However, Web sites generated from databases invariably have all sorts of other signals embedded. For example, the bit after a ? is often a database prompt, while & is frequently used to separate variables.

If you are running a shopping site where pages have to be generated from a database, how do you get around these symbols so the pages can be found? If you examine the URLs of most shopping sites, you will see that all their addresses appear to be directory breaks instead of variables. So,

```
www.mywebsite.com/store?shop=disk&sku123456
```

becomes

```
www.mywebsite.com/store/disc=sku123456
```

Make sure your application server knows how to interpret this data.

Don't Change URLs in Midstream

Search engines take time to index pages. If you rename the page after they have done so, searches will bring up a blank screen.

If you are forced to change URLs, it makes sense to keep the old pages in place so they will be found. Search engines can take a long time to purge old entries. Put a redirector in the old location to load the new page automatically.

But remember, it improves your ranking to have a single URL address regardless of whether you are using static or dynamic pages.

Other Useful Meta Names

There are three other types of widely used meta names, not currently used by search engines. The first allows you to insert the company or author's name between the last quotes:

```
<meta name="author" content="author's name"/>
```

The second meta name allows you to insert the name of the program used to create your Web page (substitute your program for *program* in the following code line):

```
<meta name="generator" content="program" />
```

If you are using an editor, it will usually publicize itself for you.

You can also insert the name of the copyright holder, together with the span of years for which the copyright is valid:

```
<meta name="copyright" content="&copy: Company Year">
```

Body Copy or Meta Text

The heading (title) and the copy (description) should both be about the same thing. If you embed keywords judiciously, each will help the other to inch you up the list.

Descriptive text resides within the HTML header. Look for a line like this:

```
<meta name=Description" content="..."/>
```

It is important that readers can learn something from the descriptive content on every page.

Search engines may raise the ranking of your page according to how you write your descriptions.

Try to limit the body copy on each page to 5,000 characters. Two hundred to three hundred words is ideal. Some search engines will support much more copy, but the type has to be squeezed too small for most readers. Remember to make your body copy appealing and embed the keywords. Body copy should hold the information the search engine displays when it hits your page.

In practice, the summary a search engine provides does not always match what is there. Some engines simply repeat the meta name description; others only show them if the keywords have been repeated in the body copy. They may, on yet other occasions, reproduce some random snippet from an `Alt` tag. Because of this, it pays to keep your key words running through the body copy so the search engine screen shows what you intended.

Including Testimonials on Your Page

Nothing gives potential converts greater confidence than a strong endorsement from someone they respect. These should be categorical statements from known people; companies are best used to make one point. Quotes can be legitimately edited to fit into available space, but the recommendation must not be manipulated, exaggerated, or distorted.

Obtain the endorsee's permission in writing in advance. Show the endorsee the quote in the final form in which it is going to be displayed.

Incorporating Images and Animations

While search engines can read text fairly easily, deciphering graphics and animations is a much tougher task. Until recently, search engines ignored most graphics. More recently, the analysis techniques are still in their formative stage. If you rely heavily on animation, it is vital that each page of them be accompanied by text the search engine can index. Having just animation on a home page is not recommended.

I recommend putting an Alt (short for alternative) tag to provide alternative text for any non-trivial image. The alternative text then appears as a tooltip whenever the user's mouse is over the picture. This also adds a phrase that the search engine can chalk up to your credit. But keep the Alt text short and strictly functional. Remember, too, to fill in the Alt information. Not only will you please the search engine, but visually impaired readers using text-to-audio decoders will be able to make sense of these pages as well.

Address the Visually and Audibly Impaired

The Web may be a visual medium, but this hasn't stopped the visually and audibly challenged population from using it with great success. When designing your Web site, consider how this section of your market will access your site.

A common technique is to use voice boxes that convert text into spoken words. These boxes typically tab from link to link, so to facilitate fluent navigation, your tabbing has to work in a consistent, logical way that is easy to grasp.

It also helps if information is organized into small, manageable bites. Make sure your layout is consistent throughout. Including a site map helps everyone.

Another technique to consider is Cascading Style Sheets (CSS). This text format has compound advantages. As well as making life easier for those with visual or hearing difficulties, CSS produces a higher ratio of text to code that search engines appreciate. Cascading Style Sheets also make it easier to link sites with non-PC devices such as handhelds, personal organizers, phones, Web TV, and in-car browsers.

Finally, if your site has to use large audio files, consider providing transcripts for the hearing impaired.

Step 7: Submit Your Site and Monitor Progress

Your Web site is about to be your shop window to the world. It now needs to go through the same rigorous testing process you used for your software. Put it up on a closed Web server and get colleagues and potential users to check it over thoroughly.

When you have done everything, give your entire site a final check. Make sure your site reads well both for visitors and engines. See that all the tags for crawlers and spiders are in place. If you are using frames, check that you have duplicated the redirector in every frame.

You are now ready to put on a searcher's hat and try to find your site.

Each search engine has its own protocol and filters to analyze the signals offered. Unless you have the time and inclination to try and find your site from all the main engines, it may be a good move to employ a specialist firm to do the posting. For a small fee, professional checkers will normally repost your data regularly and monitor your search ranking as key phrases are changed. Providing they are, it is money well spent. If the contractor is new to you, seek recommendations and check references before signing.

As the Internet becomes increasingly commercial, more search engines are touting for paid entries. If you want quick recognition or want privileged status, be prepared to pay extra.

Although the vast majority of visits will almost certainly come through the major search engines, remember to submit your site to all and every relevant directory.

Finally—Be Realistic

Unless you are an undisputed leader in your sector or are prepared to spend millions on search engine positioning, you will never be top of your tree. Yet if you have done everything well and your product or service offers a genuine unique selling proposition (USP), you should rate quite highly.

✦   ✦   ✦

Index

Continued

Continued

Continued

Continued

Continued